T0193150

Saints of Hysteria
A Half-Century of Collaborative American Poetry
Edited by Denise Duhamel, Maureen Seaton & David Trinidad

Saints of Hysteria
A Half-Century of Collaborative American Poetry
Edited by Denise Duhamel, Maureen Seaton & David Trinidad

Soft Skull Press

Cover art: Good'n Fruity Madonna © 1968 Joe Brainard
Used by permission of the Estate of Joe Brainard.

Credits & acknowledgments for the poems begin on page 389.

Soft Skull project editor & book designer: Shanna Compton

*A note on the text: Because the poems in this anthology were created over seven decades
by more than 200 authors, certain idiosyncrasies of style, orthography, and form
have been preserved in order to present the works as their authors intended. These
variations are characteristic textural effects of the collaborative process
and should not be interpreted as errors.*

Soft Skull Press
New York, NY
www.softskull.com

Printed in the United States of America

ISBN: 978-1-933368-18-4

Cataloging in Publication information for this book is
available from the Library of Congress

Contents

Introduction

Collaborative poetry is perhaps as old as song and story. It has flourished for
centuries in oral traditions. It served as an integral source of entertainment and
competition in Japanese court life as early as the twelfth century. It's an
honored and a healthy practice, mysterious to many who think of writing as a
solitary act, and a bastard branch to those who hold that solitary act sacred. We,
the editors in this historical volume of duets, fugues, and polyphonic word
inventions, bring our biases with us, of course: for us, as for the multitude of
poets who inhabit these pages, poetic collaboration is part holy, part hell. It's
intimate, insane, it's love, it's the Fool of the Tarot, it's the path to Oz, it's
terrifying and postcoital. The twentieth century resurgence of collaboration fas-
cinates us. We're hooked bad and we're deep in the impulse—to connect with
each other, to stymie the purists, to transgress aesthetic boundaries. We're no
saints, it's true, but our relationship to these poems is certainly one of spirit
and awe. And our laughter, in many cases, can be called hysterical.

A Brief History:

In the 1930s, a group of Japanese poets called the Vou Club began to create
collaborative poetry and translate it into English for a pamphlet published by
New Directions (New York City). In 1940, American Charles Henri Ford adapted
this practice into what he dubbed the "chainpoem," which he defined as an
"intellectual sport ... an anonymous shape laying in a hypothetical joint imag-
ination." Ford and his collaborators mailed their lines all over the world. As the
poets continued to pass on their lines to other poets, they believed that the
chainpoems would "revolve to completion." Anyone could decide to write the
concluding line; that poet would then make copies of the completed chainpoem
and send one to each chainpoet ·on the list. Because chainpoems were
coauthored by different poets, they found their way into obscure literary
magazines rather than into solo collections.

The chainpoets and the Vou Club were preceded by (and perhaps inspired
by) the French poets of the early 1900s who defined Surrealism and were
among the first in the West to create collaborative poetry on an ongoing basis.
Surrealist "chain games," used as prompts to create impromptu poems, included
Exquisite Corpse, Syllogisms, Echo Poems, and the Game of Variants.

In the late 40s and early 50s, Beat writers began their collaborative experiments; among them was "Pull My Daisy" by Allen Ginsberg, Jack Kerouac, and Neal Cassady. This poem also inspired the underground film of the same name by Alfred Leslie. Some of the Beats were included in "A Special Issue of Collaborations" of the now defunct literary magazine *Locus Solus*, the first attempt to gather a substantial amount of collaborative poetry. Edited by New York School poet Kenneth Koch, the issue included some very early renga by Basho, Bonsho, Fumikuni, and Kyoria, and "Cadavres Exquis" by Surrealist Paul Éluard and others containing the now-famous line, "The exquisite corpse shall drink the new wine." In his foreword, Koch described literary collaboration as "a usually concealed subjective phenomenon . . . jar[ring] the mind into strange new positions." He cites the Japanese poets as inspiration–"Japanese poets wrote together as naturally as Shelley wrote alone"–and traces the sketchier history of collaboration in English-language poets through the Metaphysical poets (Abraham Cowley, Richard Crashaw, Sir John Suckling, and Edmund Waller) and the Romantics (Coleridge and Wordsworth).

Collaboration was to become a main feature of the New York School–the first and subsequent generations. The collaboration issue of *Locus Solus* includes "Crone Rhapsody," a sestina by Koch and John Ashbery reprinted in this anthology. In addition to fulfilling the formal rules of the sestina, every line of "Crone Rhapsody" contains the name of a flower, a tree, a fruit, a game, a famous old lady, and the word "bathtub." This is an example of how poets can "up the ante" while collaborating, creating ingenious ways to both entertain and outsmart each other.

One of the most prolific collaborators of the New York School was Frank O'Hara. The title of this anthology is a nod to his work with Bill Berkson, a series entitled "Hymns of St. Bridget," written from 1960–1962. In "St. Bridget's Neighborhood," Berkson and O'Hara wrote:

She

Is supposed to watch over them   She is a lamp
Their feet are blue   hee hee   She is the Saint

of Hysteria

In the 60s and 70s, there was a flurry of collaborative activity among the second and third generation New York School poets. Ted Berrigan and Ron Padgett collaborated with each other and each also collaborated with a number of their other friends and peers. In 1971, Berrigan and Anne Waldman wrote the book-length poem *Memorial Day* for a reading at St. Mark's Poetry Project. Waldman in turn collaborated with Eileen Myles, who in turn collaborated with Alice Notley, who in turn collaborated with Bernadette Mayer. This particular "chain" is of historical interest: these poems are some of the earliest examples of women writing with other women. Such a chain also illustrates the infectious spirit of poetic collaboration. For the poets in the St. Mark's Poetry Project scene, collaboration was a way of life, some good stimulating fun in those pre-careerist days, a means of fostering literary fellowship. This spirit of generosity and playfulness continues to inspire younger poets who are drawn to the Poetry Project milieu.

Feminist poets have engaged in collaboration for a more overtly political reason: as an attempt to find a collective female voice. In the 80s, Olga Broumas began to experiment with Jane Miller in *Black Holes, Black Stockings.* Her second collaboration, *Sappho's Gymnasium,* was written with T Bègley. She has said in an interview in *Provincetown Arts* (1993) that she now "only writes with others, never alone." Jane Miller notes that the process of collaboration, "[a]nimating one's privacy with another person's magic," can lead to "the creation of a third participant, the 'us,'" and has stated in a 1996 interview in the *Electronic Poetry Review* that this process enabled her to begin to trust herself as a writer. Other female "teams" in this anthology—Lyn Hejinian and Leslie Scalapino, Denise Duhamel and Maureen Seaton, Veronica Corpuz and Michele Naka Pierce—have also sustained book-length collaborative projects, continuing the trend.

Collaborations often arise out of close relationships. In the 1980s David Shapiro and David Lehman wrote poems with their young sons. This tradition continues into the present: Susan Wheeler has collaborated with her young niece and nephew, and Jim Brock wrote a road-trip poem with his teenage son. Other road-trip collaborators included in these pages are Tom Disch and Marilyn Hacker, and Terri Carrion and Michael Rothenberg. Stephen Dunn and Lawrence Raab wrote the collaborations compiled in their chapbook *Winter at the Caspian Sea* over a three-year period, during week-long summer vacations with their wives at Cape May Point, New Jersey. In their introduction to that chapbook, they describe their method as one of Exquisite Corpse with this variation: "the person who hadn't started the poem would complete it with a single line." And while we don't know the precise number of collaborators represented here who were in love at the time their poems were written, we know of at least seven couples who were married or soon-to-be married when they wrote collaboratively: Maxine Chernoff and Paul Hoover, Dodie Bellamy and Kevin Killian, Sam Ace and Margo Donaldson, Stacey Harwood and David Lehman, Amy Gerstler and Benjamin Weissman, Lisa Glatt and David Hernandez, Violet Snow and Sparrow, and Anselm Berrigan and Karen Weiser.

The majority of the poems in *Saints of Hysteria* were written by two poets. A number of others were written by three, four, sometimes five collaborators. Teacher/poets Allen Ginsberg, Joanna Fuhrman, and Denise Duhamel have written poems with entire classes of up to eighteen people. Shortly after the September 11, 2001 attacks on the World Trade Center, New York poet Bob Holman initiated a collaboration entitled "Crisis," made of two "word towers," each 110 lines long. Adrienne Rich, Robert Creeley, and Galway Kinnell were among the hundreds of poets who contributed to this project. Though not included in our anthology, "Crisis" demonstrates another characteristic of collaboration: its group dynamic can be used to promote healing, bringing poets together during a time of devastation.

The joys of collaborative poetry, the surprise and mayhem, the experiments in wickedness, can be adapted to many philosophies and temperaments. While Anne Waldman and Andrew Schelling question the very notion of "schools" of poetry in their poem "Riparian," they do acknowledge the collaborative spirit:

> —I am not a poet of Edo
> —Not a New York School poet
> —We are not poets with any name exactly though half of us is a New York
>   School poet
> —I am not a New York School poet
> —You are when you collaborate that half
> —Collaboration was not invented in New York nor in Edo
> —I missed a beat O yes & proud of it

Poems that bicker and blend, poems with dialogue, poems in which two or more poets merge into a single narrator: all work in the collaborative impulse. Many poets in this anthology choose to write in free verse and prose blocks, while others collaborate in fixed forms. Here you will find a villanelle, a ghazal, a pantoum, sonnets, sestinas, abecedarians, somonkas, haiku, renga, and a haiku/renga hybrid called a renku. Methods, too, vary from collaboration to collaboration. Some poets alternate words, others alternate lines or stanzas, still others alternate whole sections. Some poets collaborate in person, while others exchange lines via the telephone, mail, or the Internet.

Our Madness's Method:

Because collaborative poetry is primarily published in journals or small press chapbooks, it has previously been available mainly for those who truly seek it out. Many collaborations of the 60s and 70s were published in small literary magazines like Diane DiPrima's *Floating Bear* or Anne Waldman and Lewis Warsh's *Angel Hair*, both long out of print. Contemporary small magazines and literary journals, off and on the web, which have included collaborations in their pages are the *World, Two Girls Review, Crab Orchard Review, Chain, Indiana Review, Massachusetts Review, Boston Review, Poet Lore, Hanging Loose, Prairie Schooner, Gargoyle, 5 A.M., membrane, Web del Sol, 3rd bed, Big Bridge, Hotel Amerika, MiPoesias, Nerve, Artful Dodge,* and *Painted Bride Quarterly,* among other venues. Presses such as Pearl Editions, Verse Press, Erudite Fang, Edge Books, the Owl Press, Tia Chucha Press, and Copper Canyon have published collaborative books and chapbooks. As recently as the summer of 2005, *Indiana Review* devoted an entire issue to collaboration and collage. Until now, no one has published a substantial collection in more permanent, more readily accessible anthology form.

We couldn't resist. *Saints of Hysteria* gathers some of these harder-to-find collaborative poems of the last fifty or so years. We have scoured libraries, the web, and all the literary magazines we could locate. Like many anthologists, we dread going to press having skipped over some vital practitioner of the art of collaboration. But our focus had to be narrow by design: we included only poets who collaborate directly with other living poets, and we limited the collaborations to poetry, text only. We have arranged the poems in *Saints of Hysteria* in a loose chronological order to allow for "chains" of poems by poets who collaborate with more than one partner. We have included process notes by collaborators when available and hope that these notes will serve as a springboard for future collaborators.

We would like to thank Nick Carbó (for finding the Vou Poets), David Lehman (for introducing us to Soft Skull Press), Florida International University's Office of the Provost/Foundation Internal Research Award (for supporting Denise's work on *Saints* in its early stages), and Shanna Compton and Richard Nash (for their hard work and support).

DD, MS, DT
CHICAGO & MIAMI
FEBRUARY 2007

International Chainpoem

Charles Henri Ford et al.*

When a parasol is cooled in the crystal garden,
one spire radiates and the other turns round;
a toad, the Unwanted, counts the ribs' teardrops
while I mark each idol in its dregs.
There is a shredded voice, there are three fingers
that follow to the end a dancing gesture
and pose a legend under the turning shade
where the girl's waterfall drops its piece.
Then balls of ennui burst one by one,
by and by metallic metres escape from ceramic pipes.
Oh sun, glass of cloud, adrift in the vast sky,
spell me out a sonnet of a steel necklace.

*1. Takesi Fuji
 2. Katue Kitasono
 3. Charles Henri Ford
 4. Dorian Cooke
 5. Norman McCaig
 6. Gordon Sylander
 7. George Marion O'Donnell
 8. Parker Tyler
 9. Saburoh Kuroda
 10. Nagao Hirao
 11. Syuiti Nagayasu
 12. Tuneo Osada

Process Note

From *New Directions,* 1940:

How to Write a Chainpoem

The chainpoem is not only an intellectual sport but a collective invention. However, it is not a product of social collaboration in the sense that architecture is. Each poet is architect, supervisor, bricklayer, etc., of the construction. The blueprint of the chainpoem is the anonymous shape lying in a hypothetical joint imagination, which builds as though the poem were a series of either mathematical or dream progressions.

Thus, after the first line is written, the problem of each poet, in turn, is to provide a line which may both "contradict" and carry forward the preceding line. The chain poet may attempt to include his unique style and make it intelligible to the poem as well; in which case the chainpoem will have a logical and spontaneous growth. Alternatively, using the surrealist approach, he may automatically add a line that springs from whatever is first suggested by the preceding line. After writing his line, by whatever method, the poet forwards the MS to the next on the list (which has been drawn up in advance by whoever starts the chainpoem), together with the list itself, and so the chainpoem revolves to completion. Anyone may decide he has written the concluding line, in which case he makes copies of the chainpoem and sends one to each chainpoet on the list.

CHARLES HENRI FORD

Pull My Daisy

Neal Cassady, Allen Ginsberg & Jack Kerouac

Pull my daisy
tip my cup
all my doors are open
Cut my thoughts
for coconuts
all my eggs are broken
Jack my Arden
gate my shades
woe my road is spoken
Silk my garden
rose my days
now my prayers awaken

Bone my shadow
dove my dream
start my halo bleeding
Milk my mind &
make me cream
drink me when you're ready
Hop my heart on
harp my height
seraphs hold me steady
hype my light
lay it on the needy

Heal the raindrop
sow the eye
bust my dust again
Woe the worm
work the wise
dig my space the same
Stop the hoax
what's the hex
where's the wake

how'd the hicks
take my golden beam

Rob my locker
lick my rocks
leap my cock in school
Rack my lacks
lark my looks
jump right up my hole
Whore my door
beat my boor
eat my snake of fool
Craze my hair
bare my poor
asshole shorn of wool

Say my oops
ope my shell
bite my naked nut
Roll my bones
ring my bell
call my worm to sup
Pope my parts
pop my pot
raise my daisy up
Poke my pap
pit my plum
let my gap be shut

New York, Spring–Fall, 1949

Masterpiece

Jack Kerouac & Lew Welch

The Lion said "I
demand too much"
and walked up to the Zebra
and said I want to eat you
The Zebra ran away
and the Lion chased him
    & went Pa-Wow
    & ate the Zebra anyhow

And the Vulture said
    Vuuuuuuuuuu
"Oh look what the Lion left
    Slurp slurp"
  Then the ants & the worms
      came
"Look what the Vulture left"
And then the sun came
    & said "Look
      what the worms & ants left"

And then there was dust
And then came the sun
And then came eternity
    & said "Oooh look
      what the sun left"
And then came the Lion
    & said "Look
      what eternity left—
  I think I'll make
  a little world here."

Process Note

From "A Recollection" in *Trip Trap: Haiku on the Road* by Jack Kerouac, Albert Saijo, & Lew Welch:

The section called "Masterpiece" is from Jack and Lew. I listened to them put it together.

Both Lew and Jack carried pocket notebooks, the kind spiral bound across the top, into which they jotted thoughts along the way...

The whole piece [*Trip Trap*] has the random quality of Brownian movement. It has the space of the hypnagogic state between waking and sleeping. It is offhand. It is a curiosity. It has no middle, but no beginning or end. It is neither interesting nor uninteresting, but it holds out attention somehow, for it appears to have an art after all, the fathomless art of random speech overheard through the course of a day.

ALBERT SAIJO

A Postcard to Popeye

John Ashbery & Kenneth Koch

Paolo heard the record of Brahms' Requiem in downtown Cleveland;
The mountain lion was startled by a record of a calendar falling from the
    Woolworth Building;
The hair record of George Jessel reading *Ella Cinders* is all bought up
By the lace tycoons. When will the Spike Jones record take the morning train
    for the continental shelf?
In Great Barrington a cigarette was listening to a record of the mating call of
    the Monarch butterfly.
The Dagwood and Blondie record came in three pieces—shaped like Dagwood,
    Blondie, and Daisy.
It was bought up by a ferryboat record of Mt. Etna reading the poems of
    Andy Gump.
The record of Herbert Hoover eating corn-on-the-cob was a complete sell-out,
As was the record of J. Edgar Hoover reading *Pendennis* to the Czech shoplifters.
Here, in the little town square, they are playing a record of Marianne Moore
    reading tea leaves;
It is tied on the popularity shelf with the record of the emptying of Bing
    Crosby's Christmas stocking.
A Moslem hid the record of newspapers blowing across the state of Wyoming,
    in a basket in Dundee.
Now it is time to listen to the record of *Popeye in the Court of King Arthur,*
But there is no one to listen, except the record of a ski sliding down Mont Blanc,
A sepia record of *Tiptoe through the Tulips* lay on an iceberg, waiting to be
    found by someone.
The record of whales belching was hidden in the green forest.
Ellen's record of Mel Ferrer reading the Bangkok telephone book made her
    husband shiver—
"Honey, put on that record of Rin Tin Tin eating Mel Ferrer;
You know that, next to the record of a rat trying on hats at the sock bazaar,
It is my favorite among all the records." A record of Ellen's answer
Was never made. Another record is the record of nothing, or the one r.p.m.
    record of Sonja Henie's skates.
A deer bought the first record of horns growing from an Alaskan hermit,
And the glass record of the Dreyfus trial is preserved in the Oceanographic

Institute of Vladivostok.

The record of General MacArthur eating his first beetle dinner has been turned on too loud.

Somehow a record of *Pal Joey* has escaped the gravity belt and become an artificial satellite.

That poor person over there has a record of *Cosi fan tutte* in his stomach.

How many of you know the record of *Barney Google Asleep beside Victoria Falls?*

No one? Then what do you think of the mashed banana record of Coleridge reading his life insurance policy?

Or the record of Nelson's column in Trafalgar Square?

This record the size of a nickel of Romeo's voice

Is inaudible. And the record of beer citrus fruits rolled over the hill and was seen no more.

December, 1956

Crone Rhapsody

John Ashbery & Kenneth Koch

"Pin the tail on the donkey," gurgled Julia Ward Howe. A larch shaded the
   bathtub. From the scabiosa on the desk
The maple gladioli watched Emily Post playing *May I?* in the persimmon
   bathtub with the fan.
"Nasturtiums can be eaten like horseshoes," murmured the pumpkin, "but on
   Hallowe'en when Cécile Chaminade's *Rhapsody* roars in the beeches and a
   bathtub chair
Holds Nazimova, a lilac palm plays mumbledy-peg with an orange bathtub
   filing cabinet,
And Queen Marie of Roumania remembers the Norway maple." Pitching
   pennies from the cantaloupe bathtub, I remembered the poppy and the
   typewriter,
The mangrove and the larkspur bathtub. I saw a banana Carrie Nation ducking
   for apples in the lamp.

Oak dominoes filled the bathtub with a jonquil. A crabapple rolled slowly
   toward the Edith Wharton lamp,
Crying, "Elm shuffleboard! Let the bathtub of apricots and periwinkles give
   May Robson a desk!"
"Heavy, heavy hangs over thy head," chanted the black raspberry. A zinnia
   dropped from the plane tree into a rotting bathtub. Dame Myra Hess
   slumped over the typewriter
And wrote, "Dear Madame de Farge: A sycamore, an aster, and a tangerine,
   while playing scrub in my bathtub, noticed a fan
Of yours. Do you remember the old cottonwood tree by the auction bridge?
   It's now a bathtub. The freesia is gone. And an apple placed Queen
   Victoria in the filing cabinet.
Forget me not, as Laura Hope Crewes once spelt out in anagrams while we
   were all eating honeydew melon. I write you this from the bathtub and
   from a willow chair."

A raspberry bathtub was playing leapfrog with Sarah Allgood in the heather. Junipers hemmed in the yellow Ukrainian chair.

In the apple tree Queen Mary of the Chrysanthemums shared a grape rook bathtub with her insect lamp.

The cranberry juice was playing water polo with the dwarf plum tree. Margaret Dumont approached the bathtub. A song came from within the wisteria-covered filing cabinet—

The gooseberries were playing golf! Louisa May Alcott lifted a water lily from the poison-oak bathtub: "Put this on the desk,

Mrs. August Belmont." In the poison sumac grove a spitting contest was in full swing. The bathtub peeled seven mangoes, and a petunia fan,

Known to the orchid prune as Dame May Whittle's bathtub, felt curvaceous playing house with a eucalyptus typewriter.

The Clara Barton irises worshipped a baseball pineapple. O bathtub! "A birch rod," wrote the typewriter

Of papaya (its bathtub keys tapped by Bess Truman sitting beneath the cypress— or was it a grape hyacinth?), "guided the society craps game from a red chair

To where the cherry polo faded under the holly tree." "Pear-blossom," called Edna May Oliver to the brick bathtub, "fetch me my fan.

It's over there on the Lydia E. Pinkham musical chairs." But peach ash smothered the bathtub with a calendula lamp.

"Capture the flag," whispered briar rose to mandarin orange. Standing by the bathtub, Lady Gregory thought of her spruce desk.

"A grapefruit for your tulip," Ethel Barrymore said to the cherry tree checkers. And the bathtub knew the embrace of the filing cabinet.

That was the year that a calla lily bought Colette's *Ice Hockey* in the capital of Honduras. It was the year of the bathtub Ice Age and the flowering of the stone pear. The catalpa shivered gently in the shade of the filing cabinet.

Then Barbara Frietchie skipped rope under the gingko tree, spitting buttercups on the loganberry bushes. In the dim light of the bathtub formed a typewriter.

The bathtub fell amid orange blossoms. The black walnut tree fell amid lemon soccer balls. Marie Brizard fell under the desk.

But who won the sack race? Spirea split the bathtub. Why, here is Susan B. Anthony holding up a raisin to the sequoia chair!

And here is the Joshua tree. Mistinguett thought about the tomato. The bathtub
was nailing up the rules for seven-card stud by the light of a crocus lamp.
All of these things were confided by a pine tree to a primrose in the bathtub.
Inside the pomegranate Ivy Compton-Burnett was playing hand tennis
with her fan.

In her locust bathtub Maria Ouspenskaya was playing spin-the-bottle with a
violet strawberry. The big fan
Who had once known Mary Roberts Rinehart, strangled by hemlock, wanted the
rose whortleberry to play doctor with it in the bathtub. A tiny filing cabinet
Was reading Harriet Beecher Stowe's *One Potato Two Potato* to a blueberry in a
room that contained no furniture other than a bathtub, a poplar, and a
dogwood lamp.
Cowboys and Indians brought the shasta daisy to watermelon Eleanor Roosevelt.
In the meantime a horse-chestnut tree had gotten into the bathtub with the
typewriter.
"I saw Lily Muskmelon and Tag Football just now. They were on their way to
Margaret Sanger's new place, The Baobab Tree," chorused the bathtub.
"When I think that that chair
Once held Alice B. Toklas, I don't give a fig for what I catch from the live-
oak tree or the cowslip!" Then the bathtub became silent as a desk.

The crabapple tree screamed. The carnation said, "I am a hundred years old!"
The breadfruit fell onto the desk. In the post-office bathtub an Edith
Sitwell fan
Muttered, "I want a bathtub." Forgetful of contract bridge, Alison Skipworth
pulled up a chair to the yew tree and looked for *heliotrope* and *blood orange*
in its filing cabinet.
The gentian finished chopping down the linden. The kumquat typewriter was
attacked by Grace Coolidge. She wrote, "When I play cops and robbers I
need a bathtub lamp!"

The Car

Jane Freilicher & Kenneth Koch

Choke: I am a bloke. My name is choke.

Wheel: I am a wheel, central feel of the automobile.

Gear: I am a gear. You all fear me.

Tires: I am the tires, a raspberry is filled with sins.

Window: I am a window. I know everything.

Windshield Wiper: I am a wiper of window that shieldwiper.

Crank: I am a crank.

Crankcase: I am a crankcase.

Nurse: Bottoms up.

Transmission: I am the transmission, ever close to you.

Trunk: I am a trunk, full of personality.

Dashboard: I am my setting sun, a dashboard.

Clutch: I clutch. We like each other.

Brake: Brake, brake, brake.

Shift: Shifty me you like to see.

Roof: I am roof, the winter's tooth.

Throttle: They call me throttle. Relax everybody.

Backseat: I am the backseat. Climb up and down.

Petroleum: I am petroleum, love's dream.

Doctor: Where the hell is that nurse?

Nurse: I am in the glove compartment.

Glove Compartment: I am the glove compartment, your love department.

St. Bridget's Neighborhood

Bill Berkson & Frank O'Hara

Her shoe fits today   It is St. Bridget
turning the corner   She wears blue Maybelline

on her eyelids and in a streak on her hair
She will never have a baby, thank goodness! Her hair

brushes the sidewalk where all is dusk   The
afternoon is leaning toward drinks   I am getting

myself one right now though I shouldn't   Would
you like one, heaviness of the compost thresh-

hold?   No, I want the plants to have it, for
they have died   Sometimes the streets are full

of snot sometimes the traveling ferris-wheel
pulls up in its truck singing like a Good Humor truck

sometimes the street gets soft as taffy
and feels nice to the green foot sneaking along

Hee hee and the tea bags are drooping from ledges
and the droops are drooling like spoons   She

is supposed to watch over them   She is a lamp
Their feet are blue   hee hee   She is the Saint

of Hysteria as Dvorak steams along over QXR
and in the mood you're in you're lucky you're here

but so am I it gives a kind of neighborhoodliness
to everything   I like to go around with attractive

people it makes me feel humble like her up there
on the floor down here   Only the lonely

is a wish afforded the ice cream person   I have
a headache, I want to have a heartache   (to begin:)

My heart is corresponding oddly and with odd things and I
sometimes wonder if the future holds nothing

but the Surgical-Dental Supply Co. and Disney
the light is getting dim and a softness is settling

over the aluminum appliances and the fire escapes
and a fresh green paint over my royal flush heart

There is nothing like a comrade in one's journey
toward the bathroom   Cleanliness

is next to godliness, so we clean it up!   It's saintly
to come from anywhere but from where you're going

St. Bridget I wish you would wake up and tend my bumper
It's cracked it is like the thought

I had of you when I cut myself shaving "O steeple
why don't you help me as you helped the Missouri islanders?"

But I know it is missing (my belief in you) although
I love you because I feel you are the only thing

that cares or wants me in its thoughts But I guess
I am there anyway   But how wonderful when someone lets you know

Yes we have games on our street too though the little girls
think a ball game is throwing the ball through my window

and I rather like these minor attentions when I
am not alone and it is nice for me when you are not alone

An orchestra is never alone   St. Bridget is never alone
although she must feel lonely when we ask her such questions

Is the nest an animal too?

1960

Song Heard Around St. Bridget's

Bill Berkson & Frank O'Hara

When you're in love the whole world's Polish
and your heart's in a gold stripped frame
you only eat cabbage and yogurt
and when you sign you don't sign your own name

If it's *above* you you want and you know it
and the parting you want's in your hair
the yogurt gets creamy and seamy
and the poles that you climb aren't there

To think, poor St. Bridget, that you never got to see an Ingmar Bergman movie
because you were forbidden our modern times
but you're not as old as all that, you're not a mummy
you saw the Armory Show and Louis Jouvet
and Mary of Scotland and ANCHORS AWEIGH
                                       and we're sure
that you've caught up with La Vie et Esprit poetically pure
and are indeed quite contemporary and just as extraordinary
as ice cubes and STONES and dinosaur bones and manure

When you're in love the whole world's a steeple
and the moss is peculiarly green
you may not be liked or like people
but you know your love's on your team

When you're shaving your face is a snow bank
and your eyes are particularly blue
and your feelings may be fading and go blank
but the soap is happy "It's you!"

1960

St. Bridget's Efficacy

Bill Berkson & Frank O'Hara

The basic problem of Latin America
is that you're here, St. Bridget
how they miss you and your crooked
nose and your calming influence
they're all stirred up! I think
of you as climbing the arroyo
like a bandito in your rage   you are
the true war between money and despair
Bread is responsible for you and you're here
a short pause for statue identification
what if you were once Rosa de Lima?
what if you were an earthquake? or a bull?
The secret of your force is that you're ugly
the secret of your ugliness is your love that storms
the pampas like the dust that's dry and convinces
it's human   You are the real Communista
you are attractive and poor   you are a horse
become a cloud of grey that bores us   it's brown
whenever you sit   What if you were once Bolivar
in Central Park?   Or the Southern Cross which we remember
as a gas station?

7/3/61

PROCESS NOTE

Updated from *Hymns of St. Bridget* by Bill Berkson & Frank O'Hara:

One autumn afternoon in 1960, Frank and I were walking up First Avenue [in New York City] and suddenly noticed something odd about St. Bridget's Irish Catholic church on the Avenue B side of Tompkins Square Park, across from Frank's place at 441 East Ninth Street, near Avenue A. The left-hand steeple of the church was curving inward. This flaw (on account of which, apparently, years later, the steeple was removed) struck both of us as hilarious. Later that day, I went home and wrote "Hymn to St. Bridget's Steeple," the first of the "St. Bridget" series, in rather clunky imitation of what Frank later called his "I do this I do that poems." Most of the hymns were written, taking turns at the typewriter, either at Frank's or at Larry Rivers's house in Southampton. Frank's keyboard attack was fabulously quick, so most of these—as well as most of the other collaborations we did—are mostly by him, and the parts by me are mostly me trying to keep up. [. . .] Whenever the exact date of writing is indicated on the manuscript I have included it (the dates are cumulatively October 19, 1960 to April 1, 1962). Otherwise, the set is pretty much in the order as retyped by Frank for a possible book manuscript (he thought Grove Press might be interested) in 1962.

"St. Bridget's Neighborhood" was partly in imitation of Robert Desnos's "Quartier San Merri."

Note: The name of the eponymous Irish saint is actually spelled "Brigid."

BILL BERKSON

Reverdy

Bill Berkson & Frank O'Hara

Reverdy is not Chopin. He is a long city street with small musical houses on it.

There is a word, *rédacteur*, in French, of which I cannot recall the meaning.

Here are two cups, a Keats, a comb and a brush, four packs of cigarettes, an ashtray labeled "Chance," two boxes of matches, a rope, *Always Love a Stranger*, a wire brush and a carved piece of wood, which I cannot understand. This is where Reverdy still lives, inexplicable as ever.

What strikes the eye hurts, what one hears is a lie. What is written struggles through, and then has struggled through and is white. The snow lasts because of the sun. Never letters, always messages.

Here we are, getting ideas like the French, yippee!

We discovered many years ago that in French you *can* say anything . . . Except certain things which Eliot, Valéry, Claudel, Béranger and others have said. Yippee!

Reverdy is not a cubist. Who ever was? One hundred Americans a day are accused of cubism. "The pubic area of the male is not a thing of beauty." "The public area of the female is not a thing of beauty." (These are two American sayings showing a lack of Reverdy.)

Picasso is fire, Reverdy is flint. In America flint is used for arrowheads as well as tinderboxes. Do you like to hunt for what you eat? Are you a cannibal? Is there order outside of insanity or just a maelstrom of velleities and mistakes?

Je suis las de vivre dans le pays natal. When you get to the maelstrom let me know. If you have to pick the ashes off your cigarette, you are born to any given work of modern art. We no longer know what wires are wrapped around us than what air we breathe. We no longer care who is next door; we know how they feel about us. One drinks more than one thinks. There is no sense in coming home "early." We are already in the maelstrom which is why we don't "know" it. I want to get up "early."

In America there is only one other poet *beside* Reverdy: William Carlos Williams. They are both alone. How do you feel about titles like *They Are Both Alone, Wake Up and Die, You Die with Your Eyes Open Don't You?, Chair Vive, Poem?*

We have made ourselves cretins for Reverdy's sake.

We must all pretend to feel fine or get shot like a horse.

Written for the French of John Ashbery, Paris, 1961

PROCESS NOTE

In Paris, fall 1961, John Ashbery invited Frank to write something for an issue of *Mercure de France* honoring Pierre Reverdy who had died of a heart attack, July 17, 1960. Frank had the idea that we should collaborate for the occasion, and John agreed to translate what we wrote into French for the issue, which appeared the following spring. *You Die with Your Eyes Open Don't You* and *Wake Up and Die* were two of the working titles for a Horace McCoy-type lowlife novel Joe LeSueur was working on at the time.

BILL BERKSON

Waves of Particles

Bill Berkson, Michael Brownstein & Ron Padgett

Television is great. The wind blows
across a screen in Nevada, Utah. That's great,
greater than Utah. The little dots come out to play
in lines of grey and waves of gravy. Navy blue.
A physicist lights a cigarette on a horse,
although he doesn't know it
because the TV doesn't show it.
But we can see it although we can't smoke it.
Maybe that's the end of it, a little dot of light
shining its name on the great white what.

PROCESS NOTE

"Waves of Particles" was written in late summer 1969 by Michael Brownstein, Ron Padgett and me at my mother's house (code name "Brenda" in honor of the hurricane that passed through around the time the poem was written) in Port Jefferson, Long Island. As I recall, Michael Brownstein wrote down Ron's and my lines as we called them out, and his own in response, on a pad of paper and thus was both coauthor and "director" of the poem. "Waves" first appeared in *The World of Leon* (Big Sky, 1974) and then in my book *Enigma Variations* (Big Sky, 1975).

BILL BERKSON

Within the Dome

Ron Padgett & James Schuyler

There's a daisy nodding
Over my forearm
Both the sun and moon are setting into my bicep
and the bay slips onto my foot
wet, cold and blue as a sneaker
on which Mrs. Captain Jimmy Quinn just spilled a glass of ice tea
things like that happen
tidying up an island
unfortunately we are not tidying up this island we are covering it with filth
Seeing us come stickily back from the bay
Mrs. Captain Jimmy Quinn reflects, "Filth is merely relative.
Are they cleaner
or are they not?"
And here her eye is drawn out over
Penobscot
Where Buckminster Fuller is reading the *Bangor Times* and chuckling
                                   quietly to himself
ELLSWORTH ELKS DISBAND
he reads
PORTLAND FESTIVITIES MARK
ANNIVERSARY OF FIRE
                     GRASSES READY
                     ANNUAL SPLURGE
                         and
                         FULLER DOME TO RISE
"May I have that paper?" states Mrs. Captain Jimmy Quinn.
"I'm going to burn this wood."
A sneaker shaped boat toots once in the fog.
"Is there anybody there?" cries a sailor.
"Why yes," answers Mrs. Quinn.
"You're quite near to shore, you know."
Just then a great spruce reached over and slapped him hard on the cheek.
Crunchingly, the *Dora Maar* had docked on a tidal crag.

"You don't know how humiliating this is for me," said the Captain.
Buckminster Fuller joined Mrs. Quinn in a sympathetic nod.
"Who might you be?" the latter queried.
"Olaf Pedersen,"
averred the salt.
You may not remember Olaf Pedersen
Neither do I
The light is throwing lots of blue into your eyes

★

Some houseflies join me
in what has become deep shade
Yes, I can hear dinner approaching now
it is a large quiet housefly
"Ow!"
Yes, the tide of my hunger is sloshing against my gall stones
yes, as the great Joe Brainard once said,
"You can't beat meat, potatoes and a green vegetable"
So Mrs. Quinn, will you set fire to that wood?
Within the dome
Buckminster Fuller gets out the steel and the knife
as she goes about her feminine tasks.

Inner Landscapes

Ted Berrigan & Ron Padgett

1.

Why don't you tell everyone about it, he said to her,
I mean, you know, about all those terrible things, dogs
And all, and death, the terrible dying, I mean, like
In talking about it. Everyone would like it, I think,
I mean, it would be inspiring, you know, and everything.

Then John turned back to his grasshopper and sipped it quietly.
Under these harsh conditions conversation was, to put it mildly,
Easy. Here he was, alone with Edna, who had recently fallen
Victim to Polio in their rouge hut in the Arctic wastes.
He had found her, helpless, driveling on a soft bank of snow,
Being licked by dogs and the fidgety image of death.
Trying to persuade her to make use of her new-found talents
Was difficult since her jaw was immobile and hence
Her vocal abilities at their worst. "I have an idea," said John
In a queer tone of voice. "You know of course that the amount
Of space occupied by an electron as it spins around in its Atomic Orbit
Is equivalent to the space taken by a bee flying around inside Madison
Square Garden." "Gee," said Phoebe Apollo, "I didn't know that."
"Oh," said John in a rather embarrassed tone of voice. "Well, anyway,
I suggest that we organize a night patrol in order to determine
Exactly what is going on here. The three of us will spread out and
Surround everything, and you, since I am the oldest, will seize the Bee."
John demurred at this, and suggested exactly the opposite,
To which all concurred.

Years later, deep in enemy territory, John often thought about
His decision that night, and how everything might have been different
Had he acted differently. But no time to think of that now. He turned to
His desk and wrote in his tiny notebook,
"Should a drop of water be enlarged to the size of THE EARTH
Each molecule would be the size of a plum." John

Marveled for a moment, and then swallowed a memory pill, which soon
Took effect, shrinking the memory molecules in his mind
To plum size, causing him to plumb fergit everythin' he ever knew.
The only thing that he could remember was the word "plum."

Taking this as a clue to his past and the identity of his person,
He began to investigate the ramifications
Of the plumbing of his igloo, a dwelling.

His attention was disturbed by the sudden lodging of a beebee
In his aorta. What memories suddenly sprung to mind! "John!"
He said, running over to Edna and Kiki, hugging them both. Then
He made a million dollars. Then he ran into Jesse James,
A member of the B Bar B Boys. Bullets were emitted from his gun.
The bullets had been fashioned from the rotten carcasses

Of bees. One of these fateful missiles was destined for Bea,
Jesse's aged ma. "Ma!" cried Jesse, covered with whelps and wops.
"That sounded like a host of bees traversing the Autobahn," said Pop.
But outside in the bee-infested darkness the patrol silently crouched.
John wrote it all down. Then he carefully sealed it up in an envelope
Shaped like the love in his heart and tied it to the back of Edna
His faithful bee. "Now take this note to Tulsa," he said, "and deliver
It to me." With that, off she buzzed and then we left. "Goodbye," we said
And then we left. "Goodbye!" Slowly the answer buzzed in our ears:

"Goodbye, and fare thee well, from your little friend, The Bee."

2.

"In the old days it was never like this," he said. "Why when I was a bee,
A bee was a bee you could call a bee! None of this buzzing around
For us! Why, when I see these young bees buzzing around, I get so mad
I could spit!" So saying, he resumed his seat. Then mighty Edna,
Strongest of all the bees, begged permission to speak. Apollo passed
Him the baton, and Mighty Edna stood and spoke thusly: "Breathes
There a man with soul so dead, who never to himself has buzzed,
'This is my own, my native hive?'" He sat down to thunderous applause.
Years later this was forgotten.

3.

John stood in front of the Polar Gates, back to the bee,
And waved his stinger at the approaching seals. "Areté!" he muttered,
Defiantly. "Breakthrough!" they barked. Then they gently spitted him,
Turned him over thrice, roasted him up and up, and tasted his weeping
Beeflesh. Up in the interesting hive his wife and baby bees
Wept. "Honey," cried his wife, "I'll miss you." Then she dropped the honey
On the heads of the footmen in the forefront of the seal force,
Forcing the seal wave to slip and fall. They slipped, and then
They fell. They got up. It got them down. They turned tail.
Their pride was stung. They made a bee-line for home, underneath
The ice, far away; near where their mommies and daddies waited
In the pages of encyclopedias, beneath the dim watery eyes of
Henri Fabré, the last being on earth to take an interest
In "The Plight of the Bumblebee." "Honey," said Henri, "I have
A confession to make. I was never really in love with Bea."
At this Henri embraced Kiki (both in rapture).
Standing in the doorway of the conical blubber hut
They stared far out into the oatmeal which by now was beginning to boil.

Noh

Ted Berrigan & Ron Padgett

In 1935 W. B. Yeats went out to get the mail
Box before the advent of the Cincinnati glacier
In this comic strip that keeps going thru my head
Good-bye lovely comic strip of the smell of sex
Near today's bright sweet smell
The American version dropped into the icy well

W. B. Yeats arranged for a new reading at the well
He sat beside her beside the fog to get the mail
Whose smell
Became a new portent of the fiery glacier
Hello sweet glacier of the new version of sex
Everything coming that way to a head

A sudden explosion of what grows above the head
Green as the corpse of the adolescent in the well
Good-bye lovely Lolita of the burgeoning sex
Is that what Yeats thought about the mail
Box before the advent of the Cincinnati glacier
Coming under the heading of "smell"

I fell under the mild nose of the smell
Of my own head
Cold as the bed in which reposes the glacier
Hugged by a fiery girl who is boding him well
What mail
Arrives at us then! Hello lovely mail from the changing sex

Good-bye ugly mail of the broken sex
Depending on one's ability to smell
What's coming in the mail
Or to switch on the head
We shall soon set sail up the burning well
Headlong into the century of the glacier

Here are the billion cubes that were once the glacier
Good-bye phallic droplets devoid of sex
In this comic strip that keeps going into the well
So that now I think I never more shall smell
The head next to Yeats' head
A drawing of which I once received in the mail

Yeats, you have carried the mail into the glacier
On your head. So good-bye to your ancient sex
And its icy smell, that has performed so well

circa 1964

Think of Anything

Ted Berrigan & Robert Creeley

The Rose of Sharon
lights up
Grand Valley

Now
Robert Creeley speaks:

the air is getting
darker
and darker

the Rose of Sharon
moves

towards the door

and through.

PROCESS NOTE

I cannot remember very clearly the date specific, but it must have been during
the time that Ted and Alice were in Bolinas, and also Phil Whalen—and the three
of us went (flew) together to the National Poetry Festival that Robert vas Dias
had got together in that place he was then teaching just above Gerald Ford's
birthplace—Grand Rapids, etc. Very religious country, and the pukka students
disliked our gang intensely. But a few approved—as the implicit "Sharon" of our
collaboration, a pleasant young woman, like they say, who, together with her
boyfriend, found Ted especially intriguing. Did we write it in a bar? No doubt
we were sitting down somewhere in relaxed company, demonstrating our
prowess as poets. That's the only time I collaborated with Ted, or quite possibly
with anyone else either. It was fun!

ROBERT CREELEY

from **Memorial Day**

Ted Berrigan & Anne Waldman

I was asleep
in Ann Arbor

    dreaming

        in Southampton

      beneath the summer sun of a green backyard

    & up from a blue director's chair

I heard a dead brother say
           into the air

"Girl for someone else in white walk by"

        ★

I was asleep in New York

        dreaming in Southampton

& beneath the sun of the no sun sun up from my morning bed

    I heard the dead, the city dead

    The devils that surround us
never die

      the New York City devil inside me
           alive all the time

   he say

     "Tomorrow you die"

*

I woke up

       as he typed that down:

"Girl for someone else in white walk by"

       & then,

           so did I.

So my thanks to you

           the dead.

The people in the sky.

*

A minute of silent pool
       for the dead.

*

& now I can hear my dead father saying:

           "I stand corrected."

*

Dolphins, (as we speak)
are carrying on 2
conversations simultaneously

& within the clicks of one
lie the squeaks of the other
       they are alive in their little wandering pool

*

"I wonder what the dead people are doing today?"

(taking a walk, 2nd St. to GEM SPA)

(or loping down Wall St.
                                    Southampton)

★

ghost the little children

            ghost radio   ghost toast

                    ghost stars

        ghost airport
                    the ghost of Hamlet's father

ghost typewriter

                ghost lover

                                    ghost story

ghost snow   roasted ghost

            ghost in the mirror ghost

    happy ghost   most ghost

★

I dreamt that Bette Davis was a nun, we
Were in a classroom, after school, collating
The World. Jr. High. A knocking at the door, I
Went to answer (as Bette disappeared), & found my mother
Standing in the hallway.
            "Teddy," she said, "here

Is my real *mother*, who brought me up, I've always wanted
for you to meet her." Beside my mother stood
a tall, elegant lady, wearing black, an austere, stylish
Victorian lady whose eyes were clear & black; grand as
Stella Adler, but as regal & tough as Bette Davis.

Later that evening she sent me out for kippers for her bed-
time snack, giving me a shilling to spend. I went for them
to Venice, to a Coffee-House, which had a canal running right through it,
& there I ran into Ron, sitting with a beautiful boyish adolescent
blonde. "She's a *wonderful* lady," Ron said, & I was pleased.
Ron left shortly with the blonde nymphet, & I wondered a minute
about Pat (Ron's wife); but decided that Ron must know what he's doing.
    The girl, I thought, must be The Muse.

                                    ★

            She is a muse

            gone but not forgotten

                        ★

            50 STATES

            state of grace

            the milk state

            Oregon

            stateroom

            state of anxiety

            hazy state

            estate

statement

Rugby Kissick state

Florida

the empire state

disaster state

the lightbulb state

soup state

Statue of Liberty

state of no return

the White Bear state

doped state

recoil state

Please state your name, address, occupation

the German shepherd state

bent on destruction

                state

the farmer state

state of no more parades

the tobacco state

statesman

stately

state prison

stasis

status

static

station wagon

State Flower

★

state of innocence

★

ambition state

North Carolina

Jasper's state

the united state

big state

state your cause

income state

jump the gun state

Roman nose state

manic depression state

35

hospital state

speed state

calculated state

gone forever state

the body state

the death body state

                    ★

In New York State

    in 'Winter in the Country'

        at night you write

while someone

    (Alice) sometimes sleeps & dreams;

        awake she writes

22.

I dreamed you brought home a baby
Solid girl, could already walk
In blue corduroy overalls
Nice & strange, baby to keep close
I hadn't thought of it before
She & I waited for you out by the door
Of building, went in
Got you from painting
Blue & white watercolor swatches
We got on a bus, city bus

One row of seats lining it & poles
It went through the California desert
Blue bright desert day

In the country of old men I said
                            pretty good
& tho I live there
                no more
                        "you can say that again."

                Pretty good.

                        ★

It takes your best shot,
                    to knock off whatever,

so, we take our best shots
                    it gives us a boot or two

        we just do it

        we wouldn't know what to tell you

    if our lives depended upon it!

            Anne?

        but Anne's already talking

across from me   across my life

        across the mailman's
    locked box,

                over the mailman
                    I mean

where a woman is alive
                         a mailman her friend
                   as you all know
          having met the man at the Met
     introduced by Vincent,
                         & loved by Joe:

     Joe's introductions go on,

the tongue, the ears burn   on Memorial Day

          at Anne's turn:

                         ★

     Dear Mr. Postman:

          Please take this from me

                              to me

                    ★

          I'm delivered without a hitch
          to myself

                         ★

I'm a woman in the Prime of Strife

I speak for all you crazy ladies

     past & present

          & I say,

               NO MESSAGES

*

Nothing can be helped.   Nothing gets lost.

*

Blink

the eye is closed

& I am asleep
blink

the eye is open

& I am awake

in the *real* wide-eye world   nothing gets lost

*

Today was a day to remember death:

I remember the death

of Hitler

& now I think of The Song of Roland

Roland's death

& now I think to see
if there were similarities

& now I see there were . . .

*

39

& now I wonder what Tom Clark thinks

Edwin, Alex, Dick . . .

Mike?

*

A lung aching in the room

inside Mike

disease bringing you a little closer

Forget it!

Piss on it!

Kiss my ass!

he say

in his absolute way

Everybody obey

But

we are all victims

(me too)

& we all love life

(too bad)

*

I told Ron Padgett that I'd like to have

NICE TO SEE YOU

engraved on my tombstone.

Ron said he thought he'd like to have

OUT TO LUNCH

on his.

★

Dear Lewis:

I've been down but I'm surfacing

I've been lost but now I'm found

"One will leaf one's life all over again"

you say

& you are right

around & around & around go the swirling leaves

Death is *not* is *not* so horrible   today

PROCESS NOTES

The fact that Ted and I were scheduled to give a reading on Memorial Day at the Poetry Project launched this collaboration, a "meditation" on death. The poem was also an extension of, and conversation within our spacious friendship which also lead to a mimeographed edition, a performance and an "archive"– the cheap tape of the first reading at the Poetry Project that was passed around and copied. (Ted left town with the original tape and I was only able to get a copy from Clark Coolidge, years later.) It was an early performance piece–multi-voiced, with sung parts that we predetermined for the reading.

Ted was extremely focused and energetic during the entire collaboration and we sent & exchanged pages back & forth to each other regularly that spring of 1971. I took on the final task of "arrangement" with scissors, tape and paste in hand, laying cut-up sections out on the floor of the studio I was renting in Bridgehampton (later Kenneth Koch's house) to collage the poem together. The process was physical, instinctual and I remember thinking this is sort of like Pollock with words. I was listening to the flow of Terry Riley and Pibrok (Scot's bagpipe) music, hoping a sense of the seamless conversation between ourselves & others in the poem would come through. Also a sense of urgency prevailed to get the mini-epic ready for our reading at the Project.

It was a great pleasure to read the final section "The widow is closed" (which was inspired by something Chrissie Gallup–Dick and Carol Gallup's young daughter–had said) alternating lines with Alice Notley at an event honoring the publication of *The Collected Poems of Ted Berrigan* at the Poetry Project in 2005. There was also a Funhouse press edition published in New York City in 2005 with cover art by Zachary Wollard. The poem has had a long shelf life, with the earlier 1974 Aloes Edition, and was also included in the now out-of-print edition of my book *Journals & Dreams* (Stonehill, 1976).

ANNE WALDMAN

From *The Collected Poems of Ted Berrigan:*

Memorial Day was published twice as a chapbook, once in 1971 by the Poetry Project, in mimeo format, and once in 1974 by Aloes Books, London (editors Jim Pennington, Allen Fisher, and Dick Miller). For the Poetry Project edition, Anne Waldman and Ted ran off copies for the occasion of [a] May 1971 reading mentioned in the introduction. Donna Dennis did the original cover art, which was reproduced in facsimile in the Aloes Books edition. *Memorial Day* was reprinted in *So Going Around Cities*.

"I dreamed you brought home a baby": One of Ted's and Anne Waldman's intentions in *Memorial Day* was to include other voices. This sonnet by me, designated by the number "22" and beginning with the line "I dreamed you brought home a baby" is number 22 of a sonnet sequence called *165 Meeting House Lane* (New York: C Press, 1971).

"having met the man at the Met": In this convoluted passage written by Ted, the "man" is Frank O'Hara, "Joe" is Frank's partner Joe LeSueur, and "Vincent" is Frank's lover, Vincent Warren.

"It is night. You are asleep. & beautiful tears": This is Sonnet XXXVII from *The Sonnets*.

[...]

During the time that Ted was co-writing *Memorial Day*, he was listening obsessively to two record albums, Mississippi John Hurt's *Today!* (which contained "Talking Casey") and an album by the Byrds. His composition process involved being interactive with the music, as if there were something about "voice" he wanted to get from actual singing. And the finished poem is for alternating voices, Waldman's arrangement of the text alternating sections by the two of them.

"The windows are closed": The final litany [not included here], written by Ted, was read by the two poets in voices alternating for each phrase ending with "is closed." After the reading at the Poetry Project, Ted obtained a copy of the tape and listened to it as obsessively as he had to the John Hurt and Byrds albums. He continued to learn from this collaboration for many years and in the early 80s occasionally asked me to read the final litany with him, as a separate piece, at poetry readings.

ALICE NOTLEY

A Crown of Western Sonnets

Tom Disch & Marilyn Hacker

I

The flat red earth stretched out on either side
taps out the rhythm of Route 66.
On the turnpike where the lanes divide
we stopped to ask the distance to the Styx,
and he said, "You cannot buy cowboy boots,"
beside a patch of parched grass where we once
had drunk with publishers and prostitutes.
Day followed day, demurely as the Lunts
in *Sleeping Beauty*. She admonished him
to draw a parallel between this trip
and water wings for Charles, who cannot swim.
He spoke his lines; *she* bit her lower lip.
We saw, among the heaps of junked-out cars,
plain folk in Texas, but in Vegas, stars.

II

Plain folk in Texas, but in Vegas, stars
collected photographs of murderers.
Policemen chewing on wet black cigars
recalled to him those nervous tics of hers
which restaurants serve in Frisco with French names
which burn his eyes and spoil his appetite.
The road is bumpy, the air is hot; she blames
casuists who probed the tripartite
species of plants and animals we've seen
in a Polish poem. The yucca flats
stop at the green seacoast, not in between
truckers' cafes and all-night laundromats.
The toughest part of everyday is when
Albuquerque entices us again.

III

Albuquerque entices us again
to buy bullwhips and hunting knives, gunbelts
and rented formal wear for gentlemen
for Charles, who has the fair skin of the Celts.
Between the mesquite and the fallen slabs
we scrawled GOOD FOOD in letters ten feet high
and wondered if the itching came from crabs
or sparseness. Long white lines across the sky,
the product of a schizophrenic brain,
plunge ahead to Arizona as
aborigines inflicted pain.
We've bought a hundred dollars worth of gas!
If we are neat and quiet and polite
perhaps poor Charles will freeze to death tonight.

IV

Perhaps poor Charles will freeze to death tonight
and crystallize into the canyon's rim.
The paranoid delusions of the Right
lure and devour poor travellers like him.
"This is a landscape for geometers,"
she said. "All right, I'll feed it,'" he replied,
"but I will need a pair of silver spurs."
The Hopi goatherds on the mountainside
grow cold as ice cream, red as cherries. Shoot!
When will my red begonia and my cat
grow lean and skinny living on a butte?
Not while I'm so concupiscent and fat.
The grandiose is inconvenient:
they won't get all the postcards that we sent.

V

They won't get all the postcards that we sent
from dried-out riverbeds and sandstone cliffs
recalling our original intent
to faint from hunger after just a whiff
of Charles' sun-reddened profile at the wheel.
If goats and cows find munchables out here,
why can't we tell our mothers how we feel?
I'd pay ten dollars for a glass of clear
Texaco Hi-Test. He wanted to shit
in Reno on a dare. She doffed her hat
and said, "You're so vulgar you're exquisite.
I've got to take off forty pounds of fat."
When friendship is subjected to a strain,
our bed will jiggle, and the clouds will rain.

VI

Our bed will jiggle, and the clouds will rain
horrific torrents into Morro Bay,
where, having said good-bye to Charles, a pain
followed the freeway traffic through L.A.
Above our heads is hung a copper sunburst
which keeps us from becoming movie stars.
Today we'll pay to see the wealth of Hearst
and leave our manuscripts in rented cars.
We have escaped the smogs of Hollywood
but haven't picked up any hitchhikers.
Where are the little cubes of breakfast food,
thorns, nettles, gnats, mosquitoes, ticks and burrs?
The road reels by in billions of white flashes
like checks from out of state that no one cashes.

VII

Like checks from out of state that no one cashes,
the hills of iceplants swoon down to the beach
where the ice-green Pacific Ocean crashes.
The sea was warm. "Let's sail until we reach
Howard Johnson's," the park attendant said.
One can legitimately wonder how
he flails his arms and legs around in bed.
Unfabulous, a zebra and a cow
covered the upholstery with gritty
imitation turquoise Art-Nouveau
figurines of the name-saint of the city
that had been all the rage some years ago.
With shades of sea and sky, the cars deride
the flat red earth stretched out on either side.

PROCESS NOTES

The way we wrote the sonnets was—we didn't see the previous lines, but told
each other what the next line would have to do syntactically ("I've ended with
a preposition indicating direction," "I've made a statement you might qualify
with a simile," "I've ended with a transitive verb but not given the object.") They
are Shakespearean sonnets, so each person was doing his/her own rhymes,
except for the couplet where the person who did line one told the partner what
the rhyme sound was. Which produced, my favorite:

> The road reels by in millions of white flashes (Tom)
> Like checks from out of state which no one cashes. (Marilyn)

MARILYN HACKER

The chapbook that contained these sonnets, *Highway Sandwiches,* consisted of
sonnets by Marilyn Hacker and Tom Disch, and Marilyn Hacker and Charles
Platt, and also included the following note: "There are no sonnets by Charles
and Tom because Marilyn can't drive."

EDITORS

Freeze the Moment

Maxine Chernoff & Paul Hoover

Beings right in your face.
The sound of three O's
as distinguished from two,
about all your mouth can hold.
Sounds like someone rubbing the pipes
with a comb,
and you feel like you're going to sneeze,
but only yawn instead.
(They're cousins.)
There's batter in your heart
sometimes more than others.
So freeze the moment
when you look good.
Love means being right in your face,
little black and blue marks (ink).

1972

Slow Flurries

Maxine Chernoff & Paul Hoover

Like walking on ice
or pancake batter,
some days it takes all your energy
just to say three words.
The next day: more words.
Sensational snow flurries:
a breath tonic.
My arms are flying out,
yours "mushy," lost in
the bed,
meaning "I'm broken!"
You and I, we see,
do a lot of things at the same time
standing on the same patch of grass
often at different times
or different patches of grass
at the same time.
Two birds on the same stretch of air—
two leaves, different trees.
But pinching someone else's skin
is very different from pinching your own
a different shading.
If we pinch each other
at the same time,
we're doing the same thing
and we're proud.
Proud means happy.
Why is it, when I toss two rocks on the water,
one of them floats and the other sinks,
like two olives in a Martini,
or different Martinis.

1972

Process Note

Maxine and I met at the Body Politic reading series in Chicago in 1972. It was Halloween and everyone had to be in costume to read at the open mike. She was dressed as a football player, and despite my height of 6'5" I was dressed as a little boy, with a beanie on my head and a strap of books over my shoulder. The following week, we met again at a reading by Philip Whalen and went out afterwards. The poems were written in that year, before we were married. It was the year of Watergate and the Nixon impeachment hearings, which along with Cubs games we religiously watched on a black-and-white television. Much of the rest of our time was taken up with reading and writing poetry. Neither of us taught poetry for a living. I worked in management at Wesley Memorial Hospital, and Maxine waited tables at a bar in the Drake Hotel, where her customers included actor Forrest Tucker, the great conductor Sir George Solti, legendary White Sox. announcer Bob Elson, gossip columnist Irv Kupcinet, and Judge Julius Hoffman of Chicago Seven fame. She was also a University of Illinois Fellow. The local poets were Gwendolyn Brooks, Paul Carroll, Ted Berrigan, Bill Knott, Lisel Mueller, and Haki Madhubuti, among others. The idea of collaboration was in the air because of Berrigan, whose collaboration with Ron Padgett, *Bean Spasms,* was so much fun.

There was no special methodology to writing the poems. We simply took turns writing lines, handing the paper back and forth. They are the oldest poems either of us has in our possession, so old that they survived the conflagration when, in the belief that we could transform our work through a purification rite, we tossed our poetry manuscripts (we had one each) into a drum fire in the alley and solemnly watched them burn. This was our romantic vow to poesy. Twenty-five years later we collaborated on a double acrostic cento to present to Marjorie Perloff on her seventieth birthday. In the summer of 2004, because we both had some German, we translated seventy pages of poetry by Friedrich Hölderlin, with Maxine doing the first draft out loud and me writing it down. Then I would do several drafts at the computer before checking again with her. Our translations are our most extensive collaborations by far, and we plan to do more. At the same time, working with Nguyen Do, I translated the work of seventeen contemporary Vietnamese poets. I know virtually no Vietnamese, but Do is a wonderful poet and we worked well together. My task was to transform his English versions into a poem in English that would communicate the original intention of the work. It's fascinating to see into other minds, especially across culture. It has given me the impression that experience and perception are much more commonly shared than doctrines of cultural difference often suggest. The same with Hölderlin, who was insane for half of his life and wrote at the time of Napoleon but saw into the essential.

PAUL HOOVER

from **Polar Ode**

Eileen Myles & Anne Waldman

BLUE!
moon coming up in Aries this October 16
over Cherry Valley New York, slightly overcast
slightly wintry, starting to feel it in the marrow

Cherry Valley, home of the massacre about to be reenacted
on the very same spot with real live Indians. There's some
       history . . . . .

but about your history, Eileen:
    where were you before you got to be here?

      walked in the back door
         hugged Gen,
          my mother
    thought, Ma, you look like
         Gertrude Stein.

          Actually my mother was always
           fairly foxy
       painting walls, wallpapering rooms
         very physical
             it was a turnon to
             watch

      we drank coffee in the morning
      she read the *Boston Globe*
          picture of Allen Ginsberg, Andrei Voz-
nezensky

told Gen how Voz
            chased me around
                a room & she liked it.

she never figured out
what it was
I did

            so she appreciates these
            little jokes

my brothers son Joshua David Myles
the little Irish Jew

            I ate a revolting number of desserts
            as the micks ate mince pie,
                & squash, the jews
                ate jello mold &
                    debbie's cookies
                        & I'm against these sort of stereo-types.

                        Dear Sagittarius: Aries here
                            in a baroque phase
                        I'm working on this rash, a permanent tone
                    it's red for anger and aggression and sex and sunset
                        & transmute the chill in my fingerbones
                            type confident, now,
                                to spell the chill away

            I need a secretary to do this

Where is the White Winter Goddess?
            putting on her panty hose?
        her icy bangles?
                her winter pearls
                    & glitter?
        gaze on thee, til my eye-strings crackt with icy loves...

            need more jewelry in this poem

53

I suppose in the ancient druidical past
        Wasn't Stonehenge some sort of
    giant wrist watch to the
        stars and *today!*
      Maybe a dawn
        all the creepy little druids
        huddling around the hulky rocks
        and *Lo!*   Sun lines up with
          earth or
          pointy rock and
            Eep!   a vision
          the eye of winter
          is bright & white
        this morning
            something like that
    I mean thats the
            history of the situation.

    "a manifest fissure between thought and sensibility"
        seems as good a definition as any
            for you, Winter
    —something T. S. Eliot remarked about J. Donne, I think
    in "A Garland for John Donne"
        I mean
            my thoughts are warm—
                senses, cold

                which reminds me
    I've gotta take another oatmeal bath for strange hot rash
        it's hard, Eileen, keeping the body together
            & warm
        in the years of the coming plagues

more costume jewelry!

        and you should see
    her move in sleep &
      take her arm from
      me & turn her

back. O
 I gasp,
  it is the *Book I Read*
  in bed.

and you should see
 his body melt the ice
  reading THE TOWN AND THE CITY

this day has a way
 of being spent in bed. Heat's on:
  THE AWKWARD AGE
   and
  MUTHOLOGOS where Olson
   speaks
  Under the Mushroom:

it's a true love fest and a truth pill
 but you people are so literate
  I don't want to read to you anymore!

blue acara, blue alert, blue andalusia, blue eyed yellow macaw, blue anemone, blue angel, blue ant, blue asbestos (crocidolite), blue ash, blue ashes, blue baby, blue baby operation, blueback, blueback mullet, blueback salmon, blueback trout, blue bag, blue ball, blue basic lead sulfate, blue bass, bluehead, bluebear, bluebeard, bluebeard tongue, blue beech, bluebell, bluebells of scotland, blueberry, blueberry ash, blueberry maggot, blueberry root, blueberry thrips, blue bice, bluebill, blue billy, blue bindweed, blue birch, bluebird, blue biskop, blue-black, blue blazer, blue blazing star, blue blindness (tritanopia), blueblood, blueblossom, blue bonset, blue bonnet, blue book, blue bottle, blue brant, blue bream, bluebreast darter, blue-breasted quail, blue birch, blue brush, blueback, blue bug, blue bull, blue bunch grass also bluebund fescue bluebunch wheatgrass, blue bur, bluefish, bluecap, blue cardinal flower, blue catfish or blue channel fish, blue cheese, blue chip, blue coat, bluecoat boy, bluecoat school, blue cod, blue cohosh, blue collar, blue comb, blue copperas, blue copper ore, blue coral, blue crap, blue crane, blue creeper, blue crevally, bluecup, blue curls, blued, blue daisy, blue dandelion, blue darner, blue darter, blue devil, blue dicks, blue discharge, blue disease, blue doe, blue dog, blue dogwood, blue duck, blue duiker, blue earth, blue elder, blue ensign, blue-eye, blue eyed babies, bluets, blue-eyed grass, blue-eyed Mary, blue faced booby, blue false indigo . . . . .

> & there are a few more
> (show ended here)

Process Notes

Anne I think was very into collaborations. I mean everyone was at that time and it had mainly to do with staying up late and drinking with someone and whether you would have sex or not unless you were not of the right genders or whatever. It was definitely part of drinking or getting high. Having time. Anne I think proposed the collab. I give all this history since Anne, different from most people, seemed to publish her collaborations. I had seen her do this with others. I was part of a line. So we started out writing letters since she was mostly in Boulder, or Boulder and NY. Jim Brodey had a reading series at a club called Zu and we were to read there on the day of the winter solstice so maybe the collaboration came out of that. So finally Anne came over to my apartment one night (in NY) to finish the poem in person. I did want to have sex with her, so I asked her on the typewriter and that was the end of the poem.

EILEEN MYLES

I wanted to get to know Eileen better. I loved her dynamics on the page, her candid spirit, her magazine *Dodgems,* thus initiated the project which seemed to extend over a good chunk of time. I seemed more formal in retrospect and it's her contribution that keeps the poem from taking itself too seriously. O sleeping with Eileen, what a great fantasy, I was probably too scared. Greg Masters did the mimeo edition.

ANNE WALDMAN

Masters of Suspense

Susan Cataldo & Susie Timmons

Say you, say.
You're Joe Williams, aren't you?
Joe I simply can't believe it's you
After all these years!
We had a few good times back there,
Didn't we, old buddy?
What happened to your face?

We are Masters of Suspense.
We are Masters of Suspense.

We snuggle up before a warm fire
And begin to get to know each other better.
Snapping logs, roasting marshmallows,
What comes to mind is Paul Newman
Getting his head stuck in a gas oven
In *Torn Curtain*.

We are Masters of Suspense.
We are Masters of Suspense.

Free at last from the shackles that bind us,
We fall into each other's arms
And trembling, embrace.
My trembling increases.

We are Masters of Suspense.
We are Masters of Suspense.

The entire party is poised
Waiting for your arrival.
As you descend the winding stairs
Our eyes meet midway.
And beautiful, I think, beautiful,

You are more beautiful than ever before.
The immediate horror becomes painfully apparent.

We are Masters of Suspense.
We are Masters of Suspense.

You look so handsome in your uniform,
My daring, bold leader of the band.
You turn your head over your shoulder.
That's the last thing I remember.

We are Masters of Suspense.
We are Masters of Suspense.

2/2/79

Driven North by Poverty

Susan Cataldo & Susie Timmons

You fail to understand the uniqueness of our city

I see, I see
a mighty bird
& there's a priest
& there's god
& the virgin Mary
& God is holding up a tiny baby
& they're all sitting on a big cloud

Maybe not God.
How can you tell?
A salesman from Alabama
is wearing a red satin gown and blue cape
fashioned from peau de soie.

His swarming companions emerge from the reeds
to complete the ensemble of historic buildings

Machu Picchu
a dwarf cathedral
"viva el Peru!"

How serious those Indians are
with their fierce loaves of bread babies.
I'm not depressed about John Lennon;
at least he found the peace he sought.

It was only a year ago, by pickup truck.

PROCESS NOTE

The poems included here were written along with several others in the early 80s—probably 1981. Our decision to write them was about as impromptu as a plan to get together and go see a movie. I don't recall our collaborative process in precise detail but I can visualize in my mind's eye our four knees side by side beneath the table and can also hear Susan reading various lines out loud in a ridiculously portentous tone of voice. I certainly remember our glee escalating until we crumpled over the typewriter, too incapacitated by laughter to continue typing at all. We would then slide the machine back and forth toward each other along the tabletop. Once it flew right off the end of the table onto the floor. When Susan and I read "Masters of Suspense" at the Poetry Project, our dear friend Ann Rupel participated by singing an eerie thereminesque tune after each repetition of the chorus.

I feel really lucky to have belonged to a time, place and community where sharing such amusements was a commonplace occurrence among friends.

SUSIE TIMMONS

Today the Nuclear Bombs

Allen Ginsberg & Kenneth Koch

AG: Today the nuclear bombs arise in mind
KK: Allen sees danger to all human kind

AG: Kenneth delights him, feels but a flower
KK: I only think it, though, at a late hour

AG: But morning comes, and dawn with a ruinous blast
KK: Revives me, and makes me worry very fast

AG: Evening shadows steal with radioactive shadow
     Evening shadows steal with radioactive shade
KK: Full many a tune on this machine is played

AG: The hydrogen jukebox repeats the old prophecy
KK: And many a poem's writ by you and me

AG: Continuing for the generations yet to come
KK: I think to go on more like this is dumb

AG: Yet I came to this most absolute trial
KK: I think I'd like to give first lines a while

AG: Again, again, Kenneth, I will shut up
     And now it is your turn to wake it up

KK: Sweet are the uses of adversity
AG: And many are the dungeons undersea

KK: And many are the octopus inside them
AG: And flowers that upon their brows bestride them

KK: And many are the mermaids dancing, singing
AG: And the seaweed to their ears and ankles clinging

KK: How clean an image you produced, I thought
AG: Rather than continue Armageddon, which I brought

KK: To this our audience tonight, yet still
AG: [inaudible] . . . joyful will

KK: To get back to the ocean, and its depths
AG: Where we were before, before we got our trips

KK: I won't use orange, and I won't use silver
AG: Well, I'll try to keep it outside of quicksilver

KK: Those two are words for which there is no rhyme
AG: Well, we call that off-rhyme, or pseudo-rhyme

KK: Returning to our story—Wednesday evening
AG: New York City, in the gloaming
        New York City in the darks are gloaming

KK: Am I supposed to get the rhyme now, roaming?
AG: I thought I was rhyming at your scheming? Evening?

KK: Well, now you've got it so we'll start all over
AG: Well, let's begin again and go on, rover

KK: A dog may bark but seldom barks in verse
AG: Ourselves, both old dogs, can bark worse and worse

KK: A bird however, sings in rhyme and meter
AG: Gregory Corso sometimes sings with his peter

KK: You scared me, Allen, he's not here tonight—
AG: Why Gregory is here, imbibing wine most bright

KK: If he were here, I think we'd hear his voice
AG: Oh no, he's vowed himself to let us have our choice

KK: Well, I think that it's time we brought an end
AG: And so another poem doth portend

PROCESS NOTES

This poem and "Hilarious Sestina," which appears on the next page, were composed live during a reading at St. Mark's Church in May 1979. Both were later published in *Making It Up: Poetry Composed at St. Mark's Church on May 9, 1979* (Catchword Papers, New York, 1994). The conversation below, in which Ginsberg and Koch decided what to do next, took place between the poems. "Ron" and "RP" refer to Ron Padgett, who was in the audience.

EDITORS

AG: What now, sestina?

KK: OK. That'll be relaxing. A sestina, in case anyone has forgotten, is a poem in which all the lines end in the same six words. Ron has sadistically chosen the six words: *hilarious, spirituality, although, gatecrasher, slam,* and *dreaming.* And Allen and I will just make up the rest of the lines. The lines in the sestina are all set in a certain order and I suppose the person who will enjoy this poem the most will be the tape recorder. Anyway, if we're fast enough, you'll get some sense of the form. We've got the words written here, and we'll say the lines that fit them. Could you wait a minute till I get a drink?

AG: The sequence will be hilarious to dreaming and then the beginning of the second stanza will be dreaming, just rolling around, taking the last end-word of the previous stanza for the first end-word of the next stanza, and the last end-word of that stanza for the first line of the next stanza and the coda will have three lines with *hilarious, spirituality, although, gatecrasher, slam, dreaming*—all six words.

KK: OK. Do you want to start, maestro?

AG: I'm scared. I don't know how to go with this hilarious poetry.

RP: You have to end the line with the word.

AG: I didn't know the rules of the sestina.

A Hilarious Sestina

Allen Ginsberg & Kenneth Koch

AG: I'm scared! I don't know how to make my sestina hilarious

KK: Well, you just have to give up for a moment, Allen, your spirituality

AG: It may seem like that's in order, Ken, although

KK: Thus doing so in the poetry of the New York School you would be a gatecrasher

AG: Well, in any case, upon my face the door they'd slam

KK: Allen, if you think that, you must be dreaming

AG: Well, Ken, you know I'm a poet and I'm always dreaming

KK: Yes, I suppose you are, and sometimes your dreams are hilarious

AG: Until I find myself waking up in the morning with a headache in the slam

KK: Well, that's I suppose when you get in the mood for spirituality

AG: No, meditation on the railroad tracks at Rocky Flats like a great gatecrasher

KK: Yes, your lines are getting a little more characteristic, although

AG: It seems that I might continue meditating until permanence became an although

KK: And I, until the red inkwell unsteadied, some dreaming

AG: And I continue with my meditation until at the Gates of Heaven, they look out and say gatecrasher

KK: At which point, not only the angels but clouds seem slightly hilarious

AG: Will, implore me for once and for all, Ginsberg, give up your spirituality

KK: It is at this point that we both got the nickname, Slam

AG: Stewart who was a guy I once heard of in the forties, he also had the name Slam

KK: Jenny is another one who had a nickname, although

AG: I once had a guru who claimed to have some kind of spirituality

KK: That he only felt at night when he was not dreaming

AG: I think probably all poets, gurus, Jennys, Kenneths, Ginsbergs are all hilarious

KK: Only, I think, when trying to erase the word gatecrasher

AG: Well, I guess you'd want to erase the gatecrasher if you were already inside heaven I'm sorry

AG: I guess if you were already inside heaven you'd want to erase the word gatecrasher

KK: I suppose I'd have to agree with you there, Slam

AG: Well, it's a pretty funny situation for those who aren't in, especially hilarious

KK: Yes, yes, yellow, orange, red, green, permanent, heaven, albatross, raspberry, although

AG: Kenneth, I know you're in heaven but how come you keep on dreaming?

KK: It's the only answer I have to a certain kind of spirituality

AG: Nothing is the proper answer to any kind of spirituality

KK: I think actually that every mystical thought in the most serious sense is only a gatecrasher

AG: Well, every sitting Buddhist would agree that materialism in the form of spirituality is only dreaming

KK: I don't think any of it is quite as convincing as a slam

AG: Well, there are people screaming the window, they want to get in heaven too, although

KK: The prospect of everyone now living plus all the dead being in heaven, you must admit is really hilarious

AG: Being at St. Mark's Church and then going to heaven is a hilarious form of spirituality

KK: It's disturbing to think about the fact that although a gatecrasher

AG: Is slamming his voice through the window

AG & KK: We're both dreaming

Breaking Up Is Hard to Do

Maureen Owen & Rebecca Wright

The point of departure is   always a fantasy really
and then again   fantastically real
                    leaving like this unprepared   Nothing

packed or ordered   and the time   not right

stealing out at midnight
for the piers   for the tungsten mines   for the Orient!
carrying the broken heart in a suitcase   badly fastened
luckily to hurry   is not necessary now
We will arrive at the appointed time regardless
it doesn't exist   in fact.
            To think that I might arrive!
            instead of this passing through
            oceans and strangers   opening
            like the Red Sea . . . .
Eternally on the voyage now   walking backwards on the
speeding train   descending laterally the   yellow plastic
escalators   leaning and laughing!   towards the top
we see   the sky & beyond that   more escalators in gaudy
contemporary colors   on time   late   almost early   &
too soon   and before that   passing beyond this world
which smolders for closeups   into What
now beyond usefulness   beyond pleasure!
            Energy   you directionless Goose!   You
have tempted me too far this time
I close my eyes   prepared to perish   for another ideal
but when   I close my eyes I see you   who have
become a stranger to me   my point of departure

Seven for Roy Rogers

Maureen Owen & Rebecca Wright

The catalogue opened: it *was* a banister!

lilac expanded on the hillsides of the unfamiliar.

Slug! it appears and slug it will remain.

Browsing darkness programmed to fit in around the trees.

Arching with the curves of the distant hills, he sneezed.

So while we are stuck between floors, we suck.

Process Note

Rebecca and I worked by turns, one of us writing a line or two and then the other. We composed our line without looking at each other's preceding line and then by reading that preceding line and manipulating our new line to be a kind of opposition to it. On our one-liners we worked in much the same manner with each of us creating half of the line. We collaborated in person and worked without hesitation to keep our ideas moving at a fast pace.

We always drank Japanese Bancha tea out of delicate elaborately painted Chinese teacups while we wrote.

Maureen Owen

Milk Punch or Whiskey?

Tom Carey, Helena Hughes & James Schuyler

The sun was shining or the moon at night
smiled shyly behind a cloud.
The look alikes danced by two by two
dancing the waltzes of the last fifty years.
The moon, could it make up its mind?
The coins jingled in his pocket.
"I keep worrying that you've been
run over." I keep whistling through my
gap tooth. I whistle "Rio Rita" and "Honey"
but the atmosphere without the moon is lacking.
Don't die you must finish reading this poem!
To speak in half sentences is to ignore the
three graces. I'm the upstairs maid.
Let me wash the dried milk from your mug.
The distractions distracted me
so I turned on the t.v. and got myself
an ice cold beer. "Your hair, Tom, is
a regular rats' nest." That's because
I'm a regular guy.
Just then Helena arrived with the Hollandaise
sauce. "This is for the sea bass, I think."
The moon withdrew into its covert again
time for a private sulk. The steam rises
from a nearby swamp—you are in the shower.
The moon came back in a leather jacket
he was rehearsing for a part in Orpheus!
The stars were all atwitter. The Orang-utan
sang "Baboon moon." The look alikes came
round again, along with the weird sisters
and the raggled-taggled gypsies. I wish
they would come and take me away the moon
sighed and put his head inside a sack.

4/20/80

70

PROCESS NOTE

The problem with this section is that I have only the vaguest memory of writing the collaboration, as I believe I was addicted to heroin at the time. The vague memory that I do have is a picture: hot summer day 1980, Jimmy Schuyler laying on his bed at the Hotel Chelsea, me at the typewriter a few feet away, alternately typing and figuring out how to get money, writing a few lines and then hurrying off to attend to the "real" business at hand.

TOM CAREY

Full Moon

Helena Hughes & James Schuyler

The full moon shining on the scintillating city.
There was no need for old obsessive dreams.
The moon put on its underpants and shut the French
window shivering a bit in the cold night air.
The moon took off its underpants and did a dirty
little dance celebrating the desires we do not
dream of. And yet we do, we dream of them constantly.
We leave the money on the mantle and loose the door.
"Let's pay a visit to the Mozart's," the moon lisped
mopping his brow with a handkerchief of Swiss lace.
He mopped and mopped and mopped and mopped,
then opened the windows to see the minarets of
the city more clearly. "You're not wearing your
high heeled boots tonight!" the moon exclaimed.
"No, I'm wearing my little purple dancing shoes."
As though to prove her point she danced a few
steps then disappeared into the seductive folds
of the city. The moonlight cast a gloom upon
them as they fled along the winding streets of
Fez. "I think I'll call it a day," the moon yawned.
The sun was shining sulkily it had its reasons
for its sulks. A ladder ran up her new silk stockings.
"Damn!" she said. "Another day another dollar and these
cost plenty." In a lyric tenor the moon sang
"Strutting on down" and fell behind the eastern horizon.

4/30/80

Debris

Helena Hughes & James Schuyler

"I will guard this cup of coffee from the demon to
my right with a leather tongue." Helga stroked
her swollen ankle and winced. "A little practise,
a little discipline and this is what you get," she
moaned quietly. Edith Wharton made a cameo appearance,
how she loved the stage! She wore a cloche hat with a long
curl of shiny black feathers clustered by a diamond pin.
The feathers made her sneeze but she wore them
anyway. Elegance like exercise has its price.

A new stanza, a fresh start, the alarm clock rang in
her left ear. Time to be up and doing, so up she got
and did. Like her grandmother before her she had the
habit of taking forty winks after lunch. But today
the forty had run into many, many more. It was a hot
day and the heat led her to self-indulgence. Never mind
what kind of self-indulgence. "I need to get my hair
fixed," she thought, and sighed with pleasure. It was
a long soft sigh which turned into a summer breeze.

Helga pretended not to see the monks that were looking
on and waded on out into the cool lake waters lifting
her arms above her head. The monks broke into a plainsong
which accompanied her breast-strokes. Her long hair
fanned out behind her in the waters. "Enough, enough,"
Helga muttered and swam ashore. Dripping she walked
up the beach flinching from a twisted ankle. The monks
had vanished from the scene. And Helga sat to nurse her
little foot and croon. "Good-bye," she crooned,
"all you readers, good-bye!"

5/27/80

Little Chinese Box

Helena Hughes & James Schuyler

Her heart was like a little chinese box
and when it beat her adam's apple throbbed
and lent a delightful hue to her cheeks.
Her box was like a little Chinese heart
with compartments inside which she had
opened all but one. Now she opened that
one. There was nothing there. And this
became her favorite. The little Chinese
box was lacquered black with designs in
red and gold. She told it all her secrets.

"Time," she thought, "to cut some peonies
and arrange them in a vase." Thoughts
were weighing on her mind. Her purple legs
flashed in and out the knife slits of her
skirt. She ran her fingers caressingly
over the shiny lacquered top of her little
box, a movement soothing to her worried mind.
The box shuddered and said "Ooh!"

She picked a secret out from underneath
her tongue. It shriveled in the light
and vanished as secrets will. Then
she pulled a petal from the peony.
The peony said "ooh!" "Ah! my beloved
possessions," she sighed, "I must leave you
now and go out into the rain to buy some
Diet-Pepsi for the great being."

6/4/80

Black Mink

Helena Hughes & James Schuyler

She put on her black mink and swirled around the room.
Then pausing in front of the full length mirror she
lit a cigarette and blew a smoke ring at her image.
The question uppermost in her mind was: "It's black mink
but is it Blackglama?" Either way she felt like Vampirella.
It was August: funny time to wear black mink: though it
might be Blackglama. The late afternoon light shed
prettily upon the leaves of the tree outside the window.

Is this a poem? Is this a poem?

She turned from the window to the coffee table where
her two girl friends were drinking tea. She returned
to the window and scrutinized the fur. It *was* Blackglama.
The girls were discussing where to score. Hetty said
Union Square, Nancy had other thoughts. The trouble with
Hetty was that her ideas were too butch, while Nancy was
an incorrigible romantic. (In fact one might even call her a
"femme"). She knew that if she wanted anything it was but
a phone call away. *Quod erat factum.* Anything that is except
Italy, and now in this black mink the canals of Venice tugged
at her mind filled with unrelinquished desire.

Some time passed but
our three heroines aged well.
Now they were like three quiet snails.
Well not *snails* really, more like squirrels.
The Blackglama mink had begun to molt.

6/18/80

Thundering Undies

Allen Ginsberg & Ron Padgett

Passing through Manhattan's sodium vapor sidestreet glare
with pink electric powderpuffs overhead,
mmmmm, that Catholic churchwall's old as Science
tho Science is older, but O please don't tell me about it tonight,
no pain please in the strange spring light,
tho my baby's waiting on the corner with 160 pounds of meat
on her 148 bones all for sale for 25 bucks.
Furious & Aurelius, now that we're back in town, tell her
to take cosmetics from the air, and let the dark blue city
sift slowly down to where lamplight shadows her cheeks
& her lips shine dayglo purple moist with sperm of her 300 adorers
—O come let us adore her, weird Madonna of the street
and not in real great shape, though we're in far-off Elsewhere
with our sad souls and aching teeth! Too late for old loves,
but a little nosegay of pansies cut by Time's tractor where
the pasture meets the dirt road and my heart meets the flower bed
dug up years ago to make East 12th Street, where you float
a little off the ground, thinking of the withered posy of pussy-
willows cox-stamens & rosepetal lips dumped in the garbage can
by unthinking lovers I used to sleep & giggle with,
crazed, hateful & disappointed, Catullus.

21 April 1981

I Got Easy

Eileen Myles & Alice Notley

Easy River

a piece of cake

even

still some dough

In the shape of

every bathrobe you

loved

you walk around in a

messy room,

a Saturday morning in her thirties.

PROCESS NOTE

I was in [Alice Notley] and Ted [Berrigan]'s house almost constantly circa 1975–198– (until Alice moved to Paris). At one point Ken & Ann Mikolowski gave Alice and Ted about 500 postcards to write poems on and I did several with both of them, and this was one.

EILEEN MYLES

From a Continuing Collaboration

Bernadette Mayer & Alice Notley

I have great wonder, be this light,
How I can live, for day nor night
I may not sleep
I sleep in a room in the snow
With the god of sleep in a cave of stone
Who sleeps with songs to make sleep less death
I have so many idle thoughts
That all things alike seem good to me,
Sorrow or joy or whatever it might be
Bewilders me and I fall down
All I have is this imagination
I dream in this ecstatic room we see
Heights of frescoes in Venetian villas
Full of sons and daughters
I would make a pathway in the disrepair
To the glories through the genius of the story
Our sleep is corrupted by scenes of snow
We are the double impostors you're warned of
Resting intransigence on poetry's head
Like a warm predicted storm of love of stories
I lean my arm on your knee like another
You can remember the raucous exchange
Between the snow, the book and the milk
The book is in with the food
To make death more like a story,
The man who knew none, the food's with the books
And though we can't sleep, revenge for change,
There's an immodest view we laugh at.

There see the landscape of the white
Jockey-shorts-clothed erection that's no one's
Pillowed and shadowed and alone
There, the funny view of the nude with a clock
Can a naked upright woman

On a red bed be immodest
Only telling the time as she does but
When does she sleep? Oh and I
Might as well be a painting
The impostor I am now won't
She soon sing and sing me real
And in sleep Love more truly join me
And those so far away now will in dreams
Talk laugh and wander with me
Isn't this sleep yet? Aren't you near?
At 4:30 I drink flat Kirin beer
And read *A Fine Old Conflict*
The birds in the park have snow damp feathers
I can't see them can you? They
Have sisters and babies and marriages
Every day they must marry the world—
The birds in the park and the girl in my book—
But sleep is a play an enchantment
Gods, send us grace to sleep and meet
In our sleep such certain dreams
That having wandered the universe
Dimensionless, we might awake
And remarry our small given world.

I read *A Fine Old Conflict* and *Monkey Day* too
And last I read that the birds in the park
Cannot love like monkeys or like we do
Because they aren't babies long enough
And grow too fast the soft down that covers
The surfaces of plants and animals to protect them
From the coldest winds, brightest snow in the bed
I dream my sister is a lion covered with fur
I wonder how I'll be able to live with her
In the state of physical evolution when
It's first possible for us to bear children,
14 years for boys, 12 for girls, a legal age,
Small, sensitive, covered and erectile,
It corresponds to the penis of the male
The effort it takes to dream this would be equal

To lending the preposterous cab driver who left me
Stranded the dignity of all my wandering alone
Like a painting of an impostor twin on a red Valentine
Let's take a cat and foster him well with milk
And tender flesh, and make his couch of silk
And let him see a mouse go by the wall,
Instantly he forgoes milk and flesh and all
And every delicacy that is in that house
Such appetite has he to eat a mouse
Let's both only dream that we sleep,
Only that dream will marry us best
We'll drink strong wine, red as blood
And view the most modest women on the reddest beds.

The thing about milk, I prefer wine to it
My pregnant sister's a milk factory
As large modest & beautiful as a Beethoven
Sonata. But whenever I dream of Antarctica
Its topography's secretly not quite milk-
White. Once when I dreamed I dreamed
In the dream I told X in an aside from the dream, "I'm
Having this recurring dream." And then he said,
"Who isn't?" Later Y said, "Alice needs
To know what to say about it."
I've done my Milk Time and still I dream
I nurse the baby and feel milk come down
In my left breast. Bernadette, do you think
It's possible to die of daily drinks, in
Modestly large amounts, of wine?
The modest woman gets her nourishment
From...fostering? I'm sleeping drinking and
Singing, having no peer but thee, as
Death has no peer. It's too beautiful!
I dream a woman lies in a crib, how compact
She is! I dream I write a lament and a
Lai and they nourish the very sun who makes
Day I dream I'm waiting I'm 12 and childless
And want no child nor nothing but trance
I dream I'm a hundred wanting nothing but

My trance, and all is always potential as the
Birds sing again the song we help write
In ink of wine as well as milk, while spellbound on the bed.

If it isn't spring yet like milk it's alot like spring
I guess we might die and all of practically nothing,
I don't know, I daily drink an awful lot of beer
We can't get wine up here, milk is more like whiskey
Fostering I think what we cherish like the dictionary does
Remember we'd nursed hopes we'd be speaking of Chaucer
His lines ripe as wine and full of hops, what's a Lai?
My grandfather used to rest his stein in a saucer
Like a jovial moon in the draft of the room, is that silly?
If we were together in Antarctica today or tonight
We might be in total darkness in a trance like he was
At a table in the milk-white night reminiscing for fear
Of the elements about our child-bearing years or something
With the order of confidences as milk for the night's sonata
Where you say you can feel the milk come down, & I still say "let"
Yet it's still immensely still as you said in your letter
There's a moon reported in The Times to which we're getting closer
It appears through densest radiation to have been a wetter body
Somebody even said it had looked alot like a pizza pie
When, less displayed, it was viewed at first more modestly
Now close up this moon is dry yet still red, maybe I
Will get to have the same trance as you to dream or sing in
I think beer is more like milk than wine is, wine is old
But beer's cold, I did dream I did all I was doing twice
Then I flew on a plane where the cocktail menu was hung
With all kinds of tiny whiskey bottles both to choose from
And to signify the memory of lactation in this flight
I saw everyone I ever knew while I flew to Chicago's loop at night.

Hey when I said wine I really meant beer
But when I said lai I didn't mean lay but
When I said death I meant death "SABRES
SLASH WOOZY ISLES." How much beer, and
How much did your grandfather too, do daily
You drink? You tell me and I'll tell you or

Do we nurse vice as number (how much how many) like other
Americans? Am I losing my sense
Of the beauty of tonight, but temporarily, I
Think, for white nights always have fluctuated
Moonlight river rush rapture pang sweetness sudden
Busyness again, Chaucer attending to the data
Of clothing or of dream, the which are many
Of the guise one is only the genial host to, do
You think? I wear a dark blue tee-shirt under a light
Blue pure silk shirt and what was bothering me was
The knight who can't come to know she's dead see
If I'm the knight and I am she, can't I sleep to awaken as I?
Perhaps that can't be—though perhaps I have
And often, but I feel like the knight's bewildered again
That's the meaning of this long night, full of
Lovely sleepers but devoid of sleep but shapely sweet
Here's a sort of a short sort of lai:

> O earthly lady new lady—
> In your service always with 2 kids
> Plus my poverty my impatience
> My vices my blind spots—heal me
> A minute really it's time to.

Strategy

Bernard Welt & Terence Winch

The buttons are the size of nickels
and black like your eyes. Your teeth
are the size of fingernails and white
as paint and the whites of your eyes.
The body is better than the clothes
that hold it. The box is better
than the music it plays. A man
is playing a gold saxophone in the rush
hour. His hands hold the gold saxophone.
His fingernails are the size of nickels.
The violins are hanging on the wall.
The barometer drops. A man is holding
a gold sax. He is naked. He won't go home.

PROCESS NOTES

Process: In the '70s and '80s, I and a lot of my friends, who were also poets, lived in Dupont Circle in D.C. Michael Lally, Doug Lang, Diane Ward, Phyllis Rosenzweig, Bernie Welt, and others all lived in the neighborhood at one time or another. It was not unusual for an evening of hanging out to include collaborating on poems. Someone would put some paper in the typewriter and get a line or two going, then someone else would pick it up. Usually you'd stop in the middle of a line or phrase, leaving it for your collaborator to complete. My most extensive collaboration was a sonnet sequence of thirty or forty poems with Doug Lang, which we called "Take the Qua Train." It's hard to tell, especially years later, who wrote what in any of these collabs. "Strategy" was written on June 16th, 1981.

TERENCE WINCH

What I liked about the collaborations was they were sort of like working with verse rules: they started you off with a constraint that made you focus on the language, so the process was often about funny rhymes, perverse turns of phrase, rhythm. I don't remember how we did this one, but if it followed the general pattern, my guess is that Terence did most of the work.

BERNARD WELT

from **Black Holes, Black Stockings**

Olga Broumas & Jane Miller

Enfleurage

As from a water lily, *periplum,*

not as land looks on a map
    but as sea bord seen by men sailing

successive ferries, my toy boats, leaf, song, heart. Or again, I step into a street and, commensurate with its width its bazaar breaks into range, wares, voices, steam float distinctly in unequal units closer. A blur of relations and then synchromesh: rachet, whistle, bulk, cold, scallion bitter, fish heads, city dock. Out of the midst of the city the country, forested one by one into many, alert like the tops of trees with inexact news about an imminent arrival; I tilt until it becomes time and there she is, most beautiful come upon from behind, where she is waiting for a moment, discouraged her message never arrived. And as she turns, her sunglasses glint and she brushes back her braid where her hair was loose before, and since; there is no one of them that does not see her, unconsciously—and, white birds casting a dark shadow, fly out of themselves.

We parked and hiked and climbed over the wide sleeve of the Atlantic. Below and between, the beach where even in season the many travelers rested or tossed far apart. In perfect September I sent them to be alone. Without mission or admonition. Feeling as we did then about each other, already relaxed, how would two wed the fall of summer, speechless for three days, how far from the other? Satin shorts and roller skates at night in the streets of the village, transvestites. Perrier and pistachio. The fabulous dark divulging day, deliberately provoked. Saran wrap and plexiglass about the night and the day, the membrane between them. I thought we might lap and here at the great magnet meet. I unmade my bed, wind torn from clouds, massaged by distance, and slept. We pull on cords from the earth where we are joined. We the plural.

She liked to be in the middle. One of them was taken by how close her heart beat to the surface like a robin's and how she landed with a light touch. If the sheets were white and the sun glanced on them, blond had more red. Another was olive with almond eyes, who liked to wake slowly and fall back. She lay beside the row of windows and rolled out into the night on their long wooden oven spoons. Sometimes they came for her and woke her, kissing the corners of her mouth. The long hairs in the bed, the very curly, the weighty and the subtle, lit an arabesque. When they were wet they were very very wet, and when they were dry they were funny. Excited, the candle burned like cry-breath. Who called out and where answered and when became thirsty. She reached for the lucky pitcher sailing across the sky. Tissue, tissue, kiss you.

She didn't think we were married in any traditional sense so didn't hesitate to apply first to one and then the other the awkward silences which her colorful beauty could be felt to fill, as in panavision, setting a slower mood for the spectator perhaps but quickening her pulse. *Don't leave,* she didn't whisper, nor *stay with me,* but rather shifted her hair as one shifts an entire pose left to right close-up, taking a minute, triggering the free association where every promise lost or denied finds its place. Blue skies, tawny beach, sea-green and berry stain. By year's end she would bring us one of her first architecture assignments, in the manner of the Japanese masters, the arrangement of dots in disorder. Impressionable and expressive, she lined the corridors with butcher paper, unable to avoid herself and, hence, design—wool-bodies, lace, the infinite destinies of flakes, ceramic porosity, wormwood. She would hide sea, sand and boat by hanging the sheet upside down. Told to watch water boil, stray rain, to unrehearse them, she did it many times and in her mind, until by ear first fathomed disarray.

the only cool day of summer
kids at bullfights
yellow and purple
green olives under an almond tree
a trapezoid smile
indoors without a flash
two aunts and an uncle
avocado vinaigrette
a bath with no hot water
a spoon and a fork
illuminated hands of a clock on its side
the hidden side of an arriving train
Paris at night
a face appearing at different windows of a big house
the last half of April and the first of May
one other

Like shower over the heart muscle and, after rain, summer. Peaches and rose. A steam bath for the earth, Chinese massage, long silver pins drawn the great distance of daylight from handclouds into trees standing on their heads, roots. Waterwheel over the terraced vertebrae, earthface rosé tanning toward the many the long the most generous hours of light that today rain, yet light, the lightest gray, gray apple-green, gray lilac, white. Solstice of pins, of verticals, into the haunches of horsehills. Tongues in puddles. Hours in twos and threes, hours in elongated seconds, thick sentences taut and thinning into words and finally breaking into alphabet, moments without shadow, the long spaces between lights in a countryside going to sleep in even daylight from the rain, and the different lamps meeting in the evening making gold the gray, buttering the houses in small swatches as if they were children holding out their pieces of bread, watching the last light perforate the darkness and not admit to it, no it shall never, happy soul, winter.

Round Sunday. Wooded plains underwater, seaweed, urchin, seahorse, and the gelatinous os implanted on the rock. Its rose madder flowered—the myth of the toothed—a sunrise of tresses to cilialike ease in its prey. The rose flash sweeps the waterwind. And when the mouth puckers, cordovan, doorless, it confounds. Smoke-moon enamel from a distance, traversed by speedboat the sea jells into membrane, petrol green on descent. We thought silverfish until the boat stopped and we saw seaweed reflected as silver-leafed poplars. Cricket island. White flowers of summer like winter, milksnake feeding on the paproot. Nimble light we crack diving. The horn of the troubadour is forced outside the self in shape, where we bob a brief note in the after-dive. Allowing someone else to panic where I was playing, taking the whole hillside for a friend from far asea, the sea grapes, emptying its vacuum of charged bubbles from a double-prowed cruiser, both wakes. Day necklace, night glass unwobbling. The first inch is forgiveness. The noun that is cleaned disappears. Putting up with their manifestations like smoke in our faces already turned from that elegant perfume, like flamingos who wandered north from the tropics, we concentrate on abiding. Our body casts out a cypress root as logos while the unharnessed gray whale escapes the muffle of the ocean wash: fattest cows and youngest heifers, beautiful electronic images, the loneliness of their small good hearts. All the nights go on by hand, journey of a thousand knots, milk again learning nothing. Ha! Priests! Red lamp poles, muscadet sky: upside down. Parakeets in the afterlife, silverpious, pass to slope the world. Pre-Alps, perched villages, memories, as when you fall asleep god exists. Some visible keeping still, opium, oyster, the unswirling of the smoke unswirling the mollusk, signals us to daily with the frail. The sound of a nut opening, brain-wake.

Since I dreamt of a lion with a cat on its back, the tear which is glass which is stone in a ring in its eye, I lay on the beach dimly and therefore elementally, taking the pearl from her mouth back into the mussel, irregular, tearlike, breaking it down. Dissolve the pearl and remove the irritant carefully to the sea floor where the crystalline, faceted, rocks and fits. The whole bar shifting clouds in the water. Deeper, a sun-ray shower plummets to a plateau below which, unirradiated, free-form masses of water tilt and lug to the basalt and its schism, oiling their sides with black molt oozing from crusted chimneys, cellar fire. Fantastically weeps the eye of fire.

A gram. How much?
Are you married?
Yes.
Is she?
Of course.
Where are your men?
My husband is arriving later.
Will he let you go?
Of course. Where are we going?
I will meet you here at 4 o'clock.
How much?
He will let you go?
4 o'clock.

Blue of rainforest green, of moss, ultramarine of closed eyes, evening pearl, berry black, blue of earth cerulean in space, royal, prussian; porpoise blue and whale gray, slate blue of metal, enamel; iridescent trout, blue of fungus and mold; sky, pacific, mediterranean, aqua of translucent blues, blue stained with yellow; iris, silver, purple, rose blue, military, grape; in the shadow, violet or port; pool blue, quivering; church-stain, red madder, octopal; ice blue; blue of sighs, bluebird in twilight with a white stripe; polka dot, blood blue, nordic, light; diamond, meteor; parallel lines, density; powder, red, white and blue, blue concerto, island.

Process Notes

From *How(ever)*, January 1986:

We undertook to coauthor a book through a desire to transcend personality and its aggregate of habits, to sidestep these into what we hoped would be a more sensual intelligence informed by our studies of subatomic physics, its implied philosophy and methodology at play in the macrocosm around us, South Greece and France. We agreed on two rules: write every day, which, life being distracting or spectacular, translated to four to five out of seven and don't look back til it's done. We wrote pieces together, wrote separately and revised together at day's end, composed aloud (Barthe's writing aloud), spoke to a tape recorder, one meditated and the other wrote in her aura. We put the first draft away for two years, and then, in a dramatic two-week period, performed a drastic final draft.

OLGA BROUMAS & JANE MILLER

From "An Interview with Jane Miller," *Electronic Poetry Review*, 1996:

Black Holes, Black Stockings is the first and only time I've done collaborative work as a writer. I've fooled around with other musicians, but this too has been largely in the company of Olga. She really introduced me to, and guided me through, the wonderful world of self-effacement. Everyone should consider disappearing for a while into another voice! Very liberating! I suppose it works when the collaborators are emotionally disposed toward such a project. Our goal was to come up with a voice that sounded like neither of us, so that the pages Olga wrote were indistinguishable from mine. It must have worked to some degree because to this day, we delight in arguing about who wrote what. In allowing someone else into my work, I realized that composition was more dynamic than I'd thought before, and that what was sacred about language, for me, was not so much its genesis as its transformation. I now revise more freely, and the process itself has become more pleasurable, less self-conscious. I hesitate to admit that collaboration is the place where I began to trust myself as a writer, but in fact, at least part of the confidence I have comes from trusting the creation of a third participant, the "us," which, in turn, led me to recognize the many selves who compose my work. When I lived in my imagination, I held vainly to a code about creation: that it took place in a silence that was private. Animating one's privacy with another person's magic was something beyond me until Olga persuaded me that there was nothing to lose. Indeed! Art is stubborn, and says what it has to say.

JANE MILLER

S.O.S.

Dennis Cooper & David Trinidad

If lucky, you might capture that
elusive flight of ideas which involve you
when you're "in love" with the chosen one.
One fine day, in other words, your
fleet might come waltzing around
your door. With luck you'll be looking for what
it implies about truth, beauty, and gratitude—
that kind of stuff. You are my kind
of guy. I am the lucky one. I am
awaiting one sign, or this romanticized look in my eyes
has a way of throwing its dead weight around when
you keep me at arm's length.
The longer I wait, the more I want you.
I'm in love with you, you big galoot!
Put simply, if I'm allowed to lose total control of my-
self for a guy, as if you didn't know. Don't go.

1/9/85, NYC, 5:54 p.m.

PROCESS NOTE

I was visiting Dennis in New York; we wrote "S.O.S." in the living room of his apartment on Twelfth Street (just off of Second Avenue). A few years earlier we'd written, while driving from San Francisco to Los Angeles, a poem called "The Ordeal," so this was our second—and in my opinion more successful—collaboration. I don't think we ever wrote another. The title is from the ABBA song; I'm sure it came from Dennis, as ABBA was one of his favorite groups. I remember that we alternated lines, and that Dennis was responsible for the ending, which I liked, which I still like. "One fine day" in the fourth line had to have come from me: I was obsessed with 60s girl groups at the time; "One Fine Day" was a hit by the Chiffons. I also remember that I had a big (ultimately unrequited) crush on someone in Los Angeles; this kind of wistful energy fueled not only the poem with Dennis, but many of my own poems from that period as well.

DAVID TRINIDAD

Strawberry Blonde

Bob Flanagan & David Trinidad

At last there's proof: we can talk to the dead!
I'm doing it now. And guess who talks back?
Liberace? Rock Hudson? Marilyn?
There's more to life than has-been movie stars,
but this voice I hear sounds so familiar.
Far from the hollowness of Hollywood,
the larger-than-life image that flickers
before me is a projection of my
own secret dream of immortality.
A close-up of my mouth floating in space
speaks for itself: "I am the spirit of
lost words, paying lip service to what was."
What was isn't worth remembering, but
I miss it. And that's what matters: the hurt.
Not to mention the pain and the drama:
boy meets girl; girl beats boy; boy gets hard-on;
boy sticks hard-on up ass of other boy;
the end. In the meantime, the real meaning
of this underground film remains hidden
between the lines of these silly actors.
Jayne Mansfield reclines in her pink mansion.
"Beautiful, ain't it?" she whispers to me
as I wait in line at the checkout stand,
her sweet voice thicker than the jam I just bought.
She follows me out to the parking lot.
The jam hits the pavement and suddenly
I'm splattered with preserves. It looks like blood.
What a sap I am to be so careless,
especially with something this precious:
the confectionary embodiment
of the dumb blonde—another sex goddess
fallen prey to my insatiable lust.

And now I'm lost in a cloud of stardust,
scattered lint from the fabric of one's life.
I stand naked in front of you tonight,
a star in my own right, about to go out.

Anger Turned Inward

Bob Flanagan & David Trinidad

I am the God of Hellfire and I bring
incense, peppermints, and green tambourines
to delight and titillate the senses
that I've neglected for such a long time.
But, try as I might, I'm still a numbskull,
a bona fide nincompoop, a nothing
in a world where everyone wins but me.
I suffer from entropy and a mal odor.
I myself am an eyesore and should be
treated far worse than the Elephant Man
for I am not even a human being.
I am the God of Hellfire and I bring
myself into every conversation
about sex and death. Though you're not aware,
I'm stealing from you and I'm fucking you
in the face while you caress your pet rock—
that's about as much life as you can stand.
Nonetheless, I have come to answer your
need for love and your hunger for someone
with a big dick and excellent credit
so you can buy, buy, buy and fuck, fuck, fuck
in order to feel complete and make life
appear to be more than the maddening
mishmash of morbid misinformation
you've had forced down your throat ever since birth.
Instead of lies, you now gag on a prick—
the biggest lie of all. Now you see it
and now you don't even want to see it.
But see it you will, and taste it too, each
glorious inch of stiff, uncut Godhead!
You need it! You are the God of Hellfire
(not me) and you have brought me down to earth,

down to my knees, up to your expectations
of the kind of blow job you dream of
where at last you swallow seed and bear fruit
in the flickering red flames of Hellfire.

PROCESS NOTE

Bob and I alternated lines. We wrote one poem a month for a year, ending up with a chapbook of twelve poems, *A Taste of Honey*. We often left our lines on each other's phone machines (this was before cell phones). And it was often a tug of war, each of us trying to pull the poem our own way, only to have it yanked right back. I remember we purposefully tried to irritate each other, in an affectionate way (for instance, I'd throw in some 60s reference, which I knew would piss Bob off; he'd reply with an explicit sexual or S & M reference, which he knew would make me squirm a little). Thus would we goad each other along.

DAVID TRINIDAD

Graphic Winces

Allen Ginsberg, with Bob Rosenthal
& Brooklyn College MFA Class

In high school when you crack your front tooth bending down too fast over
the porcelain water fountain
or raise the tuna sandwich to your open mouth and a cockroach tickles your
knuckle
or step off the kitchen Cabinet ladder on the ball of your foot hear the
piercing meow of a soft kitten
or sit on a rattling subway next to the woman scratching the sores on her
legs, thick pus on her fingers
or put your tongue to a winter-frozen porch door, a layer of frightening
white flesh sticks to the wooden frame—
or pinch your little baby boy's fat neck skin in the teeth of his snowsuit zipper
or when you cross Route 85 the double yellow line's painted over a dead
possum
or tip your stale party Budweiser on the window sill to your lips, taste
Marlboro butts floating top of the can—
or fighting on the second flight of the tenement push your younger sister
down the marble stairs she bites her tongue in half, they have to sew it
back in the hospital—
or at icebox grabbing the half eaten Nestles' Crunch a sliver of foil sparks on
your back molar's silver filling
or playing dare in high school you fall legs split on opposite sides of a high
iron spiked fence
or kicked in the Karate Dojo hear the sound like a cracked twig then feel a
slow dull throb in your left forearm,
or tripping fall on the sidewalk & rip last week's scab off your left knee
You might grimace, a sharp breath from the solar plexus, a chill spreading
from shoulderblades and down the arms,
or you may wince, tingling twixt sphincter and scrotum a subtle electric
discharge.

December 8, 1986

PROCESS NOTE

Collaborations seem to come out of the idea of two or more writers becoming a group or embracing an idea. I have collaborated to create the fictional "bad" poet Derek Steele to spoof the campus literary review (with success). I have typed on a hassock pushed around the room at Actualist parties in Iowa City. Buzzed through nights with friends all on black beauties creating reams of gibberish never meant to be read. That was precisely what we were doing as the 1977 Blackout in New York City slowed the record of Jimi and stopped. Most fun were the collaborations done in the office of the Poetry Project to create *Caveman,* a mimeo scandal sheet always edited by Simon Schuchat although he was never there. Most of *Caveman* was written directly on the stencils leaving no possibility of revisionism. Occasionally Allen Ginsberg had a universal idea about the groin area. "Graphic Winces" was offered to his friends and his class at Brooklyn College and he collated the responses. Recently I have found IM'ing to be effective way to create a collaboration. Collaborations lift the need to be great and reveal the need to just be together.

BOB ROSENTHAL

Cataract

Allen Ginsberg, Lita Hornick & Peter Orlovsky

I'm having a cataract operation this October 20
My Russian father had cataracts & vaguely said don't
    play with yourself & rub your eyes
I grew cataracts myself, a senior citizen
    with no playmate for years
I'm very nervous about it, I've always
    been phobic about eyes.
A pair of reading glasses coming up, not just
    to read NY Times all day
But Surongama, Lovhavatara, Prajnaparamita
    & *Dharma Bums.*
I don't mind being a senior citizen as
    I'm happy with the poets.
And we're going to leave out Politicians Whoops!
    we almost forgot to vote in the Primary
So rush downtown eat Macrobiotic eyeballs & pull
    all the levers to save the world.

September 9, 1991

White Mink

Lita Hornick & Ron Padgett

I am wearing my new white mink tonight
Liberace had one with a train
It made him feel that the right
Thing to do was live all the way outside his brain.
Clothes are my weakness, poetry my strength
Because it covers my body's and my soul's length.
In the deliquescence of the year came Christ the tiger
Wearing a robe the color of the River Niger.
I've always loved the sea
And I'd like to have its colors all over me.
A child, I swam out past the last rope
And now, grown up, I'm dressed up like the Pope.

January 23, 1992

Hot Pink

Alice Notley, Douglas Oliver & Ron Padgett

I dreamt I was mugged
by Lita
No I didn't I mean
I thought it was Lita but
it turned out to be
John Ashbery
wearing some of Lita's best
jewelry, because
he had just mugged her!
He knocked me down and
demanded I give him my
hot-pink vintage forties dress
But I ran away from
him because I had to
make it to Lita's party I had to
wear that dress to one of
her fabulous parties, in the
seventies, it was nineteen
seventy-seven in this dream
And then when I woke up it
was 1965, a new issue of *Kulchur*
had just come out with a Joe
Brainard black and white cover,
the 8th Street Bookshop was still
on the corner of MacDougal, and
no one could figure out how
such an amazing magazine could
be issuing from Park Avenue!
Then John Ashbery became John Ashbery
and everyone else flew up into niches
in the weird pantheon of New York
what-do-you-call-it cultural life?
"You've got to hand it to Lita," Morris
Golde once said, "she did it when no
one else did."

Then another moment of the dream came back:
fuzzily, bookshelves, perhaps at Gotham,
and Ashbery reading somewhere there,
everyone wearing hot pink dresses.

All Ears

Keith Abbott, Pat Nolan, Maureen Owen & Michael Sowl

After rain the freeze
gnawing at the wall
hands over heater all ears

after rain the freeze
gnawing at the wall
hands over heater all ears
leaves cut into a steel sky
or the gray in photographs

leaves cut into a steel sky
or the gray in photographs
when we started we
knew the sun was at our backs
that's all we knew

when we started we
knew the sun was at our backs
that's all we knew
such a strange bird call no
only a crowbar stubborn nail

such a strange bird call no
only a crowbar stubborn nail
a tree gets a shave
take my word for it moon-cut
razor strop cold snap

a tree gets a shave
take my word for it moon-cut
razor strop cold snap
morning's frost warmed to froth
mist beards a fir studded hillside

morning's frost warmed to froth
mist beards a fir studded hillside
　　　front door opens
and all the hall doors open, too—
　　　　drafts and vacuums rule

　　　front door opens
and all the hall doors open, too—
　　　　drafts and vacuums rule
old men's still raging hatred—
"time don't do shit for some wounds"

old men's still raging hatred—
"time don't do shit for some wounds"
　　　mild late winter
many strange birds pass through
　　　Adventists go door to door

　　　mild late winter
many strange birds pass through
　　　Adventists go door to door
shirt sleeves rolled back to elbows
whose arms emerge like white fish?

shirt sleeves rolled back to elbows
whose arms emerge like white fish?
　　　blue ocean calm blue
ocean calm blue ocean
　　　calm blue ocean calm

　　　blue ocean calm blue
ocean calm blue ocean
　　　calm blue ocean calm
out my window fountain and
rain sounds separate then blur

out my window fountain and
rain sounds separate then blur
　　　all bets are off now
we talk late into the hour
　　　no one knows us here

all bets are off now
we talk late into the hour
            no one knows us here
a crowd of dead leaves and
their shadows wait to be let in

a crowd of dead leaves and
their shadows wait to be let in
            for years the neighbor's house
seemed abandoned desolate—
            their first grandchild

            for years the neighbor's house
seemed abandoned desolate—
            their first grandchild
forget-me-nots everywhere
I can't believe you're not here

forget-me-nots everywhere
I can't believe you're not here
            are you still yelling
about those tickets, Blanche?
            sky blue with yellow eyes

            are you still yelling
about those tickets, Blanche?
            sky blue with yellow eyes
what a mess—who expects the cat
to read a Wet Paint sign

what a mess—who expects the cat
to read a Wet Paint sign
            Cairo video
"What's the sound of one million
            swarming Egyptians?"

Cairo video
"What's the sound of one million
          swarming Egyptians?"
a blackened nail turning ·
over and over in the soil

a blackened nail turning
over and over in the soil
          bare feet on cold tiles
peek out at morning
          leaves plastered to damp pavement

          bare feet on cold tiles
peek out at morning
          leaves plastered to damp pavement
arms at the side of your head
I've been in love all night now

arms at the side of your head
I've been in love all night now
          a huge firefly
wicky wacky wicky wacky wicky
          passes by

          a huge firefly
wicky wacky wicky wacky wicky
          passes by
warning–keep all body parts
out of window openings

warning–keep all body parts
out of window openings
          frequently the crowds
were so thick a car halted
          horn vainly bleating

frequently the crowds
were so thick a car halted
          horn vainly bleating
each night a new figure's
added to the Nativity scene

each night a new figure's
added to the Nativity scene
          now in winter
it's always the same river
          flowing nowhere fast

          now in winter
it's always the same river
          flowing nowhere fast
"nah, you shouldna mailed them bills—
we're flat broke until the first"

"nah, you shouldna mailed them bills—
we're flat broke until the first"
          too wet to view the moon
rain veined window reflects
          her tear streaked likeness

          too wet to view the moon
rain veined window reflects
          her tear streaked likeness
sound of a car door slamming
just someone who lives nearby

sound of a car door slamming
just someone who lives nearby
          distracted he asks
the empty bus driver's seat
          for directions

distracted he asks
the empty bus driver's seat
for directions
volleys taps flag folded
ceremony for a plain man

volleys taps flag folded
ceremony for a plain man
the puppy howled
into the neighbors' front rooms
crepuscular songs

the puppy howled
into the neighbors' front rooms
crepuscular songs
easy quiet way of chi
snowflake's wet kisses eyelash

easy quiet way of chi
snowflake's wet kisses eyelash
sumacs run crimson
river of hawks cut the ridge
what more needs telling?

sumacs run crimson
river of hawks cut the ridge
what more needs telling?
on this fresh black asphalt
shadows of power lines, of smoke

Process Notes

I liked the noise levels in "All Ears." And the range of emotions shown throughout the poem. And the way, as Pat remarked, all my collaborators altruistically tried to end this poem for me. I think the passage of links from 15 to 19 are as wonderfully complicated and various as any I've ever seen. It was inspiring to read this improvisation by my collaborators. It reminded me of a really tight jazz ensemble passage. Maureen's flower stanza was especially wonderful, opening up what had been somber wintry imagery to summer, love, and humor.

KEITH ABBOTT

Most impressed with Maureen's #5 (a tree gets a shave), Pat's #21 (bare feet on cold tiles) and Keith's #20 (a blackened nail turning) as free-standing stanzas. Like the linkage, also between #20/#21. And Maureen's #30 (sound of a car door slamming) to Pat's #29 (too wet to view the moon). And Keith's answering the question with smoke and shadow in the ageku.

MICHAEL SOWL

Thought it was wonderful the way Pat took the last stanza of mine ("the puppy howled") and carried it into the great center of being, chi and nature's gentleness. Reminding us of the natural order of birth and death and the calm of it, the true understanding. Also the difference of the view the East takes vs. the view the West takes. And then, Michael's lovely hit of nature keeping the connection and then Keith taking it back into the city, the congestion and pollution, but also keeping the line taut by addressing the urban as a modern day natural phase of life.

MAUREEN OWEN

Keith is right about the jazzlike quality of the links; those were some of the squarest, most brilliant corners I've ever looked around. Each stanza linking with the following stanza created a unique five-line poem. That they appear in sequence contributes to the illusion of a plot. There is no plot, only narrative, lyric narrative. Maureen, however, deserves the credit for adding a quality that the old fogies hadn't dared broach: love. Romance is a very important aspect of any renku. Stanza 18 and 35, the second flower stanza, speak for themselves.

PAT NOLAN

"After rain the freeze"
Hokku. On winter nights when the temperature drops below freezing, my little room is a source of heat. Nothing like little animals trying to chew their way in to get your attention. –PN

"Leaves cut into a steel sky"
Waki. Standing in the yard as a storm moves in. The roiling clouds in ten thousand shades of gray. Noticing the way the leaves jag out in relief against the gray and that darkening, thinking of black-&-white photographs and those levels of gray with objects sharp, knifelike, everything so clear and definite. Suddenly so full of power. –MO

"when we started we"
Trying to follow a moose track in the former Laurentian Mountains (now hills)– we got lost–and then "found" ourselves by walking toward the Sun. Basic Celestial Navigation. –MS

"such a strange bird call no"
I can't remember when I wrote this, or where. It seemed appropriate for a renku titled "All Ears," and with Michael's link about being lost, about making mistakes. –KA

"a tree gets a shave"
First moon stanza. Thinking of an old friend, a kind of woodsman in his own right, who had an old leather strop, well-oiled and gorgeous, as I watched the moonlight fall full-faced on the hemlocks. Saw him shaving the moon off the trees, his razor strop snapping in the cold night airs. –MO

"morning's frost warmed to froth"
The problem with shaving is that it always grows back. Maureen's crystalline baby faced moonlit night by morning has its stubble in froth ready for another scrape. –PN

"front door opens"
When I went outside to see what was in the mail, I found the link from Pat. When I opened the front door to go back in the house, nothing like this happened, but I imagined that it did, so I wrote it that way. –KA

"old men's still raging hatred—"
An old friend and fishing partner of mine—seventy-five—railing against his
father's treatment of the family. His father now long dead. Doors slamming
open instead of shut. —MS

"mild late winter"
Perhaps the mildness of the day and the birds, harbingers of spring, can lighten
the spirit. Then the people in suits carrying briefcases show up. —PN

"shirt sleeves rolled back to elbows"
Reading Miyazawa Kenji while walking along the beach seeing a stranger fishing,
his untanned arms flying out of his rolled sleeves stark and slippery like the fish
he was hunting. Miyazawa's big white feet motif. —MO

"blue ocean calm blue"
Marcy's mantra (Al Bundy's neighbor). —MS

"out my window fountain and rain sounds"
Being given an almost impossibly huge samsara link by Michael, I dove in. My
stanza was originally experienced on a rainy day in a pensione in Venice over-
looking a little courtyard with fountain. —KA

"all bets are off now"
That highly charged, mysterious first encounter when you feel wildly attracted
to someone and can't help feeling you've known them before. The possibilities
seem endless and pointless; it's impossible to even consider the odds. —MO

"a crowd of dead leaves and"
Second moon stanza. I can't remember where I was when this poem occurred.
All I can remember are the leaves and the shadows and the grain of the porch
boards. I might have been up in the country, perhaps Inverness, at a friend's
house. In this link, the moon is alluded to. —KA

"for years the neighbor's house"
Even though it is Keith's moon stanza, there is a heavy sadness about the scene,
of something abandoned or forgotten. But then a child's melodious meaning-
less babble erases the gloom as if it were the light of life. —PN

"forget-me-nots everywhere"
My backyard a sea of blue. The sudden death of my younger sister. Desolate.
—MS

"are you still yelling"
First flower stanza. One of our luxuries (my son, Kyran, and I) is to get our hair cut at this rather expensive salon in New Haven, Galaxy. It's run by a couple of really cool people and the people who work there are great. Also, the scene alone is worth the price. I was having coffee there waiting for Andy to finish cutting Kyran's hair, listening to the crazy wild dialogue and overheard the first two lines. Then added the flower image to match Blanche and also Michael's forget-me-nots that he generously provided my first flower stanza. —MO

"what a mess – who expects the cat"
The cat had just rubbed up against the freshly painted baby furniture–those brazen remorseless yellow eyes! —PN

"Cairo video"
What a mess. The Cairo earthquake. The news video. What at first I thought was a background noise of machinery was the huge roar of voices all across the city. Probably audible to ships in the Med. Number closer to ten million, I suppose. —MS

"a blackened nail turning"
Earlier that day before I received the link in the mail, I had been tilling the back-yard, turning over the fireplace ashes where the corn was going to be planted in a few months. I suppose this could be an example of what the renku masters in Japan called a distant link. Its connection to the previous stanza being entirely metaphorical. —KA

"bare feet on cold tiles"
Don't you remember what your mother said about stepping on rusty nails? And there I was in my bare feet! —PN

"arms at each side of your head"
A friend I love deeply who when I wake him in the morning has his arms over his head. He has beautiful cream arms. —MO´

"a huge firefly"
This is a free translation from Issa. The Japanese in the second line reads, "yurari-yurari to." In his gloss on this line, D. T. Suzuki says there is no equivalent in English for this onomatopoeia. And then goes on to say much, much more. Originally, I assumed he was right, then one day in an idle mood, I remembered the poem and thought, naw, and spontaneously rewrote it from memory. The business card I wrote it on migrated as a bookmark through a few books. When I found it a few months later (by turning it over), I couldn't remember where the original translation was. I thought Buson and searched through all my Buson translations, but no dice, so I checked Issa translations, too, no. I then assumed that I imagined the whole thing and it was an original poem. A year or so after that, I was researching the tea ceremony and rediscovered its source in *Zen and Japanese Culture*. –KA

I'm fascinated by Keith's Issa information. It's quite exciting to think of my simple lines being traceable through Issa to Keith's business card bookmark and on. –MO

"warning – keep all body parts"
Firefly flashing . . . a warning. Lifted verbatim from a sticker on the windows of a DTA city bus. A found two-liner. –MS

Michael's found poem in response is perfect. –KA

"frequently the crowds"
Reading the NY Times one morning, some vast migration of people plugging the roadways. Newscasters' cars quite stuck in the tide of humanity. Not moving but just honking. –MO

"each night a new figure's"
Maureen's stanza was almost psychically depicted on the news one night. The crowded streets of some European town during the Christmas holidays and some tiny car caught in a sea of people. It's more than just a consumer spree to them. The Feast of the Nativity has a much deeper, powerful meaning. It supercedes the prerogatives even of the modern world. –PN

Pat's stanza is a particularly fine example of a passing link, the hardest thing to write in renku. A passing link doesn't call attention to itself, displays many possibilities for further links, acts as a conduit for new themes, and yet maintains its own character. Basho excelled in them. –KA

"nah, you shouldna mailed them bills—"
A domestic argument, where I had screwed up. I sublimated my burden of guilt into a poem. But, we still didn't have any more money. –KA

"too wet to view the moon"
Third moon stanza. It was raining. She felt bad that she had paid the bills and now there was no money. And she didn't like being yelled at. –PN

"sound of a car door slamming"
It's the old lying in bed hoping the one you love will pull into the driveway, hearing a car door slam, and then gradually realizing it's the driveway next door. Hearing laughing voices. Can't help feeling disappointed. –MO

"distracted he asks"
The 43 bus in Berkeley on the corner of Bankcroft and Shattuck. I didn't get the driver's name. –KA

"volleys taps flag folded"
I was a pallbearer for my friend in #8. A survivor of Pearl Harbor. Don't know what he would have thought of the Military Honors. He didn't care for preten-sion or formalized ritual of any kind. After the funeral, we returned to his house. No one felt comfortable sitting in his chair at the head of the kitchen table. –MS

"the puppy howled"
Thinking about Michael's somber ceremony for a plain man and hearing the neighbor's puppy howling in the deepening twilight. Thinking about dogs wailing over the bodies of the dead or just how their howling for a lost master or friend is a symbol of our mortality. –MO

"easy quiet way of chi"
I had a hell of a time linking to Maureen's lines and casting about I reread her letter where I found the elements that make my lines. She linked with herself and didn't even know it! She had loud in her lines so I had to have quiet in mine. –PN

"on this fresh black asphalt"
Ageku. On a sunny day in Berkeley while riding my bike very slowly and carefully to work, the new asphalt seemed remarkably friendly and active, show-ing me moving pictures. –KA

Renga

Martine Bellen, Elaine Equi & Melanie Neilson

1.
October:
coldness or virtue—
one long line

2.
First a slump
then a glide.

3.
Quasi dye,
Routine, surprise, pines—
Comeback land.

4.
Forest White
erasure

5.
Traces map
the underpinning,
its allure.

6.
(Canny seen
Thisaway.)

7.
"Egg go home"
Shouts lord as I touch
(you are subtle)

8.

Girl Talk vs.
   The Ghost of . . .

9.

leaf by leaf
illusions of choice
work silence

10.

(a) Dangling
Palimpsest

11.

Apple Blue:
answers ripen in
morning light

12.

Lariat
Afternoon

13.

Evening sole
Thrashers without sight
   Passerine

14.

Repeating
the password.

15.

Songster once,
this knot up-in-arms
retreating.

16.

Ballistic
metaphrast

17.

Resting in
the chaos of the
Middle Ages.

18.

Eye carving
Catalpa

19.

Trumpery
. . . hid in the attic
or the spy

20.

(im)posing
the center

21.

base and backs
curls, braids, feathers, staged—
portrait self

22.

Enlarged Times
Motion Stance

23.

stutter-step
defies the image/
              obstacle

24.

spring in tears
subtle branch

25.

Second chance
Found where it was left
Memory

26.

Enshrined in
behavior.

27.

Blackboard work
summer in reader,
"a pen" picks.

28.

bored   walker

widow   planke

29.

Crossing the
border that habit
holds us to.

30.

Anecdote
Neck I rote

31.

Fixed stringed sound
Of the surf beating,
Metronome

32.

Sideshow: Ten-
Cents-A-Trance.

33.

Sometimes her
Scorchy face afield
Spectacles

34.

Mutual
Compulsion

35.

Swing in an
ever widening
arc–far flung

36.

more itself
august suite.

October 1992-September 1993

PROCESS NOTE

The three of us all used to regularly attend a lively Saturday afternoon poetry reading series at the Ear Inn, a bar in New York. Since we admired each other's work, a collaboration seemed a natural outgrowth of our friendship. Martine, who had been reading Basho's *The Monkey's Raincoat,* had the idea of doing a renga.

Renga is a form of Japanese collaborative poetry dating back to the twelfth century. It is made up of linked stanzas of set syllabic structure with a different author responding to the previous stanza.

In this poem we decided to use a syllable count of 3-5-3, followed by two lines of 3-3. Martine wrote the first haikai, Elaine the second, Melanie the third, with that order repeated consecutively throughout. In Basho's time, poets most often wrote either thirty-six chains or one hundred chains. We decided to go with thirty-six. We didn't calculate how long the poem would take us, though after a few months of very leisurely writing our respective third verse, we agreed upon a one month deadline. No one ever felt pressured and the poem completed itself in exactly a year.

MARTINE BELLEN, ELAINE EQUI & MELANIE NEILSON

Tenebrae

Dodie Bellamy & Kevin Killian

The poetry was in the gore, but in the American version the gore was cut out. Flat. How could these wet souls not love seeing through the specular glass? The blood, spattered over the kitchen cabinets.

Daria Nicolodi, a woman with a flip and a face as long as California, her raincoat flapping in the dark wind. Blue and magenta shadows bleed like what's not there. What happened?

Red stiletto heel in the raw mouth of the youth. The beach becomes a book, becomes a murder. I want to write a poem as long as California. "I didn't do it! I didn't do it!" Her body hurls through the plate glass, shards of undoing, dark pulsion glinting, the body unwound. A thousand holes like seeds, here in the seedy part of Rome. She takes a dagger in a darkroom, O heart of mine.

Revision. Victims emerge from the bath, unsane. I can't see their faces, but their sharp chemical beauty evaporates in the red air.

PROCESS NOTE

I (Kevin) wanted something a little tonally different for one of the poems I was writing for my book on the Italian film director Dario Argento, so I thought to break up the surface of the poem by asking someone "other" to write it with me. Dodie agreed to help out, even though we have rarely collaborated or even tried to without a fight, perhaps because the way we see things is so different. On this poem we pretty much made a list, like David Letterman, of the aspects of Argento's *Tenebrae* (in the U.S.A. called *Deep Red,* 1982) we liked the best, and we'd holler them out at each other until we had ten. Then we rewrote the poem to disguise the fact that two different people were writing it. Jack Spicer—or Eleni Sikelianos—wrote one line, "I want to write a poem long as California."

KEVIN KILLIAN

A Lover's Complaint

Samuel Ace & Kevin Killian

I walked through the desert to bring you a marigold
And all you did was complain about your allergies.
But I thought you said that the more we fucked the better you felt. And then
there was the cat food my doctor said to add to your meals.
My pretty kitten scratched my eyes out, one by one now I don't know where
you are.
The sounds, the sounds! Sight does not matter. Don't you remember the
reverie of crickets, and the fugue I sang for you beneath it all?
But crickets always made you think, "Pinocchio," how you felt like a puppet
when you were with me.
I was a puppet in love. The nod of your chin made me salivate. The in-out of
your breath turned me into a boy with black hair. Your blind eyes made
my cock ache. I gave you a shaving of my skin,
which you used as a postage stamp on a letter to your *new* girl. "Help!" you
wrote, "I'm a prisoner on Fantasy Island!"
Fantasy Island or not, darling, I was just leaving options open. I turned the
new girl loose in your bedroom. All along, she was always for you.
"Alas, my love, you do me wrong, to cast me off discourteously"

I bought you a diamond ring with the proceeds from my lobotomy.
I wrote your name across the sky in letters a thousand feet high, like Lulu in
To Sir with Love.
But you had become a vapid-eyed white girl, never the same after they took
out your brains.
I've known of your, your secluded nights; I've even seen her, maybe once
or twice—
I knew you were watching us down at the lake where I went to get away from
you, your yearning and your desire, your 1 A.M. journeys to the refrigerator
to (secretly) finish the pork lo mein and the devilled eggs.
The lake I bought to satisfy your need to walk on water; the eggs that weren't
devilled till you cast paprika spells on them the way I had to have
something of yours, even your poison.
But always when I tried to walk on that lake, I slipped to my knees, only to see

126

your drowned face staring up from under the ice you even took the hair
from my toes.
I braided that hair into a housecoat, for you to wear on trips in your roadster—
I gave my love a cherry, without any stone.
That was but a pretty toy, your cherry, not unlike the emerald green Z3, a nice
taste without a very long memory.
I saw you at the end of your rope, dangling down the cliff of my great love. I
drove you anywhere you wanted, but mostly, you moaned, to distraction.
Distracted is the word, not by you or your tongue, but by the lingering scent
of her hair on the back of the leather seat.

I woke to the sound of running water: you were dyeing your hair to run away
from me.
Yes, I had become that black-haired boy, pungent with musk and bleach, but I
could not get away. Your knife was true and I died there in the bathroom,
a tiny white tile and a drop of blood beneath my open eye.
For you were not prick'd out for women's pleasure, and as for me, I would
not hurt a fly!
Perhaps not a fly but certainly me. As my soul ascended, I watched you from
the ceiling, frantically washing my blood from your hands. I knew the
stain would never leave you. Never.
"There'll be days like this," Mama said, grinning, in her swivel chair rocker in
the cold fruit cellar.
Your memory is off. "Crunch crunch," your mother cackled, grinding her
teeth into what was left of my inner ear.
Gee, I guess my Long Island Lolita's not cut out for motel life, after all.
Why didn't you say so? 'Long Island,' 'Lolita,' my dear blonde thigh. The
Chelsea would be fine.
Tonight at ten.

Process Note

I (Kevin) had admired the poetry of Linda Smukler (as Samuel Ace was called then) for eons, and when Linda came to San Francisco we agreed to collaborate on a poem. It would be based on what I understood as a "call and response" format, in which I might begin a sentence with something provocative, and Linda would proceed to deflate it in the second part of the clause. Always a sting in the tail. Sometimes we would turn tables as well. The poem grew to incorporate snatches of old folk music, Nabokov's *Lolita,* Hitchcock's *Psycho,* anywhere two lovers went away to be together and get a little crazy. "'There'll be days like this,' Mama said, grinning, in her swivel chair rocker in the cold fruit cellar." We wrote this by e-mail and I remember waiting with bated breath, immense pleasure, to find out what slap I was going to get next.

KEVIN KILLIAN

from **Sappho's Gymnasium**

T Begley & Olga Broumas

Flower Parry

Clear blue temple I'm taken in
clear blue temple I'm taken in
god would talk if I did
god would talk if I did

got a mouth wants to know

I was seeing someone burst open
I was seeing someone burst open
the door she was being
the door she was being fucked

hurt as a virtue

hurt as a virtue makes me
vertigo piss-scared
seeing someone burst open
god would talk if I did

Let go your hammering
it is hot and dark in here amassing the sacraments
I can air in any direction and miss
and miss every time
with effort
I can miss with effort
back of my hand
back of my head
no matter now painful
dancing in her mirror
because it is my mirror
if it came from my heart

Among indelible black
cosmos I keep words
or sing

Walked toward the garden
I had to work to show it
then I understood the garden was destroying it
and that I should rest and not water the
shoots but wait until dark to
uncover them

Rich red euphoriant pumped by heat
at high magnification
in the lightest scan
the indescribable screams of the ego cleansing

How could I hide from talking tree
I threw that stone at the silent world
and had the sensation
of having killed

Nothing feels better
to be clear about
this within

You who are being titillated go
thrive on the tiled plaza to the sea
don't breathe our air into the dark
anti-lips eyes tongue
how come you play for maggots
when juice of air itself gives law
touch my throat I will shatter
god with restraints I'm not

I hope I go dizzy on sight
I broke no law
snip at my soul it's a relief
I know I frighten nurses
headstrong human bundle nodding
and smiling pointing to her eye
showing a picture of singing skull
less than a moment ago the fear of dying no
of killing a homosexual

Passed on by kicks its name is bad
bad doors and windows do its work
court after who courts after
I am more stupid where it strives
first it then me the power of the cage
tamper spoil and lose its asp
split breastbone that was my life

Pour down avalanche of palms
someone's pulses aim to do as soon as possible
lightening the feet dressing the lips
tenderfoot seedbed in the spirit given rights
over vast agreement
praising floor carried into fields

Practitioner without practice asylumed by her side
at first death and afterlife or even contact craving
frightened me but in commonlight at the lamphole
angel eyebright charge of dreams
shaking the vulgar tablecloth each of us
her splendid gaze mantle burning

I don't know why I serve or want to dance wake up
   be born
watching the window settle on compassion
I made a wing which we are flying
mountain covered with saints
nice of them to leave the baskets
no moral life is without
individual years creating embrace
how easily it could has changed one bit
I do myself o solitude
at the birthing of sea level
my undesired you ask undestroyed

PROCESS NOTE

Who speaks? *Metis, Outis.* But, who speaks? A voice of pluracination, heard partially, as always, gracing one of us with particulars, the other with the hallucinated breath of verbally unintelligible but musically incontrovertible dictions. That was one time, which recurs. Another is certitude of the field it requires us to serve: eros: gracious, philoxenous, augmenting, lubricant faith. We dwell, like most, in the lugubrious, cacophonous chaos of the imperial globe absorbed in its Babel complex. We don't have to sing about it. "That which disempowers you is unfit for your song," Odysseas Elytis. The lyric refuses its raptor. Sappho's legacy to her daughter Kleis, her *gymnasium*, is "Tears unbecome the house of poets." This translation honors her lithe tongue, if not the exact plurality of her meaning. The word for "tears" is *thren*, a contraction of *threnoi* (as in threnody,) which is onomatopoetic and doesn't immediately imply words (why ode is needed in threnody.) It is the sonoric and somatic act of lamentations. For "unbecome" she uses *ou Themis*, not Themis, the female god of Justice and ethics. What occurs in the simple swap is pleasure. Pleasure is infant, it too saves nothing. I mean the nothing that would have us undergo a surgery wherein "all light" is the only possible and desirable transplant. "Few know the emotional superlative is formed of light, not force," Sappho's island-mate through millennia, Odysseas Elytis. My skin is the volunteer cipher of the your emotion. Who speaks? Collaboration is compassion. Erasure of "ego" and "muse."

T BEGLEY & OLGA BROUMAS

from **A Library Book**

Norma Cole & Michael Palmer

Stanza

STANZA: Twenty-six coat hangers on a rack. Nine bottles of still water. Eleven chairs, three folded. Six ceiling vaults. Two tables parallel to each other. Twelve thousand volumes "under lock and key." Sun-flare against the lens.

STANZA: We are familiar with the phenomenon of the haunted house. We know that life unfolds in familiar interiors, gravid with fluid and astral images; images which remain linked to the place and circumstances of their birth.

As he desired, I clasped his neck, and he took opportunity of time and place; and when the wings were opened far . . .

STANZA: hesitation or stop; the dark chamber or true solar chamber.

Just when I wanted to get up to find you I found that the doors were doubly locked.

It is said, "He has many rooms for rent in his head."

exc: She spoke of the disorder of the library, but she was not speaking of the library. As the light diminished she asked, "What if a bird were to find its way in?"

STANZA: repeated measure from the corners.

This room contains three things; two are yours if you care for them. One is properly yours.

Similarly she said, "I have three words, but only the one here for you to repeat."

Two cameras on the table, one at each end.

———

Already the moon lies beneath our feet
Time is passing and there's still lots to see
Stuff you wouldn't believe

Reader

You, who are not one.

You in the corner—always in the corner?

READER: Yours, the first book, collusion's proof: wild flowers placed on the book of life and probability.
But beware of this: accidents will seduce you. For instance, baking bread will split, and the creases or folds attesting to the baker's art will have a special appeal for you.

READER: Space, penetrated by these figures, reflects both emptiness and solid bodies, having, like the solid body, dimension, but, like emptiness, being immaterial.

exc: How the body extends in space: we say, articulates space, or is read by space.

READER: Orgasm is essentially a narrative. All sexual relations are structured like a story: a one-way street, the awakening of enigma and the desire for its resolution.

III . . .the moon entangled . . .

"Here we would desire a reader with a taste for nothing but mathematics and geometry . . ."

exc: He dreamed one night that he was crossing a field, dressed only in a loincloth made from a leopard's skin, and accompanied by a favorite lion walking on his right.

Asked about certain aspects of his dream, he . . .

———

Sed cum legebat, oculi ducebantur per paginas . . . vox autem et lingua quiescebant.

> Don't ask, I won't write,
> since, reader, words couldn't say

Lens

Twenty-six coat hangers on a rack. Four bottles of still water. Eleven chairs covered in worn red velvet. Three folding chairs. Twenty-four books; two tables aligned in parallel. Sixty thrones arranged back to back along the twenty-nine arches.

LENS: A burning glass; a watery sphere; a centered system: two revolutionary surfaces with a common axis, differentiated by the thickness of the middle.

LENS: A visible boiling begins like a storm or the onset of a serious illness. Avid to paint what so rarely appears and so quickly vanishes like the lovely thing left behind in the night. A magnified image.

I will not be seeing you again today and here are my reasons.

exc: They would meet at her atelier every few weeks to discuss questions of the magazine and the press. At around eight in the evening, when everyone was beginning to feel hungry, she would appear at the table with several loaves of bread and an enormous bowl of lentils and bacon.

exc: He asked, can you recall whether the waters have always been this murky?

LENS: Any kind of thing could be the accidental cause of joy, sadness or desire.

"As to your idea of encouraging young men to polish glass—as it were, to start a school of glass-polishing—I do not myself see that that would be of much use."

LENS: These are the colors the eye prepares. Anyone wanting to know should watch my eyes.

––––––

    False attributions
    solid or liquid
    one of them infinite

    Thus the surface is a map

Process Note

From *Chain* 3.1, October 1994:

"A Library Book" is something we wrote together in 1994, at the Fondation Royaumont, after one of their collective translation sessions, an intense week. Invited to stay on and do something "else," we decided to take advantage, in all senses, of the opportunity to explore and plunder the bizarre collection of books they have as a library. These books, kept under lock and key, had never been available to us before, and once we had the key, we used them mercilessly as source, as jumping-off point, as basis for translation, for false translation, and as foil for our own writing.

As you will see, the "entries" locate under the eight "keywords" [three excerpted here], chosen from all possible words. There are different types of entries, for instance some marked "exc." for "excursus" which became in our minds "excursion." And then, at the end of each section, under a line, is an addendum.

So it's not exactly poetry or translation or narrative.

There are references also to books they must have had once, must have been "taken," abducted.

NORMA COLE & MICHAEL PALMER

Chinook, 7 Poems (Like Non-existence)

Joe Ross & Rod Smith

Chinook Model

If an insufficient
sound accomplishes
nothing, this
referral is authorized
for use for
ambulatory visits—
Hopefully the change will allow us
to move closer to the change
For I am poor,
ideal, & final
incarnation of the human
memory—you meet
in their language
The patient will experience
an unwanted resembling
We can imagine
The mutes shouldered
room, gradually feeling
an unwanted
perfect world
alone.

Interlackutal Za

earth isometric hexagon will bolt
sounds between space
hide intercepts precedence
over art.

Love, just put it in the bin over there
When the laborer who takes a surfboard wanted a bomb
you italicized the wrong hairline
talkin' to peachy peach
I don't think I'm smart Adam Smith
but what we despise may be a mystery
coping with shyness.

Chinook (As in No Other Dare Fail)

For I am poor and needy and my heart is wounded within me.
For 3 hours 14 minutes and 22 seconds.
In what language shall I address you?
For 3 hours 14 minutes and 22 seconds.
For I am poor and needy and my heart is wounded within me.

Like Non-existence

reason's Flipping through
"damn" biographical
a thing bin over ground
of over to becoming. Your
as the we are floor, or unreality
engage it
is is
sculpted. hoping for
love retreats
Fascination with
be the teaching you
makes them your will
intheswineherd board
the concept Dawson, in apparently
no the rug, tradition
without someone embarking
would find them into indestructible drop
telescreen for Zone ↔
entire budget is simply way of
but really peach about crater
is beat the resign as who takes at night
To pray don't fall on the damp, charred
and over I'm smart, smarter. We over art.
transmission. My has been
space between no longer separates thought
get over to read a problem
another. Adam
today. When
admire what

Chinook (Philosophy Patient)

Thus we have the interesting problem again within me my heart is god but that's unique in its meaning to interesting people of The Times Magazine today destroy is not one sort ceaseless & single in fact we have deductive reasoning or diagnostic tests Death is the birth of the problem of human action like chicken if you'd like foreign as it is in its unique upgrade necessary faint might save these lines if life were merely a disorderly application without me today's game to persons for what they have done to idols too deep to destroy deep idols for what we can imagine they have done to Coca Cola Classic

Reason's Over Divine

Reason's Over Divine

sentient manifest in the hexagon

        refuses Olson

dog

        Scholarship Mississippi

in the

      his reaching out   don't

sun

   most

I

   them

have

read one does

Chinook (Sonnet)

Aubrey wants special documentation idols
This isn't Germany to destroy
Sitting alone in a court
A sound accomplishes nothing
What fact more conspicuous
In modern history in the morning
The penetrating quality of the wind
It would be all very simple
If only I could forget
This portion of today's game within me
The subject of a poem dirtier & dirtier
I saw the whole thing would not last an instant
The elements of disbelief
are very strong in the morning

PROCESS NOTE

From *Membrane,* Spring 1995:

Each of us was to send the other a postcard, daily, with something read or heard, something encountered rather than something "self-generated." The words, phrases, sentences, were treated as material for composition. There was no concern for the order in which postcards arrived, and no stipulation that each card must be used or that the syntax or "content" of a thought expressed should be preserved. Each of us wrote poems with a vocabulary provided by the other. Or, more exactly, with a vocabulary encountered by the other.

JOE ROSS & ROD SMITH

The Secret

Cindy Goff & Jeffrey McDaniel

When you were sleeping on the sofa,
I put my ear to your ear and listened
to the echo of your dreams.

That's the ocean I want to dive in, merge
with the bright fish, plankton, and pirate ships.

I walk up to people on the street
that kind of look like you and ask them
the questions I would ask you.

Can we sit on a rooftop and watch stars
dissolve into smoke rising from a chimney?

Can I swing like Tarzan
in the jungle of your breathing?

I don't wish I was in your arms.
I just wish I was pedaling a bicycle
toward your arms.

Process Note

The poem came out of surrealist exercises Cindy Goff and I used to do back when we were in grad school at George Mason University. One particular exercise involved us lying on our backs with a tape recorder running and just speaking, trying to riff, trying to come up with something that had a pulse. About 90% of what we said was inane, but then one of us would stumble onto some metaphor or thread, and we'd vibe off each other. Then we'd play back the ninety minutes of tape—each of us writing down our favorite lines. We'd exchange our lists and build a poem, construct some loose narrative, or an archipelago of associations. Then we'd give the poems back for the original author to revise. The final draft of this poem is not too different from what Cindy assembled. Collaborating like that is extremely intimate. You can't just do it with anyone. You want to feel good about yourself in the morning.

JEFFREY McDANIEL

Listening to a Storyteller

Robert Bly & Yorifumi Yaguchi

In Memoriam William Stafford

YAGUCHI:

In an Ainu house an old Ainu
Woman's recital was flying like bees.

BLY:

Her voice brought honey into the room,
And the bees were preserved in that honey.

YAGUCHI:

Honey tastes of wildflowers, out of which
The songs of the bush-warblers come flying.

BLY:

There is water dripping in the deep forests;
And the gods eat the cries of the bush-warblers.

YAGUCHI:

There is a deep well covered by grasses;
And I remember the womb I was in.

BLY:

No one knows the silence of the high peaks.
But I sometimes hear Stafford's voice in the bushes.

YAGUCHI:

Suddenly silence flies up in the form
Of a bird from a bush nearby.

BLY:

I think the dead spend a lot of time
During the day in the nests of shy birds.

In the Cities of Someone Else's Anxiety

Stephen Dunn & Lawrence Raab

Black and unforgiving, the city was early Antonioni
and she its Monica Vitti, puffy-lipped and bored.
Why did it have to be this way? she wondered. Roger Vadim
would have been her choice, and here she was
burdened with the world's troubles, or one man's troubles
which were different from a woman's, especially a woman
whom Alain Resnais or someone with a soul and an eye could have
invented. Even Truffaut in his boyish way.
To make matters worse, she didn't know a word of Italian.
But her tongue, lovers had claimed, was universal
and her face was the kind Hitchcock might pursue with a crop duster.
Who could she trust? How could she find her place
in this lost world, this city of someone else's anxiety?
Her only choice was to go deeper, take it all on,
whatever it was, and this was the mood she took with her.
She cinched up her raincoat. She thought,
If you know the rules you should be able to play the game.
Those French, always so full of conundrums—
if only she'd been Japanese and inclined toward spectacle, Kurosawa
could have fashioned an ending. Now the trees shook in the wind.
A man appeared across the park. This was the moment
she felt only something black and white, perhaps Wellesian,
could properly deliver her.

The Bluest Day

Stephen Dunn & Lawrence Raab

From the beginning a grandiloquence had been missing.
The women in the next room, blonde and be-laced,
were suspect. What were they saying to each other?
Was it more whispering about taffeta, or the intolerable
absence of God? No, he decided, probably not.

Indecipherable, he thought, and moreover
they'd never tell him. Wasn't that to be expected?
Word travels through the dark corridors
until the mind is caught between one
illusion and another. On the bluest day, for example,

an airplane, frail, ablaze, falls
out of the sky into the water. But then you see
it was only a tern coasting on the blowsy wind,
another chatterer, another complainer
in the company of so much competing noise.

Or was this the lost, important bird so many desired?
Should he call the women? Would it matter to them?
Then it too was gone, missing once again. Still,
the predictable ocean lay just beyond the dunes,
its timbrous repetitions, its illusion of importance.

Anyone in his right mind, he concluded, would stop
worrying about significance, would decide
to love those women instead of listening
to what he would never hear them saying,
and perhaps someone wiser would know, as he did not,

how far to take their beautiful, unfinished sentences.

The Night She Removed Her Pearls

Stephen Dunn & Lawrence Raab

All night the fog circled their house.
He thought how easy it would be to get lost
since, after all, oblivion was just around the corner
and there was always an empty room at the inn,
the same room, its single window opening
onto the garden, weedy, adrift in fog.
She, on the other hand, saw ghost ships
riding the high waves, and wouldn't be convinced
of anything. "But can you believe all this fog?"
he asked. She shook her head, as if to say
the dark is merely your dark, and no gloom of yours
will ever be mine. Then she smiled and removed her pearls,
tossed them casually at him, which he took
for a sign, opaque, foggy, perilous.
They wished for a thunderstorm to clear everything away,
but none arrived, not even a cleansing breeze
to lift their spirits or remind them
of those days, halcyon and yet astir, when
they hadn't yet learned to care about the weather.

Sky

Stephen Dunn & Lawrence Raab

At night among the stars we see
the ever-present animals and heroes,
which preceded us. The gods
we placed there have fallen,
and the sky is thinner now
without them, lighter than
an invisible hand. It's amazing
we can touch it, that it's as close
as it is far. Turn away from it,
and still we're seen.
By whom? By what?
Only the obscurantists know.
If there's another side to it,
if we could get there,
we might understand why all
is quiet now at my father's house,
or for the first time see replayed
the lucent single eye of the moon
as it revealed a reptile
emerging from a mountain lake
without ambition or a plan.

The Other Side of the Sky

Stephen Dunn & Lawrence Raab

When God was waiting
to be invented, the sky
was thinner. You
could have touched it,
then turned away
without the fear of being seen,
gone back
to your father's house
where everything was quiet.
Perhaps the moon shone
on a mountain lake.
Animals and heroes
were the shapes the stars made
long before you heard the stories
meant to explain them.
And when you asked
your father about the sky—
if there was another side
to it, if there was an end—
he said you'd know
how to think about it
when you had to.
And you believed him.
Of all the lies
you carried with you, that one
hurt the most to leave behind.

Process Note

From the Introduction to *Winter at the Caspian Sea:*

These poems were written over the course of three years of week-long summer vacations with our wives at Cape May Point in New Jersey. All were done very quickly. The method used to compose most of them was this: one of us would write a first line; then the other would write two more, folding the paper so that only the second was visible. Pairs of lines were added until the page was reasonably full, and the person who hadn't started would complete the poem with a single final line.

Folding the paper contributed greatly to the fun, hiding enough of the poem so that we could be surprised by how it added up—how the quirky challenges of any one line would be extended, or deflected, by the next gesture. To guarantee some stability, we'd decide before beginning on at least one continuing structural element, a first or third person speaker, for example, or a man's perspective or a woman's. In "The Cities of Someone Else's Anxiety" we agreed to include the names of as many filmmakers as possible.

"Play's the thing," Robert Frost writes, and that might have been our motto, if we'd looked for one. The point always was to allow for as many surprises as possible. Coherence was, to a great extent, luck, interesting language being our primary aim. Titles were added by whichever of us first came up with a good one.

[Two] of these poems ["Sky" and "The Other Side of the Sky"] used a different and somewhat more complicated method. Each of us would write—again, quickly—four lies (one of which had to be more elaborate than the others) about an agreed-upon subject. Each would read the other's lies, and then, in no more than ten minutes, write a poem using any of the elements from both sets...Why lie? Just to avoid the ordinary, to move the material as quickly as possible into metaphorical territory. A great part of the fun was to see how we might deal with shared material.

We don't want to claim too much for these poems, but they strike us as more than souvenirs of some happy moments by the sea, after tennis and before dinner. We wanted in writing them to have as much fun as we could with words—with what Wallace Stevens calls "the gaiety of language"—and we hope some of those pleasures may be available.

STEPHEN DUNN & LAWRENCE RAAB

Dental Records Prove We Were All Children

Joanna Fuhrman & Jean-Paul Pecqueur

This poem is not a statement, nor is the soup bowl
lit by sunlight a sign of the groundhog's demise.
Some men prefer agate to mind, the path
through park cluttered with rubble.
Rubble. Cardboard. Tooth Ache. Birch.
With the picnic began civilization.
My mother said to wash the lettuce twice.
She said, "All statements are a woman in a well."
The floodlight industry destroyed my will.
I felt ashamed for trees.
Their stutter leveled artifice, that agate mind.

PROCESS NOTE

"Dental Records" was written with Jean-Paul in person. We would talk lines over
as we went along.

JOANNA FUHRMAN

To My Kidney Near My House

Joanna Fuhrman et al.

In the morning, you go to the pool
in the sky over the mountains. Kidney,
why are you swimming in a lake?
Is it because there are too many sharks
who might eat you? Why aren't you
bowling? Is it because you might
fall on the pins? Swimming in the water,
you are dressed in black because you are a clown.
Why are you falling down in hot boiling water?
Don't you know you might burn?
You'd be better off running down the street
and getting hit by a car. Kidney,
save yourself before you turn into a snake.

PROCESS NOTE

The poem "To my Kidney Near my House" was written by an amazing group of students in Nancy Sellin's class at the Manhattan Occupational Training Center High School in the West Village where I was a visiting poet in spring of 2002. My visit was sponsored by Teachers & Writers Collaborative, District 75, and PS 721M. The students in that class included Raul Acosta, Joseph Gibbs, Landen Gilfillan, Demetruis Gonzalez, David Hill, Kevin Merrill, Irene Nieves, Shaniaua Nowell, Yesemia Rodriquez, Kimberly Vinculado, and Benjamin Zisfein. We had just read Kenneth Koch's poem "To my Heart at the Close of Day" from *New Addresses*. I asked the students to make a list of body parts and a list of activities. After our list was on the board, we discussed what body part and what activity the students wanted to write their collaborative poem about. It was Kevin Merrill's idea to write about a kidney, but the rest of the class agreed. I remember David Hill called out some of my favorite lines including "You are dressed in black because you are a clown" and "is it because there are too many sharks who might eat you?" The next class students wrote their own poems about body parts. Yesemia Rodriquez wrote an interesting poem about "ears who are a machine going through a paper," and Demetrius Gonzalez wrote a poem that began "My brain is watching TV while eating poems." This is my favorite poem one of the classes I visited wrote, and I think part of the reason the students in this class were so imaginative was because of the warm and supportive atmosphere Ms. Sellin and the paraprofessional Mr. Ricky Shair provided.

JOANNA FUHRMAN

Four Attempts toward a Theory of True Names

Joanna Fuhrman & Chris Martin

1.

      There's more
to the sound of her

salvage under
coral colored

doorways, galvanized by the local juke
box axis.
   There's a holy

      set of lids slitting prurient like
rubies through the surf

                      churning stippled
   with sea doodles

and flags, and one of
     us is
     now, also
     a boy
repeating
if you want
        to run to the ocean
   turn to page "run."

2.

      Under the sterling sky, a blank banner
      of cloud swiped our eye

leaving us a negative form
to fill out, darkening

the pupils entirely
like an hour spent
    reading an article about managing
    cuticle drift and finger

nails and how to
trim them without

looking down
at one's hand.

3.

I knew that the bumper sticker labeled "the here / and now" adorned all the
broken cars in the designer / junk yard, but still I thought / by naming my car
"pain" I could keep it / from crashing.

Soon, all closed doors were named "open."

Another bird crashed into the outline of a bird on a library window, but this
time I knew enough not to call it "choice."

Another bird crashed into the wind, its wing buckling like a sail. It made a
sound you called "mogul." The sound was driven against the air and sunk
there.

4.

        We see him as he is,
blank
        spaces in a virtual cloud anthology,

a second hand ahead of the park

wolves

       an incinerated note

lit like a wet

twig.

PROCESS NOTE

"Four Attempts" was written with Chris Martin over e-mail when he was living in Minnesota (now he lives in Brooklyn like every other poet (who doesn't live in Indiana, of course.)) We would send the poems back and forth making changes to the other person's lines as we went along. Since we didn't know each other (we met virtually because of a journal I was editing at the time) we were less hesitant to erase each other's work.

JOANNA FUHRMAN

The Singing Animal World

Joanna Fuhrman & Noelle Kocot

David Lehman you are in the news.
David, go smoke some pot.
David Lehman you love to schmooze.

David Lehman your noir poems provide the clues
For what you'll have to ask the hossentot.
David Lehman you are in the news

Spouting your sexy sexy jailbreak criticism poetry muse.
David Lehman you always know which girls are hot.
David Lehman, is this why you love to schmooze?

Is this anti-De Man stuff just a ruse?
But to lose the art is to lose the master, you sot—
David Lehman do you even read the news?

Because if you do, you know we're just trying to be crude
As sexy girls from outer space take a lot
Of time to turn against Da Man, so schmooze,

Schmooze! We know you feel confused
Among the monochromal caterpillar passageways we forgot
Or didn't really know at all, not from the news
Blasting black-and-white before our times, before the noisy butterfly theories
    eked their ways across the darkened ever-growing poem which is winter
    but at the end of hibernation stretches the big paw of the anti-lion verb
    to schmooze.

Process Note

The January 2000 night that Joanna and I wrote ["The Singing Animal World"]
I was in a manic episode, totally out of my mind. I hardly remember it. I think
it was a lot of fun though. Soon after, I was taken to Bellevue hospital and
medicated; however, I have still been on fire with poetry since then.

Noelle Kocot

Enchainement

David Lehman & Karen Pepper

That afternoon he drove across the International Date Line,
which separated her place from his, about five blocks,
so he could never tell what day it was. But she could,
because she was wearing her special flowers, wanting him
to smell them tomorrow, in Japan. He never thought of it that way,
but she did, all the time. Meanwhile they wilted, turning milky.
Time remained the vexing subject of her reverie.

As a distraction, she changed her name to Judith
and took up journalism. It was tragic on Wednesday
at 4:14 P.M. "Give me a call," she said. She meant,
"give me a ring," and he pictured a wedding band
and never called her. He was on his way to Florida.
"Use some protection," she urged. "Don't get burned."
It was already yesterday in Japan.

May 7, 1997

Falstaff

David Lehman & William Wadsworth

"Look at that bum on the corner." "That's no bum, that's Harold Bloom."
If a tragic romance of uncles and aunts is the story of poetic influence
he's the voice on the phone who talks without listening, a lightning rod of anxiety.
The rest of us are in prison, but the walls are not made of words, and misprision
will not bend the bars that keep us from our freedom, as the new canon
keeps cadets in the dark on the charms of Hamlet or Falstaff.

Some have greatness thrust upon them. Then there is Falstaff,
asleep under a tree, indifferent to the charms of flowers in bloom.
Some dream of glory in combat. But he has heard the cannons
roar. The noise made him cherish the more the influence
of sack in the conduct of man's affairs. Not subject to misprision
is this self-evident truth: that we live and die alone, with anxiety

our common lot. Consider Nym, whose anxiety
was jealousy, a humor his master Falstaff
found humorous. Poor deluded Nym misread
his Mistress, believed her more constant than Mrs. Bloom.
Then under the broken-hearted influence
of too much Eastcheap Sack, he broke the canon-

ic law and robbed the Church (and took a non-
stop flight, anon, to the gallows). Anxiety
is the humor of our age, an influence
for the worse. For Dr. Bloom that old bum Falstaff
is the only cure. To be human, says Bloom,
is to be Hal, not Henry—a king mistaken

for a man by scholarly fools in whose misreading
the play's the site of a battle pitting Jill's canon
against Jack's, with Leo's old vision of a New Bloom-
usalem receding as fast as anxiety
will allow. And therefore do we turn to Falstaff
with our flags at half staff under the influence

of parents, teachers, and stars. The influence
of Falstaff is the will to live, to escape the prison
of our days, not to praise them. Falstaff
is all men, potentially (except Milton). "Yet the canon's
contradictions may doom it," Jack said, radiating anxiety.
"And well they should!" said Jill: "Doom to Bloom!"

Yet when midnight chimes, 'tis the influence of Jack's canon
that makes Miss Priss unbosom her anxiety
in the giant arms of Falstaff, conceiving Bloom.

PROCESS NOTE

This poem was written collaboratively in November 2003 by David Lehman and
William Wadsworth and was published in *Tin House* in their special "Lies" issue
(2004) under the name Jill Malley Reynolds. Her faux bio was printed as follows:
Jill Malley Reynolds grew up in Melbourne, Australia, and was educated at the
university at Perth and later at Cambridge University in England. She has lived
north of Boston since 1994 and has written a monograph about John Ashbery's
influence on Australian poets John Forbes and John Tranter: *Dear John*
(Monograph Press, 2000). She has poems forthcoming in the online journal
Disquieting Muses. The late Ethel Malley was her grandmother.

DAVID LEHMAN & WILLIAM WADSWORTH

The Literary Community

Stacey Harwood & David Lehman

Mia and Mark we want to welcome you to
the association of alcoholic aphorists
the brotherhood of bards
the congress of charismatic correspondents
the Diaspora of diarists
the ecole of ecstatic essayists
the fraternity of flaming fabricators
the guild of guilty timewasters
the hordes of horny haiku-slinging whores
the institute of ink-stained inditers
the jury of jaded journalists
the kangaroo court of critical opinion
the league of literature's loopy lovers
the maison of masturbating memoirists (e.g. Joyce Maynard)
the nation of nervous narrators
the organization of obfuscation
the prisonhouse of impenitent plagiarists
the quonset hut of quotable queers
the republic of wry raconteurs
the society of scribes
the tea party of the literati
the union of the underrated
the vault of the vilified versifiers
the wretched ranks of real writers
the Xanadu of eccentric experts
the Yugoslavia of yesterday's youthful Yaddo-goers
and the zero-sum game of Zeus and zeugmas

November 28, 1997

Process Note

David and I wrote "Literary Community"over dinner at Le Gigot on Cornelia Street. As we walked over from the parking lot on Broadway and Astor Place, David asked me to come up with euphemisms for "Literary Community" for a poem he was writing for his friends Mark Bibbins and Mia Berkman. After trading lines for a while, I suggested that we make the poem an abecedarium. We continued though drinks and appetizers. David wrote down each line as it came to one of us. I remember getting up from the table to wash my hands and returning with "association of alcoholic aphorists" and "maison of masturbating memoirists." David added "e.g. Joyce Maynard." By the time our entrées arrived, we had the poem. David read it aloud and the four-top nearby applauded.

STACEY HARWOOD

The Bus

David Lehman & Joseph Lehman

The bus, the bus, the Gotham bus. A boy sat with his mother on the bus. The bus, which they rode in the place they called Gotham City, was where they took a bite out of the Big Apple. It was a green Granny Smith apple, very tart and very cold.

It was very dark and very dank in Gotham City. A man chewing a toothpick watched the bus lurching forward into the avenue of the future. Gotham City was before them, standing right there, standing so high it could never fall down—not while the bus rode there. A beautiful dark-haired woman crossed the street, pursued by a short unshaven man with a cigar in his hand—we saw her from the window of the bus.

It was a rainy and foggy day as the bus rode through, but the black blankets of night soon circled it. The thunder roared its mighty roar. It sounded like a radio shouting its head off but in reality the roar was the sound of one hundred children humming a tune in the bus. The driver lit a cigarette as the shining moon shone on his face. He was an African-American man who used to play piano and sing, but he had to give that up when his wife had triplets. The bright and shiny moon lit up the sky so that in Gotham City, the dark, the dank Gotham City, people in the street and under the ground could see the bus. The boy and his mother were having an argument when the bus pulled to the stop. It was at the darkest place in Gotham City but the moon let people see and they all walked in the dark and dank Gotham City, waving goodbye to the bus. They missed the bus.

4/19/94

PROCESS NOTE

My son Joe Lehman, then ten years old, and I collaborated on "The Bus" one April afternoon in 1994. We sat at my desk computer and alternated phrases and sometimes sentences. The phrase "very dark and very dank" was Joe's, as was the sentence about the driver who gave up his piano playing and singing when his wife had triplets. The last sentence was mine and made Joe laugh out loud, so I will always treasure it.

DAVID LEHMAN

The Car in a Maze

Daniel Shapiro & David Shapiro

I believe the world is a maze
When you make a wrong turn
It's like making a mistake on a maze
Cars make a lot of mistakes
Angels ride along with their little xylophones
God stays where he is
Cars can get bumped into leaves
Angels sleep for the whole day
God stays where he is
The moon hates to go in front of the sun
The sun hates to go in front of the moon
I don't like to get lost in the maze you have to walk in
Angels like to get lost in God—God is never lost
I like to get lost in my house

from **Vacationland 2**

Carson Brock & James Brock

VIII. Goodbye Idaho!

Goodbye Atomic City.
Goodbye Boise.
Goodbye Couer d'Alene and Caldwell.
Goodbye Dworshak Dam.
Goodbye Eden.
Goodbye Frank Church—River of No Return Wilderness.
Goodbye Gooding.
Goodbye Hailey, sweet home of old Ezra Pound.
Goodbye Idanha Hotel.
Goodbye Juniper Basin Reservoir.
Goodbye Ketchum and Kimberly.
Goodbye Lava Hot Springs and Lowman.
Goodbye Mountain Home.
Goodbye Nampa.
Goodbye Orofino and Ovid.
Goodbye Pocatello and the lower Palisades.
Goodbye Q's Pool Hall on Fairview Boulevard.
Goodbye Rupert.
Goodbye Stanley and Soldier Mountain.
Goodbye Twin Falls.
Goodbye Ucon.
Goodbye Victor.
Goodbye White Bird and Wendell.
Goodbye Xavier Cugat Suite at the Sun Valley Inn.
Goodbye Yellow Pine.
Goodbye Zero Luck Mine.

"Goodbye Idaho!" was the result of a collaboration after a month long, 6500-mile road trip we took in the summer of 2002 in a rented Mustang. Together, we kept a travel journal, from which we wrote a sequence of poems together, sending them back and forth over the Internet after our vacation Out West. Idaho, of course, was our principal destination, and so saying goodbye to it made a lot of sense. We started with an abecderian formula so that we could have an arbitrary listing of places, both real and fantastic, to offer up our *au revoirs*. As a memory piece, then, and as a shared piece, we created this fiction, looking at where we have been, where we wanted to go, and where we could never be. The idea of Idaho, not the place itself, is what we were trying to generate together in this happy bidding.

CARSON BROCK & JAMES BROCK

The Red-Tailed Monkey

Jack Wheeler & Susan Wheeler

I once dreamed of a monkey,
one that was pink with a red tail.

The plane's pink underbelly
skeets on the air chutes, clean
in the winds hauling in.

The wind blew on faces
while the birds fell back,

the quarterback feinting at the
last, breaking his vector, veering
from helmets bearing down on him.

The bear stood up as if
he were king of the mountain –

though the scepter's short
every subject pings and glints
with Midas's sad greed.

The elf got a greedy face
as if he were to steal,

and out across the darkling road,
the dark clouds steal and,
in a row, let loose their darkest rain.

The boy rowed the boat,
even though
            he caught a fish.

And sopping wet, the soldier tossed
like a trout upon the cot,
mopped his hot-fever sweat.

Up, on the top of the mountain,
the animal showed his pride

to the palest sky, cloud hills
blotting the damp, a glint of
rainbow flickering high.

The boy was pale, so pale
he looked dead.

The Spring Years

Annabel Wheeler & Susan Wheeler

January and the wild wind whistles.
Whirrrr! Brrrrrr! go Annabel and Suse.
The sky blisters in the bright bright cold.

Then summer comes and the birds
fly high into the sky and then

the pink gum snags on the sneaker and sticks.
It creaks as it meets
the pavement of the street. Ice! Heat!

Then Annabel and Susan
go   go   go   go!

The shimmering heat in the hazy glow
pocks our skins with sweat.
Thunderheads stew overhead as we

thought about how it
would be terrible if it rained.

Birds hush. The sky is a dark green glade.
The moon is alone, says Annabel, alone now
and afraid. The wind tips in a gush.

Then we go in the sunlight
and   go   go   go   go!

Process Note

Aunt Susan lives in New York and Annabel and Jack in Chicago, so we started writing poems back and forth by mail years ago. Jack and Annabel collaborated individually with Susan, each writing a new stanza on a given poem and sending it back for Susan's stanza. Some of the first poems we tried were rengas, and Jack was about ten when he and Susan wrote "The Red-Tailed Monkey." Annabel was seven when "The Spring Years" was written. On one leg of it, she sent with the draft an excellent drawing of a girl wagging her finger and saying "Do your stanza!" Tough taskmaster.

ANNABEL, JACK, & SUSAN WHEELER

Chain Chain Chain

Jeffery Conway, Lynn Crosbie & David Trinidad

September rain
a hint of
Hurricane Floyd

razes the backs
of black gators and mini mice.

Teeth of green blades
the first leaf
falls to its death

the one Death with its
many Pick-Up-Sticks

dropped, distracted:
the ground swells, expectant:
a red carpet,

driftwood fort, highest
mound, feet frame ocean

Picture this:
Beneath the 12-Mile Reef
(Widescreen Anamorphic–2.35:1)

the sea agitated by the descent;
below the surface, fire coral, blisters

"Coach Lances Heart"
the papers read. Young stars
cry, run amok

in crayon muck,
in dried Play-Doh droppings

while Wagner lies pendant,
belly-up,
imagining Natalie dead

the bionic ear picks
up her last gasp for air

in the waters off beautiful
Santa Catalina,
primeval landscape

fruitless desiring, waves
drawn over silver fish

curtains parted, shiny slit:
silent adulterers,
uncouth, peel ripe oranges

you of the Sunkist navel,
you of the Tangerine Dream

Trained to the valence of harmonica in
"Orange Blossom Special":
of harmonica & strings

Oh Suzanna, 6th grade love
on a desert motif spread

Don't make an O'Keeffe wasteland
out of a Sapphic tiff,
e.g. Merman and Susann

scratching on the door, on your knees:
her head is wreathed with flowers.

Eve, in her happy moments,
Put hibiscus in her hair,
Before she humbled herself

in front of Phoebe: endless
drill team in Eve's likeness—fresh

maiden formed from surplus bone:
the mark of the excision shines like a misplaced
diamond; her dress of stars.

I can still hear her telling me,
"Tighter, Miss Head, tighter."

Vying to be crowned
festival queen, tiara
quite snug, she breaks wind

and discreetly fans her skirts;
Miss Poppyseed aghast

Mary Poppins gassed
Pippi Longstocking slashed
Penelope Pitstop smashed

every poodle with starched puff-
ball tails: no one rides for free

there are eight horses on the carousel
& the lighter is engraved with initials,
a tennis racket.

Perfect serve: Psycho Killer . . .
Qu'est Que C'est? Murder reflected

in the silver tray he glides around
the room retrieving shrimp tails that French
frauds have ripped from the bod with sharp teeth.

And considers their beds of ice:
his eyes closed, falling asleep in snow

like beefy Oliver Reed at the end
of *Women in Love,* his destruction
by Gudrun (Glenda Jackson) complete.

"Drop it or go down with it!"
the smart & plain Angel screams

Angel Orange & Kelly Cleopatra
drop jewelled hand grenades
& begin the war in heaven

The Olympian cloud palaces, the Pearly Gates
"Scraped flat by the roller / Of wars, wars, wars."

Of Boy George, The Doors, and low cal smores
roasted on bonfires in the moors.
The Holy compete for cash—total bores.

Last night a dream of Peter, swinging from gallows:
Picnic at Hanging Rock.

Deviled Eggs & Angel Food Cake—
No, a golden Bundt dripping
with obscene white glaze

emboldens Satan's testicles,
those profiteroles of terror

Blazing red against sheer white linen,
his Salsa a hot shimmer & I pant after
Him: a tall glass of milk

West Virginia built—lanky, blue-
eyed demon—I'd do him. Coffee?

Your Aryan bean, bright blue?
Meinkampf tea? Or chocolate,
that hot Luftwaffe Daddy?

After her fifth martini she scrawled, An oven an oven
an oven an oven an oven, for this desert fox.

not even Garbo has approached
Dietrich in Spain, for special effects
Devil is a Woman—hot, hot

The Divine Woman on Die fruedlose Gasse:
aloof, enigmatic, craving to be alone.

She is not alone but without other people,
underline this difference & look in the mirror
at what Bardot called *spoiling fruit*

"If you don't much mind a few dead minds"
being 35 ain't so lonesome

Good Lord, thirty-five! How did it happen?
You felt the same inside, but suddenly you were thirty-five
and time was racing on. One year blended into another.

What you wanted, what you wanted to look like:
the blades overlay lemon & sugar,

Sugar Ray—he's what I want,
Oh honey honey, spread out on the king-
size mattress of my sick dreams

Sweet, sticky sex with Ben
Affleck, his Oscar on top

A terse conversation with Pamela Anderson:
she tells me: it's what's inside that matters,
leaking sugar as she passes by

onto the just-gotta-haircut toupee
of Mr. Burt Reynolds. No biggy. Hey,

here comes Loni Anderson,
naked and bald in her fur,
sucking an orange lollypop

she wrested from Quentin: at thirteen he will call
his birth parents, cursing them unintelligibly

take them into the back room of the shop,
sodomize them, wear the black leather
chaps he bought for cheap at the flea market

Also for sale at the S/M booth: a pile of Barbie dolls,
naked and dirty, in the mass grave of a cardboard box.

The arches of their feet split by tiny incisors,
plastic tendon exposed. We explore the world by tasting,
then eating it whole.

True, there is a beautiful plastic Jesus,
he is molded to his plug like a chuck of beef.

Mr. Susej is talkin' to you & sho enuff
believes that He is in your computer:
Holy Electronica, the face of Veronica

(Ronnie) Spector emits this message: „i773H NI W,I−3W d73H,,
(To decipher, turn your computer upside down.)

(7!^3 noh S! hHM) 6op 'SW 'dn ap!sdn P70H moN
'Hep ap e7 'po6 we I 'sooq hueW 'sooq hueW
'S3I7 77V 'ON 'ON inoh '0773H 773M

Receiving transmissions on American Thanksgiving
from the Firebombers, with confused gratitude: a string of beads

crisscrosses Neely's breasts:
innocent kid on the
verge of monsterdom.

S   W   G   L
 H O   I R

A film more beautiful with each glass of Cristal:
on the telephone with Elizabeth Berkely last fall,
she insists I perfect the lapdance.

That E.B. is such a p _ _ _ k in a way.
Well, I guess she's just eccentric.

She took an ax and X'ed her parents.
She wore the same frumpy hairdo season after season.
She married him twice, despite drunken brawls & arguments.

ED vs EP: She dressed like a white nobody & he
gave a woman the following advice: Stay away from the large prints

"My chassis is built for comfort," he said, "not for speed."
He greeted reporters in a dressing gown over a pair of deep-dyed Chinese
    silk pajamas,
no doubt exaggerating his weight

and womanly hips, proof he was pure pre-op,
soon to be donning the dress of the Stars & Stripes majorette set.

"I was born a man, but inside I am a woman":
I am predisposed toward the home-perm,
the grooming of My Little Pony, the application of shimmering aubergine

Squeeze a button and yank it longer,
or turn the button and pull it back into her head.

"This sex aid does it all" (batteries not included).
NOTE TO EDITORIAL ASSISTANTS: "prostrate" is NOT "prostate,"
"ballsac" one word, "piss-slit" hyphenated. Let's be professional!

Porno writing largely composed of kennings, as though
there is no one hotter than Beowulf, the Wanderer

tears open his shirt, shows us
Rosie ("rose-girl") on his chest. In the metaphor,
a *recognition* takes place: this girl is a rose

whose petals have been pushed back by drunken hands.
The wind machine starts up: gown, hair, fingers flutter

as the child touches the tiny crinolines, the enamel of her face;
mechanized Swan Lake slowing down, he closes the box,
kicks it violently against the wall & hears something

topple behind it: Homily Clock, perhaps,
knocked off her vanity stool (a "borrowed" thimble)

a can of Old Dutch cleanser—he has left
the bathroom floor awash in streaks, she is just waking now
her chin-strap askew and murder in her eyes

Underneath the finest hand-embroidered organdy, underneath
the petticoats & fancy panties: large painful blisters & long red welts

depict just how hard life at the Junction can be—despite smiles
& skinny dipping in the water tank of wooden planks, the upbeat
locomotive's "Toot Toot!" (The TOWN's water? "You figure it out!")

She was whipped while lashed to the last car (filled with coal & one sleeping
boxcar jumper), her smile belying a Perilous Pauline, shark's teeth, black fin

circling the waters off beautiful
Amity Island
"when the sun makes puddles of blood on the sea"

I know the feeling well, *cuando el sol hace la sangre en el mar,* oh the
horror of it all, *mis amigos,* circling beautiful boys like a horny poodle

skirting their arms to dive below,
where the water divides them, renders them white & fair:
broken Calla Lilies, Duessa's bath: the eye of the *belle bete noir.*

fleshy shoulders, arms protruding from Egyptian milk; *en negligée*
or *au naturel,* no depth of emotion apparent in her kohl-laden eyes

Endora eyes, indeed, which watch over Sam and Derwood
all day and night (witches are genius voyeurs). She thought them
"really quite bourgeois," which explains those huge dark sunglasses

occluding avarice: she climbed into the backseat with her hand outstretched:
a smile like a jackal's, Christina thought as she moved to the next car in
        the cortege

her mind spinning back to her third birthday party:
a merry-go-round on the badminton court, a puppet show, and a trained pig
dressed like a clown: a big ruffle around its neck, walking on its hind legs

though we (squeamish rabbit, dissimulate snake, voluble dragon)
yearn for lives under the same sow spotlight, it's desperately sad, eh?

And who's responsible? I blame the dead rabbit I saw in the Saanich Peninsula;
Hugh Hefner's ascension & falling down the stairs: once as a child (sky
        lawn stone),
& this rabbit year on signing a book contract, my hands breaking the fall.

It was much pleasanter at home—cupids and roses and cornucopias—and yet—
        and yet—
when you're in the parallel universe you can also be invisibly present in this one.

Oh my gosh, I'm in it right now! It's like watching a movie on TV Mom
        wouldn't let me see when I was young.
Under the corn sits a green, nasty teenage boy with a tired-ass Biblical name
        who seems, despite bad hair,
to have power over all the other kids. The lunar cycle is high, an excellent
        aspect for winning friends and influencing people—

Contemplating this moon with mutiny in my heart:
I want to influence people with a switchblade, I want to retract it when
        friends arrive, golden & high

That's the carport where Sal Mineo was stabbed—
a spurned trick? The moon mercilessly cruising the Strip.
Next stop on the Hollywood Murder Tour . . .

would you believe—the old apartment of a trainwreck poet who, high
on shrooms, ice picked the freezer: a geyser of Freon blinded his friend.

a poem about Dana Plato, "Ma Griffe," I had forgotten
& am ashamed when I see her last picture, sick & lonely:
her last breath recorded, the choir invisible, los angeles.

Thus the wasted porn star rises, lifted
by wings of desire, to the top of the tree.

via e-mail
September 15–December 19, 1999

NOTES (BY STANZA NUMBER)

Title: "Chain of Fools," Aretha Franklin, 1967.

4. See last stanza of Sylvia Plath's "Totem."

7. One of the first CinemaScope films (1953). The aspect ratio is the relationship between the width and height of the original screen image, in this case more than twice as wide as it is high. The movie stars Robert Wagner.

9. A *Ventura County Star Free Press* newspaper article, May 1982, reports a local track star (J.C.) missing Citrus Relays meet because coach lanced blood blisters on the runner's feet (blisters he received while New Wave dancing at a San Fernando Valley dance club).

11. When movie star Natalie Wood drowned, her husband Robert Wagner was on board the *Splendour* fulminating over her dalliance with actor Christopher Walken.

12. *The Bionic Woman,* starring Lindsey Wagner.

13. Plath's "Daddy": "In the waters off beautiful Nauset." Santa Catalina: resort island situated twenty-two miles south of Los Angeles; site of Natalie Wood's drowning in 1981.

16. Anne Sexton trope.

17. "Orange Blossom Special" performed by Johnny Cash; "valence of sodium" clue in *New York Times* crossword puzzle, Saturday, August 28, 1999.

18. "Oh Suzanna"—a song easily mastered on the harmonica.

19. In 1959, future best-selling novelist Jacqueline Susann became sexually infatuated with Broadway star Ethel Merman, then a big success in *Gypsy.* Their friendship came to an abrupt end when, one night after a drunken party, Susann followed Merman home and stood outside her apartment, banging on the door and yelling, "Ethel, I love you!"

20. Reference to Susann's ardour at Merman's closed door.

21. Lines lifted directly from D. H. Lawrence's poem "Hibiscus and Salvia Flowers."

22. Phoebe—see film *All About Eve*.

23. Maiden Fresh™ and the notorious spare rib.

24. Elizabeth Taylor to costume designer Edith Head, 1949, while being fitted in a gown for *A Place in the Sun*.

25. Lines taken from *National Geographic* magazine.

28. A popular 1970s license plate frame: "Gas, grass, or ass—no one rides for free."

29. Alfred Hitchcock's *Strangers on a Train*.

30. The Talking Heads. In *Strangers on a Train*, a character's strangling is reflected in the lens of her own eyeglasses.

33. Ken Russell's 1969 film version of D. H. Lawrence's novel.

34. Kate Jackson line in an episode of *Charlie's Angels*.

35. *Charlie's Angels* by way of the wars in Vietnam and Heaven.

36. Quoted lines are from "Daddy."

38. L.C.: "Actual punning dream about apostle Peter/Petra (the rock) & Australian film of same name."

42. Overheard at David Barton Gym, New York City.

43. "Daddy" again. See also Sexton's "The Ambition Bird."

44. Ovens: Anne Sexton Panzer poem from her baroque period and Rommel.

45. Excerpt from a 1935 *Variety* article on Marlene Dietrich's film *The Devil Is a Woman*.

46. *The Divine Woman* (1928) and *Die fruedlose Gasse* (1925): two of Greta Garbo's silent films. In the latter (translated as *The Street of Sorrow* or *The Joyless Street*), her rival-to-be, Marlene Dietrich, appears as an extra.

47. Brigitte Bardot's description of her aging, as recounted by Germaine Greer.

48. Quoted lines from Lawrence Ferlinghetti's poem #25 ("The world is a beautiful place"), *Pictures of the Gone World.*

49. Jacqueline Susann, *Valley of the Dolls,* page 319.

51. Sugar Ray–a 1990s pop group featuring a severely cute lead singer. "Sugar, Sugar" by the Archies, 1969.

52. Dream, 10/21/99 (D.T.).

54. Concept of wearing a different toupee each day of the month (for "realistic" growth cycle) taken from writer Dominick Dunne.

55. See Plath's "The Munich Mannequins."

56. Quentin is the name of Burt Reynolds and Loni Anderson's adopted child.

57. Scene from *Pulp Fiction.*

58. Image from Denise Duhamel's "Holocaust Barbie": "The terror when she saw a pile / of dolls like herself, naked and dirty, in the mass grave of a toy chest."

59. Second sentence: cf. conversation with Ottawa philosopher/DJ (host of "Cabbages and Kings"), November 19, 1999 (L.C.).

60. See Sexton's "With Mercy for the Greedy."

61. Mr. Susej masculinized "Ms. Dog," a Sexton nom de plume that she adopted while using similar minstrel locutions (in the manner of John Berryman's Henry) and Beat riffs (circa *The Book of Folly*).

62. Ronnie Spector (Veronica Bennett), lead singer of the girl group, the Ronettes.

Her 1990 autobiography (with Vince Waldron), *Be My Baby: How I Survived Mascara, Miniskirts, and Madness, or My Life as a Fabulous Ronette,* describes her marriage to "tycoon of teen" Phil Spector and how the "eccentric, reclusive, and violent" producer kept her a prisoner in their "darkened Beverly Hills mansion."

63. See Sexton's "Jesus Suckles," "The Play," and "Hurry Up Please It's Time."

64. "The Firebombers": an elite group of literary terrorists, based in Toronto, Canada, and New York City. Group derived its name from Sexton poem of same title.

65. Patty Duke singing "It's Impossible" (André Previn–Dory Previn) in the 1967 film version of *Valley of the Dolls.*

67. Conversation with Elizabeth Berkely.

68. May Swenson in a letter to Ann Stanford, 12/1/71, about Elizabeth Bishop's refusal to be included in Stanford's anthology, *The Women Poets in English.*

69. Lizzy Borden, Edith Bunker, and Elizabeth (Burton) Taylor, respectively.

70. Emily Dickinson and Elvis Presley's advice to a young Priscilla Beaulieu.

71. Alfred Hitchcock, 1936.

72. Gore Vidal's *Myra Breckinridge.*

74. American Character's Tressy doll, 1964: "Tressy—Her Hair Grows!" Doll came equipped with curlers, pins, various hair-setting solutions, brushes, and combs. "Short or Long or In-Between . . . Tressy's Hair Makes Her a Queen!"

76. L.C.: "A theory I held, scanning pornography for Anglo-Saxon kennings (compound nouns)."

77. Dion, 1961. Also see Ron Padgett's description of "kenning" in the chapter on Metaphor in his *Handbook of Poetic Forms.*

78. Line 1: see Jean Genet's *Miracle of the Rose.* Line 2: see Stevie Nicks's "Stand Back" music video.

80. *The Borrowers:* Mary Norton's 1953 children's classic about a family of "little people," the Clocks (Pod, Homily, and daughter Arrietty), who live behind walls and under floorboards, and who "borrow" tidbits and trinkets from "human beans." Readers delight in the resourceful way the Clocks recycle household objects: matchboxes for storage, postage stamps for paintings, and so on.

81. Joan Crawford's behavior as recounted in *Mommie Dearest.*

82. Christina Crawford, *Mommie Dearest.*

83. TV's *Petticoat Junction.* Faye Dunaway, *Mommie Dearest.*

85. Amity Island: *Jaws,* 1975. Quoted line from Edward Field's poem "Sharks."

87. Spenser's *The Faerie Queene.* Boy narcissist in *La Belle Bete.*

88. Elizabeth Taylor as Cleopatra, 1963. Wrote Judith Crist in *New York Herald Tribune:* "Miss Taylor is monotony in a slit skirt. There is no depth of emotion apparent in her kohl-laden eyes, no modulation in her voice that too often rises to fishwife levels. Out of royal regalia, en negligee or au naturel, she gives the impression that she is really carrying on in one of Miami Beach's more exotic resorts."

89. TV's *Bewitched.* Quote from *A Woman Named Jackie:* Jackie on the Kennedy's shortly after meeting the family.

90. Jacqueline Kennedy Onassis's predatory actions in the Onassis funeral cortege ("jackal" analogue furnished by Christina Onassis).

91. Christina Crawford's third birthday party, June, 1942: "We had the merry-go-round and the clown again but this year a complete puppet show was added and for some inexplicable reason she'd even found a *trained pig!* The pig was dressed like a clown with a big ruffle around its neck and could sort of walk on just its hind legs. The pig was a big hit."

92., 93. Sexton's "The Fury of Sunsets": "why am I here? / why do I live in this house? / who's responsible? / eh?"

94. Line 1: Lewis Carroll, *Alice in Wonderland:* "'It was much pleasanter

at home,' thought poor Alice, 'when one wasn't always growing larger and smaller, and being ordered about by mice and rabbits. I almost wish I hadn't gone down that rabbit-hole—and yet—and yet—it's rather curious, you know, this sort of life!'" Also: Rex Reed's profile of Grace Slick in *People Are Crazy Here,* 1974: "Grace's pad is like Norma Shearer's bedroom in *Marie Antoinette:* Tad's Steak House wallpaper, Victorian satin drapes, flowered carpets and flowered ceilings, cupids and roses and cornucopias, gilt-edged chairs with the bottoms falling out, purses made of pheasant feathers hanging on wall sconces of melting candles, musical instruments, and suitcases everywhere with clothes hanging out." (Slick was lead singer of Jefferson Airplane; the group's 1967 Top 10 hit, "White Rabbit," was a druggy interpretation of *Alice in Wonderland.*) Line 2 from Alice Notley's poem "Dream":

> Ted has a drug which when you take it
> makes you disappear in front of
> everyone, poof, vanish into air.
> . . . .
> . . . he tells me the drug
> makes you disappear into a
> parallel universe . . . .

95. See Frank O'Hara's "Ave Maria" and *Children of the Corn* (1984; says Leonard Maltin: "Laughable adaptation of Stephen King short-short story about young couple who stumble onto Iowa town that's been taken over by sinister juvenile cultists—and then, like all stupid couples in movies like this, fail to get out while the getting is good."). Prediction from Sydney Omarr's *Day-by-Day Astrological Guide for Taurus* for Thursday, December 16, 1999.

97. Actor Sal Mineo's murder, at the age of thirty-seven, outside his apartment at 8563 Holloway Drive, just off the Sunset Strip in West Hollywood, on February 12, 1976. From a net bio: "Sal parked his blue Chevelle in the garage of his apartment complex around 10 o'clock that evening. Suddenly neighbors heard his cries: 'Oh God! No! Help! Someone help!' His cries were followed by the sound of a struggle, more screams and then an eerie dead silence. By the time some of his neighbors reached Sal, all they saw was a young white man fleeing the scene[. . .]. Ray Evans, one of the first neighbors on the scene, found Sal in the fetal position, a stream of blood ten yards long flowing from multiple chest wounds. Noticing that Sal had begun to take on an ashen color, Evans tried mouth to mouth maneuvers. 'He kept gasping and after about five or six

minutes, his last breath went into me,' Evans recalled. 'And that was the end of it.'"

99. Dana Plato's dying breath (audio tape) for sale on net (Dana Plato Cult); poet David McGimpsey's assessment of Plato's "lonely" final photograph in the *National Enquirer.*

PROCESS NOTE

"Chain Chain Chain" is a one-hundred-stanza renga, and each stanza "links" to the one before it via an image, a repeated prominent sound, a pun or play on words. The moment of our poem begins in fall, and it ends in December. David began and then e-mailed his stanza to Lynn, who then e-mailed both to me. In the middle of the poem we switched direction. The notes for the poem took on a life of their own and were a lot of fun to write. A fun moment in the poem is when David and I send upside-down messages to Lynn on Thanksgiving; I remember it because we had juxtaposed that experience with a trip to an Upstate New York Wal-Mart—the first time I had ever been in one (and we both walked out the door empty handed/hearted and catatonic, so our newly written stanzas felt like salvation). My personal favorite form in the poem is a hidden acrostic message to David and Lynn that I encrypted in my final stanzas (stanzas 83, 86, 89, 92, and 95), which reads: "D & L I heart you two."

JEFFERY CONWAY

Haiku

Amy Gerstler & Benjamin Weissman

Fuck my brains out so
I can feel my dread lift, then
descend once again.

The culprit at the
pulpit licked parishioners,
sniffed pews and giggled.

The pickled nature of
your burps disinfects me
like direct sunlight.

She rode the boy home.
He bucked for years. She soothed him,
but would not dismount.

The doctor who joined
our hips must have forgotten
to unlock our tongues.

Your feet: undaunted
emissaries: explorers,
unbooted orphans.

The cleanliness of
porn, with its attendant flames
cauterizes us.

The cleanliness of
porn, with its drippy icings,
boasts a pastry taste.

Your teeth marks: subtle
alphabet, impressed upon
the flesh of my neck.

Inseparable,
but extremely shy, the two
gazelles drank lakes dry.

The difficulties
are ticklish, endured, then
harden into gems.

Tearing your clothes off
with my teeth was my polite
first try at foreplay.

Hearing you speak sends
quixotic synaptic sparks
through this worthless hide.

Inside wormy tombs
brittle chalky skeletons
fuck for centuries.

PROCESS NOTE

These haiku, and a good many more, were written collaboratively when we were
courting. We would hand them back and forth, writing alternate lines, or one of
us would write some words in two or all three lines of the haiku, leaving key
words out, and then hand it off to the other person to complete, with blanks to
fill in for the missing words. It was a way of communicating, of keeping in touch
and of having a shared project while we were getting to know each other, but
a simple shared project that could be passed back and forth easily and wasn't
wildly time consuming. Until recently, neither of us had looked at these poems
since they were written, which is around fifteen years ago now, maybe longer.
One of us was surprised at how dark and sexual most of them are. The other
wasn't the least bit surprised.

AMY GERSTLER

from **Sight**

Lyn Hejinian & Leslie Scalapino

Only in grey the tiny birds flit in the palm tree, one lighting on a fence and singing in the grey beneath—the dark interpreted day in (whatever's) being; not with color (there'd been nothing in sleep)

where the pictures are not burned on the memory, so do occur in the vivid oblivion (but without it)

one isn't united to the colorful world and in its oblivion. One is in heavy rain meeting people just outside, outdoors: there's only grey and therefore seeing them.

Resting, they're burned in grey, at the time. At the post office mailing. Is death, and therefore knowing about memory, at the oblivion in colors

which is people's movements—is their actions—the man in the blue shirt grabbing a bug at sunset, seen only at sunset, the blue shirt ruffles in the lit air

> the blue shirt has existence by the hanging
> bright persimmons in grey
> many sights in light, in the colorful world

where one rests from merely existing. The light elation is the events in series.

(LS)

Oblivion takes the world in obverse. The colorful world there seen in negative is very colorful. Yellow plums fall into the red grass. There cannot be (in a world susceptible to oblivion) any distinction between inside and outside.

The works of oblivion hang like pictures at an exhibition in a museum abandoned by ghosts (memory).

In what country could that happen?

In my "memory" (torturously located) Spain appears (so it is not a country abandoned by ghosts)—yellow. A sacred yellow—dusty and nothing an artist could complete (it's incomplete—infinite—in the sky, too).

I "catch sight" of a grey (unverified) lizard there. But it goes into a separate fissure. Such shadows are very cold. I remember that I sprawled as if I belonged in the interpreted sun—wanting to be comprehended in a scene

(as an innocent)

oblivious, so that 'one' is not responsible for a romantic pleasure (which would put one outside it) but is seen instead and sprawling

(stalking).

(The innocent is helpful, and the innocent is helpless, too.
The visible world doesn't get swept up for nothing.)

(LH)

There's no obverse as the moon freed in one floating
the colorful world is a paradise. Not to have any conception of origin (in
it) and the moon, still, free in oneself
yellow ghosts outside only in the red grass
men sulking in a room at a party had tiny 'souls' then that were buds. The
tiny rose buds wouldn't open
the world being susceptible to oblivion, the immense slab of rose tinge of
hurling cloud-continent rushing toward me (who's on land), no moon in the
sky—either outside or within the hurling slab in the sky
would be leading the cow on the bright watery rivulets

(LS)

We would experience blindness head first (and as a vulnerability, but of the
world, too)
as moistness, breathing, or shore
(the obsolete word "bourne" comes to mind
and the figure of Lear).
The world sustains an infinity of borders and boundaries, overlapping
outlines, interstices—zones
into which we are leading. We disturb everything—being helpful
and observant.
A cow is blowing in the cold.

Bright but colorless parallel horizons fill the vista when I close my eyes.
'Behind' closed eyes I have a sensation of 'seeing' panoramically, but the view
is vertical—I see distance and surface before me from head to toe. There are
no perspective lines. Or, rather, the radials extend but not from me. I am
witnessing someone else's seeing—it's as if I were watching their perspective
from the side.

(LH)

The head of the pink tulip, bunches of them fully open are blind—and
aren't born; are eyeless and not born, or are born and are in fields where one
cow is blowing

It moves in the fields whether it's disturbing them; they're not born and are existing anyway, it moves in them

They have this peaceful but wild existence—where everything's disturbed in it, but not by them

if the cow's behind it doesn't suffer and is observant, the tulips not being born (bourne) and being pink rushes

The Red Sea not to see filled with the violent pink rushes sustains the cow to have it wade, to have it walk.

(LS)

This doesn't feel at all like "looking back" over uncertain experience. Memories (in action) (and though retrospective) seem to face forward and move.

They (these) are communiqués (chosen).

Things, one of consciousness and another just appearing, in a new place to which we have gone away.

We are looking at the town where *The Birds* was filmed—on location it's incredible. But a terrific seabreeze is scattering the light. I have a sense of illusion, one in which everything is amusing but haunting (inexplicable). This is because I am an outsider.

In the film, the outsider (Tippi Hedren) becomes an insider under unnatural circumstances which, by the end of the film, have dazzled her so that she is outside again.

A local says that people from out of town always try to figure this out.

She tells us that the familiar yellow blossoming gorse clumps in the area are ineradicable invaders. They "come out of nowhere" like "ghost-born calves." She attributes this to forces. "The things we see," she says, "shouldn't be made to jump just for the sake of jumping."

(LH)

(The (ordinary) people going to a foreign country acted (became) greedy and cruel, because of the poverty and turmoil there.

They were made ferocious so they were made to be in the place of the Ancient Mariner—where they could not be blessed.)

(In the place where there were no goods: By oneself in order not to make any change in the people at the shopping dome so as to see them, lines formed apparently silently but with the hum in the glass tiered dome as if blind bumping while in the trail, with no motion.

From all lines I would be excluded, soundless, when I reached the front of the line.

Elbowed aside, there had been no movement before the one, when I reached the head.

I felt faint with hunger and entered a line in a compartment that was for repulsive wieners and sweet coffee. I wanted the coffee.

At the front of the line I held my arms like fins couldn't be ousted.

I was elbowed away from every surface then, where people stood, though there was space would bump me silent but with a hum as of hive creatures feeding hallowed halcyon coming up again to bump me from a surface where I'd come.

I would rest with the sweet coffee in the center.

It was calves feeding in water in the protected one.

I can't be blessed in the meanness of my own. The ghost-born calves as of whales bump me. There is only the inside.)

(Being away: Ghost-born are blessed and have no existing mothers (providers).

Tippi Hedren had come to Bodega Bay wanting to date a man whose mother's sexual jealousy wanting him manifested as birds. After being attacked by birds, Tippi Hedren falls in a daze stunned.)

(LS)

I think we see things fluttering in and out of narration. We expect (expectation here is nearly synonymous with greed) things to be participants (coerced, perhaps, by our willfulness) in our way of seeing. They "ordinarily" "speak" (mean)–i.e., things are logical, and according to that logic we see in fables.

The narration is the outside of seeing. It helps with identification (of a bird, e.g., as a "black-shouldered kite" hovering over the field in the pale morning light seen through binoculars across binocular latitudes several surfaces away (binoculars also flatten the leaves and branches of the bay tree on which we later saw an "osprey"))

Sir Francis Bacon says, "Experience when it offers itself is called *chance;* when it is sought after it is called *experience.*"

He continues: "Many objects in nature fit to throw light upon knowledge have been exposed to our view and discovered by means of long voyages and travels." (In a fable such a speech might be attributed to a kite or an osprey.)

From the mud along the creek in which the bay tree has its roots, a chorus of turtles might be given Bacon's comment, "We cannot approve of any mode of discovery without writing." (The mud was covered with the marks of the turtles.)

In a country without goods, marks would have been the (almost sufficient) substitute for them. By eloquently imagining visible and palpable things, the citizens could have sustained the plentitude of an inhabitable nation.

This simulacral (willed?) nation would have been closed (self-defining) system. One might say it had been narrated into paradise. Entering with a woman of such a nation into a milling crowd attracted by a rumor of sausage, then seeing a single man in a "lab coat" wheeling a cart of such sausages toward us, I was told that I didn't understand "such things," and I was pushed out of the crowd. The "grandmothers" and the "mothers" fought it out. (You are right that the birds in *The Birds* represent, in their unnatural behavior, the possessive biological clutching of the hero's mother. Some (I haven't seen them all) of Spielberg's films (I'm thinking especially of *Jurassic Park*) are also psycho-fables about the twisted relationship between parents (adults) and children, the incommensurability of their respective desires.

Laura Dern in *Jurassic Park* and Tippi Hedren in *The Birds* both play a "ditsy" blond outsider, a cute character (very manipulative) with bouncy self-conscious courage, who expresses the hero's sexual impotence (it's a bourgeois impotence, the fear of family), while taking the side (role) of the child.

Even the audience participates, witnessing the growing fearfulness of the familiar.)

(LH)

PROCESS NOTES

The authors also collaborated on these notes, addressing each other:

We embarked on this collaboration with a very general project in mind, and one that seemed to develop many facets and suggest many possible developments as we proceeded with it. In the broadest sense, we were interested in a joint investigation into the working of experience: how experience happens, what it consists of, how the experiencing (perceiving, feeling, thinking) of it occurs, what the sensation of sensing tells us. And we were interested in knowing what actual experiences would take place over the period of time we would be working on the collaboration—what would happen in our respective lives and what would happen between us, in public (as the writing) and in private (as a flourishing friendship).

Another way to characterize the project would be to describe it as a work of acknowledgment. This is a theme which is also a prominent one in *A Border Comedy,* the work that I was writing concurrently with *Sight,* and elements from *A Border Comedy* appear in this book, most obviously in the passages which mention a "border guard" (a figure which you, at some point, change to a "boundary guard," producing a clearer trope, and one that is more "self"-reflexive).

In *Sight* we attempt to acknowledge the world simply by seeing it but also by stating that something has been seen. To do this, we carry on an activity (a continuous action); we are in motion, turning toward (things between us). Hence the inward motion. There isn't very much here that could be described as exposition—not much turning out or putting out.

From the outset, we agreed that for the purposes of this collaboration (and at some early point, do you remember just when?, we agreed that we should do other collaborations when this was completed), the question of experiencing the world would focus on sight—on the question of "seeing": seeing the world, seeing something in it, and being in it as one whose participation involved such "seeing." The thrill of acknowledgment (it is, after all, good to be alive!), while being addressed to what we saw, was also, over and over again, in real time, addressed to each other. Thanks to your suggestion that we "sign" (with our initials) our passages (poems) to each other, this is a dialogic work—a joint research undertaken through conversation, and as such it includes demands, either express or internalized, for clarification, it includes debate, and it reveals changes of view under each other's influence.

Our only constraint was that each response—each poem—would have two parts and that in each poem there should be some reference to, or presentation of, something actually seen. But we never limited the scope of what might be considered a sight or sighting. And I, at least, included occasional dream images and many other purely mental pictures, concentrating in particular on those mental pictures (sometimes logical, sometimes seemingly inappropriate) that seemed to flash into view in response to your words. This wasn't a form of mind-reading—that would have been invasive and I think we share a dislike of such mental power games. It was phenomenological—our ideas took shape for each other, though in ways that were probably idiosyncratic to each of us.

As I look at this work now in retrospect, I see it as elaborating problems in phenomenology but not in description, and this, given our topic, seems curious. Of course description is often phenomenological in intent—aimed at bringing something into view, trying to replicate for (or produce in) the reader an experience of something seen. But it seems as if our emphasis was not on the thing seen but on the coming to see. As I see it, this book argues that the moment of coming to see is active and dialogic, and as such it is dramatic.

Many things were seen during the course of our writing this book. And now I hope that some reader will see something in it—not through it but in it. *Sight* is not transparent. But the best conditions for seeing are not always clear.

LYN HEJINIAN

We agreed that the form of our collaboration was to be in doubles, pairs (such as two sentences, two lines or paragraphs, or series of these, etc.); and that the subject, being sight, should involve things actually seen. Multiple pairs and crossing the borders of these occur: which are friendship / thought / sight itself / events . . .

Crossing 'across' observation, 'argument' which is mode of extension—we tend to stay on our own 'sides' in regard to the 'subject' 'experience.' We attempt to draw each other across the sides of our 'argument' or boundary, a form of pairs, and of friendship also. We sign our segments, which are sometimes like letters as specifically referring to occasion and to writing. 'Critical discourse' as they say, in which the poetry is interchangeable as the thought in it. Sometimes, seeing in real events we had to turn seeing up to an extreme in order to see it; as if dreaming being suppressed were bursting out as luminous seeing in the waking state. Pairs of sights, become that by being placed beside each other; my dreaming speaking to you (a pairing of you), I put in as part of the collaboration.

Friendship would have to be not just 'being liked.' That one has to be likable, accommodating. One would have to 'like' also—i.e. like the other—and I think only by being oneself. Not accommodating. My need for argument in it is that you tend to view reality as wholesome; when I'm suffering you tend to alleviate to bring suffering into the currency of the 'social,' the realm that is convivial—whereas I'm saying it's (also) apprehension itself when it's occurring.

The accumulation of pairings as 'extreme' sights occurs to the extent of being as if the writing's faculty, rather than being imaginative images.

I dreamt while we were collaborating that I spat in a donkey's eye (in the future, but already known) and rushed up (before this) to tell you that all of life was void, which I knew in the dream you would want to hear. Because I was indicating that to spit in the donkey's eye (not to have to be accommodating) was the gesture, being done; that gesture also being the act of friendship and apprehension.

So, anyway—I tend to say that experience is scrutiny; that it is 'travel' in the sense of dislocation of one's own perspective (that is, not to have a perspective). You say to me then: "travel is sentimental." In other words, I'm deluding myself that I could ever not have a perspective. It is my 'doctrine' only. (You're right. I agree, it was not scrutiny enough.) When I 'discuss' "compassion," you check me. That such (in that form at least) is egotism or a 'lyrical illusion,' probably.

Then, on my part, I thought recently you described (at the university) your writing in terms of ideas—that it is "comparing cultures"—which will be accepted as description of the writing (its importance) but which are not the gesture that occurs as the writing (the mind coming up with whatever it is at that moment only). (Acknowledgment that it's perspective only.) Because you know the professors will tend not to like the 'idea' of the mind and only its action at a moment, because they don't trust that. It isn't 'any thing.' 'Writing separate from and being then people's activity' is one of the subjects of *Sight*.

As doubles or pairings: The description as what people will like is not the way the thing (the event or writing) is.

The writing that's occurring at any point is the entire body of writing. Of others, as well. So the writing of a time is everyone.

A 'time' is the work being written at the time by everyone. It is not the hierarchy of what people regard.[1] In that accumulation transforms.

I want friendship that's real, because it occurs only. (This was Lear's mistake—or maybe it was Cordelia's—?—they seem to be part of the same person. I

1. Say, the anthologizing process is to leave out the time everyone is in—that is what the anthologizing process is.

208

was rewriting King Lear in a recent work of mine, called *As: All Occurrence in Structure, Unseen–(Deer Night)*, which I was doing alongside *Sight*. I was also writing *The Front Matter, Dead Souls*. Passages of mine originating in *Sight* got into *The Front Matter* as being alongside it. In the latter, I was working on visual extremity as the writing literally as if a faculty, rather than visual being imagination.)

In such an approach–(if there's a division between description and text–you're pointing away from there being a text, from reading) you're not comparing cultures because you're indicating in a sense 'the real' is 'the social,' what is liked–else it is lyrical illusion.

Yet, to be "comparing cultures"–cannot occur from a standpoint that is an insulated one in which reality is described as (one's) halcyon/ "normal" (by such description regarded as objective in regard to culture and thought, as what is seen to be "intellectual" per se). Comparing cultures cannot occur as that, reality or cultures not being subject to 'halcyon'/ 'normal.' Apprehension as comparison isn't there then, because it's generalized. Were it there, that would be dislocating. It (apprehension /conflict–the same?) isn't there. The point is not that one is suffering because of being dislocated–but that the thought is the action.

So you're (one's) 'being removed from experience' as that being (if that's one's) definition of objectivity or apprehension itself–whereas apprehension only exists as experience?

LESLIE SCALAPINO

from **Sunflower**

Jack Collom & Lyn Hejinian

5

It has sometimes seemed to me that the best place to stand is back to back with
the sunflower,

Rubbing its surprisingly rough green length, accepting a kiss as the head hangs
over grotesquely

Sworled. From any given point (seed) it (the head of the sunflower) holds its
thought

In a rush, or so it would seem to a person from Uranus, or a person in a
golden location deftly separating orbit from spiral,

Boiling point from bubble, vicissitudes from span—or spin.

Or—why does that round yellow face follow me, into dark closets, boasting by
bursting its 212 degree shapeshift,

Leaving nothing but a world, unless to provide light, however hot and fragile

The actual is. Memory is much more solid, though you *could* say that's because
solidity is a dream

Dreamt by one who longs to see the frozen steppes and won't and remains—
reluctant to complain.

How *could* one complain that a bubble is less than "bubble"—let alone left
alone by illusions of thing ("Sacheneinbilderebeeinfluss") until—until—one
opens one's pretty mouth *pop*—

In just that one second creating and destroying a world. For isn't it just as the
metaphysicians discovered upon observing the iridescent film

Surrounding their opinions? Isn't it just? Everything has passed through an
oil stage

At an early stage before passing opinion through the prism that produces the
spectrum of opinion, the spiral from yellow to yellow.

We know now that depth is merely a flirt of the shoulders, that all (all)
composes the perfect surface of a ball

Of lightning passing through sunlight. The mud is quiet

And quite white, plopped below the riot of wavelengths pushing in and out of it

Churning shape—pots of light—which at some precise instant split

From the realization that dirty windows are works of art, and cataracts, behind
which the slatey dipper builds its beautiful sphere of soft green moss,
arched and braced with leaves.

Is there anything better than happiness?

No, because happiness oscillates in a circle, preceded by its name, bushing and
braiding memory, and then recurrently the whole idea goes poof, which
then circles back to the first circle (of oscillation ((and osculates itself)))

Merrily and meditatively. Happiness in circles is a happiness *in and of itself,*
thinking as it happens, kissing thinking,

As it happens, and looking at itself from this circle and the next, which adds
up to the O of the kiss,

The covered over noon. Fog climbs through the air, the walls disappear in a
dream, I'm patient

With the alamosa (inside that word are lines of cottonwoods); the walls come
back and are called Blanca and the blood of Christ

Which Faust at the stroke of the hour saw 'streaming in the firmament.' We
know very little about time, and yet without it 'happiness' couldn't happen.

Or do we know everything about time (since it's everything we know) and
simply fail to know it at once?

It could be this, a spontaneity or intuition, a momentary 'taking in' (this would
account for disappearance)

As if our consciousness were a kind of (gulp) amateur-night Black Hole

Around which judges have gathered to sentence sentences to poems where
they'll do less harm than good,

A bland, but dense, fate. But the harm they'll do, flailing their arms of wood,
might in time blow more "good"

Across what we call fate. Being itself, as Heidegger says, is thrown. The wholly
improbable happens:

That Heidegger (for example) is not himself! He lifts his right arm as a test, and
the left simply rests in his lap,

Until, hearing a chord, he plays a card and then, hearing a dart in the dark, he
charts an unlikely course:

Spinning a vast connotative history around a word which doesn't exist! The
rain falls, unnoticed

By a neighbor using figurative speech. But for us full of wonder for what visits
us in dreams

It seems the rain's rush-rollicking earth/sky politics thin cream of electric

Affirmation is saying *Yes* to the sunflower as to the world which *does* exist

As do, on several planes, the intriguing "pepper-spots" of counterpoint or, as
   some call them, "floating anti-planets" and others "celestial flyspecks"
And still others "cosmic parodies." Nothing itself is a reality in the cascades,
   torrents, bands and balances to which musical listeners
Attend. I am among them, cascaded, banded, in the knowledge that I have let
   a barrel of sunflower seeds grow old. It sits on my feeding possibilities like
   death, yet if I threw it out onto the earth it would sprout into a wonderful,
   bothersome life
For a spider, blown there on a length of silk attached to its spinnerets, abdomen
   up to take the air.
But my fear is that at that moment of lolling whiteness, its very indolence
   energized, as it were, to a signal, some sharp-eyed raptor would
Snatch it—a possibility like death. Yes. Between temper and delicacy there's a
   boundary but also a bond.
The boundary is the bond, a wide seam welded like a scar covering the cases of
   delicacy being the child and the father of temper, baby legs kicking from a
   black cloud, of
Delicacy, being the mother of microcosms, of which the baby is one—a great
   one, swimming through laughter
To, of course, great wisdom. Or perhaps a heart attack, although a Cherokee
   bird whispers that they are two names for the same eloquent molecule.
Of laughter, the first name designating the inner effort required, the second the
   response of the organism,
And the third (we haven't heard) is what they call themselves. It means "The
   Stuff." Its medium is more of itself, which may lead to some thing.
In a future that we know as a certainty but about which we know nothing.
(A moment's pause.) But then again, we know much about it (not mutually
   exclusive with "nothing"), in the ways we know things now, by eating
   them; as for certainty . . . the immense deer mouse just might blink its eye,
   and . . .
And can't ever be a certainty, but we take it as such, and rightly, it's the first,
   last, recurrent connector, you and I, we and the moment, the moment and
   the garbage truck and Shostakovich's mournful 13th String Quartet, which
   looks back, one might say "too far back" (into "nothing")
So that one feel caught between "the blackbird's song and a moment after," or
   preference and interference, or yet hand and foot, insurance/risk
Which are not opposites but variants, and it is spring again, instability is
   everywhere, and calm itself is an exaggeration, impatiently we caper

Into summer, so loaded with buzz that sentences never end, that is *summer* is
so loaded, but loaded longitudinally, so the vibrations are the sole motion
A man or woman can follow, though birds and the triumphant sunflower they
so admire, being given to verticality, can escape vibrations, transcend sole
motion, and –does anyone care about their being 'right'?–found fantastic
spirals in the air,
Such as Daniloff's hypothesis that the productivity of argument hinges on the
structural not only in the, as it were, erector-set geometry of the countering
proposals but in the *species* 'chosen' to perform each whirling thrust
Breathlessly. And surely it's not we who do it all. The sun turns the sunflower,
the wind brings the scent of night-flowering jasmine into the dream, and
worrisome dogs howl at the half-moon
That is just beginning to peep out from behind the awkward cupolas of
the children's library . . . . Hark! What is that prodigious Fibonacci song,
that climax run of grunts and trills?
I . . . I thought I heard it but now I'm not sure. The nights are still warm.
Everything melts together for me! Thunder becomes a cornflower.
Morning becomes electric in its very availability, its multiplication of shock
until shock's in . . . everything
Including the sunflower, which, being quotidian and fragile and more than any
other flower like a clock, measures the shock
That has, as I say, multiplied, like the multiplying days of St. Simon Stylites
blinded by staring constantly at the sun but still measuring with his
muscle movements what's happening beneath the superficiality of sight
On sunlight as it causes us to cast shadows that frighten moon-marked
butterflies into drills of misty flight,
And just where do these papillons point their lunar-bruised gyres
If not to the heart of spirals and the gist of spontaneous enthusiasms.
It's time to recognize that a darling little Nubian goat has been eating parts and
edges of our scene as he/she gradually grows
Into his/her society of goats, producing mischief and milk–mostly milk–and
very sweet milk, I should add, milk that's acceptable to the society of
humans, since it resembles the milk we humans are familiar with, the milk
of cows. Do cows browse on sunflowers?
I will answer my own question by uncovering another: do the sun's rays graze
the very whiteness they create?
In fractals of winter it seems so. The sun-saturated crystals of snow cover . . .

The collaborative procedure governing the composition of *Sunflower* was very simple; we simply took turns adding a line to the poem. Jack Collom composed the first line of the poem ("Sunflower just below gray cornucopia roof") and sent the page containing that line to me through the U.S. Postal System; he also sent a long letter on topics not, generally, related to sunflowers. We never used anything but the regular mail for sending pages back and forth, and we always sent them with an accompanying letter.

The finished poem is in six sections. There was no rule dictating when one section would end and another begin. When I happened to be the one inserting a section break, it was because the poem had come to a juncture that it couldn't cross, or a point that it couldn't surpass. That is, I just didn't know what more to say.

The section published here is the fifth. I am pretty certain that I was the one who composed its first line, though mostly because there is mention of a "mehr owl" in the last line of section four, and that was the first I'd ever heard of mehr owls.

Sunflower was the first of Jack Collom's and my collaborations. Subsequently two others have been published and six more are in progress. Of the two other published works, *Wicker* follows quite rigorous compositional rules and *On Laughter* is an extended dialogue/essay (a form exploited most brilliantly, I think, by Denis Diderot).

Apart from the sociable delight entailed in writing this collaboration—the friendship embodied in it—I learned something of particular importance to my own writing practice in the course of working with Jack on *Sunflower,* and the collaboration was directly responsible for what is, at least at the moment, my favorite of all my own books, *A Border Comedy.* In my own work, I had long been interested in the rethinking that goes by the name of memory. *Writing Is an Aid to Memory* and *My Life* are obvious products of that interest, but it has a place in all my work. The process (and the use of regular, hard copy mail) involved in writing *Sunflower,* however, got me interested in the other side of memory: forgetting. Between writing one line of *Sunflower* and writing my next, at least ten days would have gone by—long enough for me to have forgotten the line and also to have forgotten the direction of the trajectory I'd had in mind when I wrote it. And, in any case, whatever its trajectory might have been, Jack's new line would have redirected it. The process, then, involved thought, the forgetting of that thought, and a return to that thought but in an entirely reconfigured form—the thoughts were never dismembered, and couldn't ever be perfectly remembered. They were for getting, a process of continual new membering. As the sunflower turned round and round to keep its face to the sun, metamorphoses were continually underway.

LYN HEJINIAN

Sunflower was the first of many poem collaborations for Lyn and me. I wrote the first line, a simple streetside observation, and we were off, the only rule being to go line-by-line. I count 304 lines in the poem; they accreted back and forth via snailmail over a course of eight years. Incidentally, we have kept up the practice of mail collaborations and presently have six poems (varying forms) a-shuttling. Two other chapbooks have been made from "completed" poems.

I've learned a lot weaving my lines/fragments with hers. Her unremitting excellence of thought and eager exploratory attitude have amounted to a freshness that pulls me along–that I couldn't hope to match by myself. Her refusal to descent into any form of 'cheap shot' or lazy turn of phrase has inspired me to find universes of emotion within rigorous utterance.

As *Sunflower* proceeded, it developed considerably in length of line and rollicking trails of imagery–the dance of thought gained a lotta dimension.

The collaborative poem (at least with such an extraordinary poet as Lyn) is more than a statement or even a vision; it's keeping language in the air; it has "the air" of being endless. The multiplicity of "voice" is revealed. It's potentially geometry bequeathed to algebra.

JACK COLLOM

No More Linda Smukler

Samuel Ace & Margo Donaldson

I never really knew her

She had little feet

She was always just out the door

A shadow moving behind her

They said she should take the bump out of her nose

She refused knowing it did not signify

She refused to leave all at once

She was the opposite of ineffable

She lingered

She blew her nose and looked on

PROCESS NOTE

A developmentally disabled student of Sam's recognized him enough to know that Linda had disappeared. Every time the student saw him, she would say "Hello, Mr. Ace. No more Linda Smukler." She would repeat the refrain "no more Linda Smukler" over and over. The poem was written as an elegy to describe the palpability of Linda's absence, and to let her go.

We have worked on many projects together and are the co-owners of Gallery Katzenellenbogen in Truth or Consequences, New Mexico. The gallery focuses on photography, painting, and installations merging text and photography. Recent collaborative work includes *The Husband Chair*—a meditation on passionate collecting, attachment, and loss. *The Floating World* examines photographs of Coney Island amusement park, observers of modern art, and contains text about the Japanese woodblock print (Ukiyo-e), as a form of mass-produced art similar to the digital photograph. *The Floating World* explores the dissolution of self, and the pleasure and sadness contained in the pursuit of amusement.

SAMUEL ACE & MARGO DONALDSON

Social Etiquette

James Bertolino & Anita K. Boyle

When a manly man puts
his hands on another,
it should be kind of brusque.

And when a woman touches
an animal, her fingers
should be listening for
what is subtle and true.

There's something about the truth
in a child's voice that can never
be understood by a Republican,

and is always seen
as threatening
to the military mind.

Crawl Space

James Bertolino & Anita K. Boyle

The man with
Lou Gehrig's disease,
he couldn't speak–vocal
cords gone, I guess, hole
in the neck surgery–crawled
because he no longer
walked, crawled with the children
who came to his daughter's day
care center. He got down
with the children and delighted
them by placing his speaking device
to his neck. They giggled and flailed
their arms to hear such unearthly
sounds from an old man
with them on the floor.

Observer of the Obvious

James Bertolino & Anita K. Boyle

If we're supposed to be so smart,
how come we didn't keep our wings?
Why don't we have wings?

Our public school system
is the sewer system of intellect,
the septic tank and
drainfield of ethics.

I put on my glasses
and noticed the dumbfounded
look on the face of the moon.

PROCESS NOTES

From *Bar Exams:*

Sitting in a crowded pub is often too noisy for conversation, but ideal for collaborative poetry: write a line or two and pass the page.

JAMES BERTOLINO & ANITA K. BOYLE

A form of collaboration which allows for randomness, but also supports a developing sense of the poem as an intentional work, has the writers reading the prior passages before adding their own. Each writer may take the poem in a new direction, but will do so in a manner that utilizes the lines already composed. My friend Anita Boyle and I have been collaborating in this way for several years, and a number of our works have been published in magazines and chapbooks. We take the process further by doing our own revisions, then getting together to agree on which changes improve the poems. Our collaborations always carry both of our names.

An approach to collaboration I feel is fairly unique is one I've used in my graduate poetry writing courses at Western Washington University. Two or three poets pass a journal back and forth until they have what seems to be a complete draft. Then they each take a copy of the poem to revise later. By prior agreement, they focus on the aesthetic models of very different poets in their revision process (such as those of Anselm Hollo, Frank Stanford, or Anne Waldman), and feel free to make any changes or deletions that best serve their objectives. What results are poems which have some images and phrases that are recognizable, yet are significantly different from each other. Structurally, the poems may use the page, and the white space, in very different ways. One poet might add rhyme and use conventional stanzas, while another working with the original version may spread words and phrases all over the page. The collaboration element is no more important than the individual revision element, and I advise my students they can reasonably claim their final version as their own poem.

JAMES BERTOLINO

A Crown of Spells to Ward Off Susans

Denise Duhamel & Maureen Seaton

1.

Stop crying. Bring all her costume jewelry
to the oldest corner of the dark house
where rats are gnawing. Take cheese, five ounces,
preferably moldy, and write her name backwards
on a soft-shell crab. Eat it while farts
waft past that time-honored Szechuan dish,
the creamy casserole that made Susan ill.
Eat it by fistfuls, your stomach hers. Say:

Sour Cheerios and cesspool Smoothies, gray
chopmeat and the gums of old llamas.
May the double l's double over Susan.
May the pink of raw meat and mouth rip
her into puzzle pieces that tip
like a Rubik's Cube in the fat hands of God.

2.

When she denies she's flirting, slit open
a pepper and gather the seeds. Then spit
into a waiter's ear, eat rarebit
or Egg Foo Yung, release doves. Now circle
her shoe which you've stolen, its purple
laces and lime green sole. Take the tongue
of your ogling boss and, to the far-flung
noise of Nine-Inch Nails, wave it high and yell:

Goddess of Toe Nail Clippings and Bad Smells,
pluck Susan from each potential suitor
and stick her with a corsage pin saying: "For-
ever clumsy." May she wander dazed

through malls where she works for minimum wage
in stores where my lover would never shop.

3.

Razor the bristles off her wet toothbrush,
collect her saliva and plaque in a pouch.
Throw a carton of organic eggs, loud
and unfertilized, into her pancakes.
Now pee on a lamb's tongue then into a lake
where your power will do the most harm. Lick
the crispy raisin moles that dot your sick
mother's stomach and you're through. Ready? Say:

Goddess of Wheatgrass, keep Susan away
in the state of Kentucky where lovers
sleep in slop of pigs and fowl. May she hover
over the Jersey turnpike at rush hour
as she spends her years alone. May admirers
find her breath bad and her clitoris lax.

4.

Cull the sickest-looking fruit from the scarred bowl.
Mashing, drip something green from your mean face
into a stew of awkwardness and baste
until Susan is the shade of your eyebrows.
Stir until she is the shape of five cows—
never before has broth tasted so bossy!
Walk into a forest, bicycle or ski
where you can spin near wild mushrooms, singing:

May the angels toll for you, Susan, ring
creepy Alleluias into sex and dream.
May your days be dark and stained as red beets
as you crawl to find your dusty contact lens.
May the skinny ghost of Ichabod Crane
carry you, cashless, into K-Mart.

5.

Gather stereotypes who look like Susan.
Bring them, insipid and limp, to the cliff
where you saw her kiss your sweetheart. Don't mind if
the pain in her loins is stronger than rum.
Sing "Hey la hey la my girlfriend's back." Bum
a funny cigarette from a famous queen
whose danger is unknown. Sauté a cat's spleen,
if you can find one, and while you're cooking, say:

May the half-moons of your thumbnails slay
your future offspring, may their sharp white teeth
bite the TV cord during Ricki Lake week.
May safety pins leap through your ears and tongue
and lacerate you, Susan, the thin rungs
of your career plans ladder you into hell.

6.

Turn on the ceiling fan and imagine
her neck cut off by each whirring blade,
her spine collapsing like a blanched and frayed
embryo in the clinic's light. Pour urine
into the mouth of a North-flowing river
while drowning five blue newts in the creme bleach
she used to lighten her moustache. Eat
the dandruff you snatched from her collar. Holler:

May your leather be stolen at Girl Bar.
May your pee be green, may your hair be cut
by untrained stylists who highlight your bald spot.
May everyone who meets you say "Who?" May
you grow as lonely as rope. May you fly
into traffic begging my forgiveness.

7.

Now go to Penney's and hide in the smallest
dressing room until you see Susan's feet.
Stretch her toes until they resemble eels,
then bruise them with rocks or small furniture.
Take your brother's old odor-eaters,
the hair of a plucked nipple, and repeat.
Slip her photograph into a hive of bees
and as they sting her image, say out loud:

May you live to bowdlerize your proud
operas into fanny songs, your cinched
waistline into suet. May your rhinestoned hand
grow arthritic, and may your whiny voice
whine over the last prairie like a toy
airplane before it screams into flame and melts.

PROCESS NOTE

Our "Spells" do not adhere to the traditional rules for a crown of sonnets, although there are seven of them and they are, at least in our collaborative minds, sonnets. We were simply unable to resist the vision of "crowning" Susans. We played the surrealist game of Exquisite Corpse to give ourselves both strategy and surprise. We planned a crooked, dissonant rhyme-scheme, a loose ten-syllable line, and agreed that the gruesome lists of the octaves would set up the spells of the sestets. We gave vent. We felt fabulous.

DENISE DUHAMEL & MAUREEN SEATON

Madame Bovary

Denise Duhamel & Maureen Seaton

What was the point of marrying a doctor
who couldn't even cure a clubfoot
or withhold orgasm until his wife could float
in ecstasy? She missed the word *ecstasy*,
stuck with Charles' insipid snoring every
night. Not only that—he was dopey
about everything French: the kiss, the sloppy
cheeses. When Emma pretended orgasms,
no one could tell—Charles, Rodolphe, even Leon
was sure each squeal, giggle, and sigh was true.
Emma often felt like a martyr to
fidelity, like Joan of Arc or Anne Boleyn.
She plied the wet nurse with vodka again
and again, then bolted with a new lover.

Madame Bovary 2

Denise Duhamel & Maureen Seaton

If anyone ever needed Debtor's
Anonymous it was Emma Bovary.
She loved aqua lamp shades and hosiery
made of pink silk. Her husband was clueless
re: the big A. Brazen cuckolds slept stress-
free in Charles' own examining room.
"Why don't you go shopping with Leon?"
Charles said, the ultimate dummy in love
and finance. Thank God no shopping channels
existed in that part of France. Or Lotto.
The Medical Convention was not
where Emma wanted to go for kicks. Paris
was cruelly tempting with its frivolous
pastries, its crudités, its Eiffel Tower.

PROCESS NOTE

In our collection *Little Novels* we attempted to shrink novels of the canon into sonnets. As in "A Crown of Spells to Ward Off Susans," these sonnets were composed using the method of Exquisite Corpse and the rhyme scheme: abbcddeeffa. We hoped to subvert content as well, especially in regards to gender.

DENISE DUHAMEL & MAUREEN SEATON

Caprice

Denise Duhamel & Maureen Seaton

From the day she met you-know-who, Olive Oyl was tortured by spinach.
She'd made a thousand green soufflés before she gave the sap the boot,
whipping eggs with spinach, splashing everything with oil, cold-pressed
    and virgin,
then sliding the pan into the oven with Popeye's stern orders
to make it snappy. Why didn't he like her honey-baked hams? He preferred
    skinny
sausages, strung link to link like necklaces. Their lopsided kitchen was no haven

for Popeye's lanky paramour. Still, she was used to the shenanigans of zany
    Sweet Haven,
her sailor breakdancing on the linoleum, peeking up her skirt, catching spinach
leaves like wet confetti on his tongue. Only Olive knew the skinny
on Popeye's perversions, the way he loved to spit-polish her big brown boots,
tap his pipe on her bony back, lower his voice a scratchy scale or two, order
her to kiss him. There was nothing Tammy Wynette about Olive—

more than once she'd shrunk his bell bottoms, then sucked the pimentos out
    of his olives.
She beat him at bowling, despite the snickering from his cronies on the
    Sweet Haven
League, despite the fact that she sometimes liked all the butch-femme stuff,
    ordering
and submitting, the kinky games they sometimes played with spinach.
He'd wrap her in foil so she looked like a can, arranging spinach leaves
    around her boot-
tops, a few green stems in her hair. He squeezed her silver middle until she
    popped, her skinny

abs twitching and rippling like a filly, all the pencil-sleek and board-skinny
parts of her hardening to attention. Sometimes he called her "Olives"
and she'd slap him, sure he was making fun of her breast size. He'd call her boots
"bootsk" and she'd kick him, waiting to see if he'd smile. Sex was a haven,

something they rowed into after Segar, their creator, died and they could
    finally fuck. Spinach,
on the other hand, lost its slimy appeal during the Bobby London years, the
    chaos and order

of pro-choice battles smudging up the strip.[1] Olive filed a protection order
against iron-enriched greens. No matter what he bench-pressed, Popeye's
    biceps stayed skinnier
than the duct tape on Olive's nipples when she marched in the pride parade.
    "Spinach
sucks" read the sign she held over her head with an anarchic gleam in her
    eye. "I love
Sour Patch Kids," gurgled Swee'pea, unused to the protests surrounding the
    usually safe haven
of his basket. Without warning, Olive whipped out her laptop and booted

into space, a full-figured Cyberella-star in the spring sky: Virgo, Boötes,
Ursa Major. She entered the chat rooms of large women, browsed
    amazon.com and placed orders
for every book published by Firebrand Press. Sweet Haven now felt like
    McHaven,
a fat town full of gristle and greasy-bottomed paper bags, where only the
    french fries were skinny
and size fifty-six hips switched charmingly down the boardwalk. Olive
kissed a girl in cyberspace. They both loved Tracy Chapman and despised spinach

in any of its forms. Their boots left deep footprints all over pink clouds' skinny
wisps. They ordered each other around like siblings. "Oh Olive,"
bounced along the rooftops of Sweet Haven, the heavens sailorless and
    spinach-free.

1. London was fired by King Features after penning an episode in '93 in which Olive was perceived
as pro-choice by the anti-choice owner of Popeye's Fried Chicken.

The Origin of Olive Oyl

Denise Duhamel & Maureen Seaton

1.

When Olive was an embryo, she curled her thumbs
into the "o," stretched herself into an obelisk,
tall as a coconut palm, stately as a saguaro.
Legends crisscross at this crucial point:
Sweet Haven lore has Olive as princess of knobby-kneed
school girls, while King Features lists her as kitsch witch.
She used to spin on the playground until she fainted.
She used to pull herself up and scare everyone.

2.

Olive drew her own face, then her mother's
rose full-moon over her daughter's rubbery china bones.
Orzo, Ooze, Oulipo—
as though the whole world were one big O![2]

3.

She rose from razor shells and the abiding anorectic
wombs of the gods of Italy and vinegar.

4.

Olive saw the ad—*f u cn rd ths u cn gt a gd jb*[3]
and sent her resumé to a P.O. Box,
the thin lines of her qualifications
like squiggles of a Basho
or tiny flecks of light that have passed through crystal.

5. (The Origin of Popeye)

Only Olive owned ostentatious orgasms;
the puerile position of pomp belonged to Popeye.
Olive, it is said, created him when she slipped
on a slimy spinach leaf and landed on a pipe.
Ceci n'est pas une pipe,[4] some said to negate the narration,
the way Olive's body looks sideways, blending into the vertical
horizon we call the end, dead end, sweet dreams.
Olive, so many dots of color, rearranging herself like nomenclature.

2. Frank O'Hara's favorite form of punctuation was the exclamation point.

3. If you can read this you can get a good job.

4. Sometimes Olive smoked a pipe and sometimes she didn't.

PROCESS NOTE

"Caprice" and "The Origin of Olive Oyl" are from our collaborative collection *OYL*. We wrote "Caprice" as an Exquisite sestina with all the normal rules of the surrealist game. We picked the six end words beforehand. We wrote "The Origin of Olive Oyl" in couplets with the title as inspiration, responding back and forth to each other's lines. The original was completely dismantled, however, the couplets cut up and rearranged, the footnotes added for luck.

DENISE DUHAMEL & MAUREEN SEATON

82 Reasons Not to Get out of Bed

Denise Duhamel et al.

I fear dented cans,
the ones with their labels torn like a pantyhose run.
I fear dented cans even though I know
bulging cans are the ones that cause botulism.
I fear small caskets, and I fear small pox.
I can't be vaccinated because I'm allergic to the serum.
Check my arms—I don't have any of those vaccination dents
like everyone else. I fear going to a new hairdresser
or gynecologist. I fear people with authority who look nervous.
I fear any box big enough to hold me.
I fear the number 4 for no reason.
I fear this bad habit will catch up to me.
I fear being awake in the middle of the night
when everyone else is asleep, even that yappy dog Peppy,
and the baby in him. I fear the dogs that do not recognize
my smell or care. I fear the whirr and rattle of the tail.
I fear the front door slamming when the bedroom window is locked.
I fear strangers who do not know my strength.
I fear the laughter I do not share.
I fear not living with the fear of dying,
the threat of mortality that moves us.
I fear that hell is a cold place.
The way they told it to me in Sunday school
sounds a lot like Miami Beach.
If I keep it up, I'll be shoveling snowy driveways for all eternity.
I fear that maybe I am wrong. That we are all wrong.
Love is bad. Hate is good. Germs are good.
The Hare Krishnas are right about all of it.
I fear the Wicked Witch of the West peddling
on her bicycle in black boot shoes not yet melted.
I fear M.S., anthrax, cancer, AIDS, herpes,
the common cold, Ebola, and salmonella.
I fear my heart might stop while I'm in the kitchen
chopping garlic listening to an old Marvin Gaye tape

on my Wal-Mart boom box.
I fear the man named Rodger
with an old green Ford and a rifle rack
and tobacco juice dribbling stupid from his mouth.
I fear zombies and their long lovely fingers,
those teeth that are still growing,
how what even they loved becomes a meal,
a memory that taps at me like fingernails on glass.
I fear losing the thread, losing a clear vision
of what makes the grand machine grind forward.
I fear the thread ends of chance, they boil up
in one whenever—king doubt—and I have to put them in corners,
under boxes and forget them until something happens
and I can hunt them out by the map and catalogue,
I've lived my life by them.
I fear distance, not for its outstretched hands
that I can't reach—but because through its veil
I don't even know the hands are trying to climb up
to where my name is.
I fear mildew on my words, worse, the bleaching rewrite.
I fear that words will leave me like a one-night stand at sunrise.
I fear I'll have to go back to my old job
stocking shoes in a dusty warehouse at Sears,
cutting my hand with the razor I use to open boxes.
I fear that I have grown to love
the burning, stinging pain of alcohol on a fresh wound.
I fear being God in my universe of one.
I fear that I'll wake up one morning
and there will be six of us
instead of two.
I fear that you'll always beg for those children's stingy love
their numbers multiplying each year.
I fear the wrinkles between your eyebrows when you're mad.
I fear the eyes of big dogs, the way they track you
with viper-shaped heads when you walk past.
I fear the end of sidewalks.
I fear that first step off the curb, always a little further
than you think, that much closer,
fear the breath of the red Mercedes as it squalls past.

I fear the rest of my hair will fall out and leave me with a turtle-shiny head.
I hate hats and scalp sunburns.
I fear I won't hear that thud in my chest one night
and there won't be time to finish my beginnings before the dark
crawls in bed with me. I fear the loss of beginnings, how fast they recede.
I fear the no man's land between awake and asleep.
I fear the roar of planes unseen, their thunder without lightning.
I fear the lurch to the left,
the pilot's interrupted announcement,
and the five minute fall toward the hard ground.
I don't think it will feel like flying.
I fear my hard drive will explode, and when I lose all my poems,
I won't care. I fear my computers.
Were those heartbeats I heard this morning,
or just the E. A. Poe website left on overnight?
Will I come home to see smoke curling up from the keyboard,
a few Marlboros missing, my coffee cup drained?
I fear the creak at the top of the stairs will one day disappear.
I fear the gestures I make in my sleep,
my inability to fall asleep when everyone else does.
I fear the little house lizard that wandered
into my room and scaled the walls until it reached
the ceiling will fall. I fear the suction cup staying power of his feet
will give way and he will land on my half open lips as I snore.
I also fear cockroaches. One of them wrapped
its legs around my big toe and squeezed as if trying to extract nectar
while my mother tried to pry it off with her bare hands.
I fear never understanding why my fearless
mother became afraid, because I have not had a child,
and I think that is when she began to be afraid.
I fear losing the love of two persons,
two different people, two very different kinds of love.
Why are so many people focused on just one?
I fear that I will die before someone tells me I love you—
someone who meant it and just wasn't trying to sleep with me.
I fear that I may never get to make love to you.
I fear that my looks will fade before I have the chance to settle down.
I fear I might be wasting my time with Alex.
I fear I will have a potbelly when I grow old.

I fear I'm wasting the best years of my life.
I fear not having enough time to finish whatever my life's project is.
(This is not the same as saying I fear death.)
I fear making beautiful things and having them dry out from lack of water.
I fear the humanity, or rather, the inhumanity of men.
I fear the part of my countrymen who have no tolerance
or understanding for anyone different than themselves.
I fear my parrots' resentment, their chirping
and squalling about their cage, the shambles it's in,
how they miss their mother and hate Felix, my tabby.
I fear my son, so smart, so stubborn, so creative,
so fast in my car that he loves like a pet.
I fear the white cloud of anthrax billowing in my imagination
when I keep my children home from the mall, the movies, from Disney World.
I fear the crisp-edged thought that sounds safe and Republican.
I fear taking a stand so hard it's all I can see.
I fear betrayal in friendship and love that blindsides me
and leaves me raw and confused.
I fear lies that I tell, those sweet white lies:
Yes, he loves you. He'll call soon.
What's twenty pounds, you have a beautiful face.
I fear losing my mind. I fear being forgotten by God
or not remembering my way home.
I fear losing my books,
softened by the Florida dampness and eaten by bugs.
I fear losing myself to fear as much as I fear overcoming too much fear.
I fear the mirror's indifference, not its honesty.
I fear eloquence that declines, starving on its own security.
I fear the role of the number 1 in a countdown.
I fear not knowing the back of my hand as well as other things.
I fear the casual malevolence of drivers who think I'm in their way.
I fear anything that reminds me of pain I already buried.
I fear the way two problems in a row conjure new problems,
one after another, generations perfecting themselves.
I fear how mundane my fears become, that too many sun-filled days
are simply a poor reflection of a great storm to come.
I fear the cerulean sky for what could follow such bright color?
An unhappy forecast—and no ridiculing the weatherman
to take our minds off the rain.

PROCESS NOTE

Lines for "82 Reasons Not to Get Out of Bed" were written on October 24, 2001 by the members of Special Topics: Trends in Contemporary Poetry—Literary Collaboration and Collage, a graduate seminar I taught at Florida International University. Mitch Alderman, Terri Carrion, Andreé Conrad, Kendra Dwelley Guimaraes, Wayne Loshusan, Abigail Martin, Rita Martinez, Estee Mazor, Astrid Parrish, Stacy Richardson, Sandy Rodriguez, Jay Snodgrass, Richard Toumey, George Tucker, Jennifer Welch, William Whitehurst, and I wrote individual lines. Rita Martinez took the lines and rearranged them into the final version of the poem. Stacy Richardson, the only undergraduate in our class, passed away in 2002. This poem is dedicated to her.

DENISE DUHAMEL

Five Orgasms

Bernadette Geiser, Zoe O'Banion,
Sarah Odishoo, Maureen Seaton & Ginny Sykes

1. Circus Orgasm

I saw an orgasm at a circus once.
It was wild and they had it caged—
orgasm furioso.
It couldn't be tied, it couldn't be chained,
it was a beam of light undone.

2. Orgasms Are Mysterious Slivers

Finding orgasms is a lifetime work
beginning in ovulation (the presumed first site of the orgasm)
and ending in obituary (the last revenge of the orgasm).
What if all the dead people in their coffins
rose up and had orgasms?
When it rains, the flowers (especially the roses)
in the garden have multiple orgasms.
They tell all their friends about it
and the neighborhood is scandalized by orgasms.

3. The Deliciousness of Mother Bundling You in Your Snowsuit, and That Cold Zipper on Your Tongue

I had my first orgasm at 4.
In their dreams, an orgasm, in their skies
the orgasm blooms like an iris in their eye.
It swells to the heft of a thousand orgasms.
The orgasm crashes down like coconuts.
A juicy knot, the orgasm is unchained,
sliding and gliding, freefall orgasm,
like sledding—a tobogganistic orgasm—
or snow—that unaffected orgasm.

4. Lies Flies

An orgasm in every line,
She said with exuberant orgasm.
Eddie didn't have his first orgasm till 17 or 18—
Isn't that old for a man to have his first orgasm?
A first orgasm is a lie—it grows from day to day
until it blooms out of your body and into the skies.
An orgasm flies.
An orgasm lies.
Sometimes an orgasm crucifies
and cries for its mother, oh orgasm,
where are you?
Do not be afraid, little orgasm, little one.

5. Orgasm Civil Rights

The color of the orgasm is orange
and the motto of the orgasm is "Oh, yeah!"

Could Houdini orgasm in his bonds
or a genie orgasm in a bottle?
Please pass the bottle of orgasms.

Can you imagine if the word organization,
abbreviated to org. really meant orgasm?

You can have a whole bunch of orgasms
on a bobcat, without even trying.
An orgasm is as an orgasm does.

Orgasms find their own levels
and their own depths and heights—

We shall over come!

Process Note

Composed using Exquisite Corpse at Woman Made Gallery, Chicago, Illinois, during the "Deal with It" Exhibit and Workshop, June, 2001.

MAUREEN SEATON

Gay Parade

Lisa Glatt & David Hernandez

Four stories up we watch the whole shebang
from the balcony: first, a fleet of women
in black leather thundering down Ocean Boulevard

on motorcycles, then shirtless boys on blades,
followed by the smiling mayor in a yellow Caddy.
We hoot and holler at the men dressed

as cheerleaders, their hairdos like giant scoops
of sherbet: orange, berry, lime. At the corner
a boy stands beside a lanky transvestite, waiting

for his friend to snap a photograph.
We are relatively happy, but the married couple
who joined us are nitpicking and blue.

They assess the situation from opposite ends
of the continuum. He'd *never;* she isn't
so sure. They stare glum-faced at the parade,

their love for each other as fragile
as the soap bubbles lifting from below,
filled with the breath of someone with pursed lips.

Mercy

Lisa Glatt & David Hernandez

Every bird she sees wears her
dead mother's face, a tiny handmade dress.
She will not speak about pigeons or sorrow,
and only now, with him, whispers love.

Before they met there was a desert
stretched between them, a vulture gliding
in the air above him like a black kite.
In its claws, a one-word note from her mother:

Mercy. Now they drink water from the bowl
of each other's cupped hands. Now they twist
the sheets into a nest, bending together
in a blue and merciful bed.

Process Note

We'd been dating for a few weeks when Lisa showed me a collection of collaborative poems by Denise Duhamel and Maureen Seaton. I remember perusing the book and wondering how it was done, who wrote what, and if egos ever got in the way. While talking on the telephone days later, Lisa suggested that we write a collaborative poem. Now? I said. Get on your computer, she said. I sensed that it wasn't going to work, that we were sure to bicker or disagree. There was some wheel-spinning at first, but eventually we were able to drive the poem forward, each with a hand on the wheel.

After that first experience, we decided to write more together. The poems typically began with one of us typing the first two or three lines on the computer while the other person sat and waited. The edits we made were minimal because we were mostly pleased with each other's lines. On the occasions when we weren't pleased, we were surprisingly open to criticism and happy to change what we'd written. There was little of the protectiveness that sometimes inhibits the poem in progress or the poet in progress. I welcomed Lisa's suggestions and she welcomed mine. Meanwhile, our egos seemed to stay out of it, which was a sort of lesson learned for the two of us—one that we've hopefully carried into our individual poems, our own writing.

DAVID HERNANDEZ

Waiting for the Cat Food to Come

Violet Snow & Sparrow

We're lying around,
It's Saturday afternoon.
You're looking at me,
I'm looking at you.
We're waiting for the cat food to come,
Waiting for the cat food to come.

The cat food's supposed to come
Between 12 and 2,
And now it's noon and
We have to decide what to do
Should we have sex,
Or wait for the cat food?
What if it comes
Before we do?
Waiting for the cat food to come,
Waiting for the cat food to come.

Each time you put your hand on my thigh
Or I put my thigh on your hand,
We have to try to understand
If we're about to hear the cat food man
Carrying the cat food cans.

Now we're lying on the bed,
We've had sex and it's still not 2.
I've come and you've come, too,
But where's the cat food?

Waiting for the cat food to come,
Waiting for the cat food to come.

Process Note

How we wrote "Waiting for the Cat Food to Come":

"Waiting for the Cat Food to Come" is based on a true story. For ten years, we lived in the East Village of Manhattan. A local pet store, Little Creatures, would deliver food (for our cat, Gummy). A brawny fellow would climb the three flights of stairs to our apartment, bearing a case of food tins. Of course, with such deliverers, one is never certain of the exact time they will arrive. They say something like: "We'll be there between 1 and 3 P.M."

One day, we wanted to have sex—but this was between 1 and 3 P.M., and the cat food man was on his way. Should we wait for him, or just hope he would arrive closer to 3? One of us—probably Sparrow—decided this would be an apt subject for a song. We began writing, each taking one line. If one of us was inspired, she would add the following line. For example, Violet wrote:

If we're about to hear the cat food man

then continued:

Carrying the cat food cans.

This was 1990, or thereabouts. (This became a song for our band, Foamola.)

SPARROW

Dollar Store

Sparrow & Mike Topp

Peggy Jo and I love shopping—not just going to the dollar store and buying coin-rolling wrappers. We love also to buy big ice creams and Serenity Pills.

PROCESS NOTE

The story of "Dollar Store":

Mike Topp and Sparrow were in the habit of sending each other their recent poems, and little stories. Sometimes they would rewrite each other's poems. (Mike Topp began this practice.) One day (April 3, 2002, to be exact), Mike e-mailed this paragraph:

DOLLAR STORE

Peggy Jo and I love shopping—not just going to the dollar store and buying a change purse and some coin-rolling wrappers. We love going to the big stores that sell things which cost a great deal. I don't care if I don't have a penny in my pocket—I can just plan what to buy when I get some money.

Sparrow rewrote it as it appears above.

Sparrow can no longer remember why he wrote this. (Although he does like all writings short.)

SPARROW & MIKE TOPP

245

The New Prosperity

Thomas Fink & Timothy Liu

We're not "against" the river per se,

just the way you say it. How the Hudson
absorbs other energies like a trooper—

so why get tanked all the time? A hearty

baptism. What the portfolio declined
to mention against the Dow surging to

new gravy. But who's in clover? Pushed

to give our pacifiers back—borrowed
dent in the plush icon. You cad, flaunting

caviar loss and excess. Brace yourselves

for the overripe lifestyle. Never mind
the drab-suited octopus: you just don't

career off plankton without that hard-on.

Art in America

Thomas Fink & Timothy Liu

As serious as cash plunked down,
a greasy flash goes off. Okay, you

win the kewpie doll, the magpie.
Senators, don't pronate your wrists.

Don't think of snarfing the whole
pie. Peace, already! Washington's

crapped out while the Popemobile
cruises the Golan Heights—AK-

47s saluting his white target, his
Jasper Johns riddled full of holes.

PROCESS NOTE

In the case of both poems, we e-mailed each other a few lines at a time. Then,
when we agreed each poem was finished, we each suggested revisions. Once
these changes were agreed upon, we brainstormed to find a title.

THOMAS FINK

Derivative of the Curve: 2

Kendra Dwelley Guimaraes & George Tucker

Put the first derivative = zero: you have a critical point.
My sister's robotic heart went critical when
She walked into the room where Mom microwaved
Canned peaches in a plastic bowl.
Lisa pissed herself and fell on the floor, kinda jiggled
Like a hooked fish for a while. That night at dinner
Her fingers were rusty with peach juice.
Mom had lost the owner's manual so Lisa didn't
Know what not to do. Red wire #47
Slithered like a bloody tear from under her left breast.
One night while she slept I touched the red snake's copper tongue
To a nine-volt battery—her eyes stayed closed but she quivered all over—
Turned a little purple.
After that, at mealtimes when no one talked, you could hear it—
A high-pitched flutter like a hummingbird's song—
For the rest of her life my mutt Savage hid from her.
To him she sounded like Budweiser cans tied to the bumper of a Volkswagen.
To me, across the dark six feet that separated our beds,
She sounded like my own mortality.
In the end, the coffee machine killed her, indirectly,
When she tried to wash it. Still plugged in.

Robotics

Kendra Dwelley Guimaraes & George Tucker

The Cheshire cat was a matter of robotics and the grin was red wire #47.
Alice Alice Alice
There is a groove in gigabyte 30,101,010
The mad hatter had a robot in the
Kitchen armed with pink rubber gloves
To rinse the tea dregs
Alice Alice Alice
When my mother was twenty-two she went to a Jefferson Starship concert just to
Hear the song White Rabbit.
Alice Alice Alice
With the mechanical heart
Lewis Carroll with the Sanity Transplant
From too much opium
Red wire #47 a copper binary tangle.

PROCESS NOTE

These poems were written over the course of an evening after much sushi, beer and one strong cappuccino. George and I worked individually to invent four "lies" which were bits of fictionalized biography, creative facts and/or bizarre ramblings. We jotted these lies on separate pieces of paper. Each group of lies was based on a theme assigned at random from a dictionary, a thesaurus, or the latest issue of the *New Yorker*. Then we read all eight lies and used them to create one poem in the time span of ten to fifteen minutes. We chose not to edit the resultant poems much, because art is freedom, man.

KENDRA DWELLEY GUIMARAES

Cereal Monogamy

Maureen Seaton & Terese Svoboda

A bagel chipper in Excalibur!
A simple flan exfoliated

sets off. Tis Huns hunting rabbits,
starched, a-steamed, and poofed,

soft and sticky, tis milk.
Preggers of glips of crispy.

Melody remote as island
juggery, brewed buggery

beckons. Rising depthwise,
an expletive from itchy tits,

the bread-noughts frame the sun
slanting like a line of brow,

which, sinking, they Arizona
the e-motion, an electric

wheedling kettle, a kind of
pulse from brain to tongue-tip.

Hun-shunned and Birkenstocked,
biscuit-toned and floatable,

impregnable, shuckable
and incorruptibly

eerie in milkdom, a big
bumble bowl of blah blah

breakfast food saves several,
saves the toppled highchair.

A shadow from bottom,
an omphalos, a take five.

Hear the cheerio, the Quaker
breathing in air? Who can blame them?

The wheat, the golden spoon.

PROCESS NOTE

I started out with the title and a draft playing on the punnishness of it and
punished M. with it, that is to say, I found a cul de sac that we could meet in
and do the play part together. M. culled and I sacked.

TERESE SVOBODA

Somonka

Jacqueline Johnson & devorah major

Grey hairs—those bitches
show up everywhere. Talking
about "we don't care
what color you put over us
we showing our asses anyway."

(JJ)

vegetable dye
henna or shaved oiled head
temple mascara
or a night of wild loving
will tame those fickle tresses.

(dm)

PROCESS NOTES

The first part of this somonka was initially sent to Denise Duhamel at the bottom of the packet as a tanka hanging on its own. As time would prove this tanka had more power than the poems I sent in collaboration with others. Denise gave me an opportunity to seek out a collaborator. I sent out a call to devorah major who is a novelist and poet whose work I respect. For me respect is the key ingredient in the art of collaboration. devorah major's novel *An Open Weave,* eloquently tells of African-American women seeking to survive with mind, body and spirit intact, and she [has been] the Poet Laureate of San Francisco.

devorah responded with a humorous but deliciously wicked tanka proving women of all ages are resourceful when it comes to grey hairs. devorah had never written a tanka but knew the haiku form and was willing to go for it. I decided these tankas could now form a somonka, which is the old Japanese letter writing form of the court poets. Several of the poems I have in translation have tankas with two responses, thus allowing for a varied experience. For me, the fun of this collaboration was bringing back a form and giving it a contemporary twist.

JACQUELINE JOHNSON

In this poem Jacqueline Johnson started the "conversation" and I tried to be a good listener, responding to and countering her ideas.

devorah major

Somonka

Patricia A. Johnson & Christina Springer

Mint's lilac blooms
swing down, waft their perfume
like a church lady
pulls a handkerchief from breasts
I draw you from memory

(PJ)

like a good woman
under Spirit shouts, "Glory!"
carried far by faith.
A dusky peach tea rose plucked.
My heart is your flower press.

(CS)

Process Note

I want to say something about . . .

Language and dialect are not just something one inherits from parents and community. We breathe tone, image, idea and spirit from the landscapes around us. We wrote "Somonka" during our own personal and private writer's retreat in 2002 in Elk Creek, Virginia after Patricia's vibrant artist in residency in Pittsburgh during the summer of 2001. During these two years as friends and colleagues, we experienced geography's impact on language. Patricia–a rural poet in Pittsburgh/Christina–an urban poet in Elk Creek. We heard the way cement makes the consonants harder and boulders soften vowels.

I remember:

Challenging ourselves to create for ourselves a sense of retreat and poetic communion. Savoring forms like an unlimited stash of Johnny Walker Blue. Sharing sisterhood with a holy woman.

Driving past Christmas Tree farms on land once cleared by slaves for other crops. Noticing the way every field, pasture and yard looked immaculately landscaped because God had expertly positioned boulders eons ago and there was nothing man could do about it.

Visiting her family's cemetery, creeping back into a stand of trees to hunt for a tombstone. Stepping through time to realize that here in the U.S. there are some people who do not deal with death by writing a check to the undertaker and the landscaping service.

Gathering our dinner from the garden. Slipping into opaque black night to blast a yellow jacket's nest. And thinking of how I felt about the Steelers.

Writing on paper with a pen.

Scowling at deer because they've crept up on the porch to eat the cherries and left processed pits behind.

Seeing the night as unmitigated blackness and understanding why some have a hard time forgiving that kind of density.

Wishing for more than the blue-yellow haze of ambient street lights
and conceiving my son two days after Patricia and I finished being
poets at communion.

CHRISTINA SPRINGER

A Game of Chance

Opal Palmer Adisa & Reginald Lockett

Year of Monkey born,
From limbs of mischief I swing.
Day and night I wait.
Throw coconuts at lion.
Tell him elephant did it.

(RL)

I am horse seeking
my tiger that craves warm meat.
I study deer's path.
A sacrifice is needed
for love to find its way home.

(OPA)

PROCESS NOTES

After Reggie wrote the first stanza, he sent it to me, and I zeroed in on the timber and sentiment of the piece and replied.

OPAL PALMER ADISA

This somonka was written via e-mail. What I thought about as I wrote it was a blending of Chinese astrology and African-American folklore. I then e-mailed it to Opal because we collaborated on another somonka while at the Cave Canem Poets Workshop/Retreat at Cranbrook, MI in 2002.

REGINALD LOCKETT

Romeo's Half-Wake

Reginald Shepherd & Gene Tanta

Was he slow lightning
poured through a smashed flute,
an oiled jade sky descending?
Or grass arm-wrestling grass

in hushes, his granite gait till nightfall? Courtier
encountered weather with its full vocabulary of line:
bright night and hunting made a pledge of him
to stay the shape of motionless, one moon

waxing with artificial swoon: one moon
turning into a god of or's browsing library shelves
trapped in the flutter of vacancy generating
a code of arms on the hunt. (Predictable and fine as

stained verdigris, the wall of what he was
where grass blades cut me green as vines
that clung there, climbed me too.) What I saw
was a woman finger-counting vows to ten,

Venus complaining of headache, of lattice-worked
azurite coastlines, of buoys past the sound.
Weather wondered when (whispered 'when' too), and how
much longer she would wait beneath the abalone

shell, iridescent, armored against inquiry or
Romeo's false waking, his laundering of irony. She finds
night wind braided with bracts, a lover's trade, all the pretty r's
folded into pearl, the rhythm-gnawed shore, a way out.

Screen Memory

Reginald Shepherd & Gene Tanta

Doubt collects in rusting rain
gutters, festers like rotting
moonlight, drains: leaves

the color it came, the size of labor-
bloated palms, fermented swelling certain
to scab. Waves feast

on late September (drowning
weather, lakewater warmest then,
most welcoming), until

Michigan's dark-infested undertow puckers up
a whole summer's worth of heat,
buckles its liquid patina, submerges cool

with absence like any window
wiped clean. The partial light
makes possible a breadth of sight

that only bees can screw through
to pollinate their brains out. Your dilated pupils
call the window streaks as evidence

on the retina: old men
playing Chinese checkers
in the park, hemp smell, sex and clove cigarettes,

Coke left lukewarm in the shade. Flattened butts
pock the asphalt rivers; the heft of city ghosts
settles on a bench. They tongue out words but

say nothing, dispute with air and disperse
afternoon, another word for stay indoors,
the inversion layer's English breaking.

Dumb with attention, the checkers fans sigh
"Whose turn is it to move?" scowling with delight.
The game is being played for cigarettes.

Coming winter weaves an acid wind
out of polluted waves, arrows
anywhere but air: even love lisps

"Stay, unclench your heart," burdened by
humid air, by fuzzy dice pressing your
cheek's chastity in the parking lot, stammer

-ing "Is this what you wanted
to see when you asked for
more light?" Without a shadow anywhere

to rinse these doubts to the beginning,
watch sunlight bow and bend, articulate
like a Schwinn spoke

broken in place, turning
anyway. Lepidoptera, Coleoptera,
Hymenoptera, Diptera, splayed-across-the-sidewalk orders,

the Jesus statue's feet kissed enough to gleam. Albert's
knuckles fail to ring the nurse
to bring his carnal hanker back, ruined, half-dressed. Five

of six, his face is finished
with insectile daylight's
being seen, finished with seeing too.

PROCESS NOTES

These two poems were written via e-mail. Gene, I believe, wrote the first stanza in each case (it was he who initiated the collaboration), and then I wrote a stanza in response, and so on until we both agreed that the poem was finished. We then went over the poems several times, sending one another drafts via e-mail, revising and reworking them into what I hope are seamless wholes. Over the course of this process the lines determining who wrote what stanzas became more and more blurred, as we each felt free to add, remove, or modify in the interest of the poem as a whole.

REGINALD SHEPHERD

For my part in the collaboration, form was not a pre-settled matter but "constantly in flux," an organic association between felt intentions. The poems were composed via e-mail in alternating lines—subverting a singular authorial narrative or lyric. The objects/poems wore their own paths toward becoming what they are and for me it seemed simply a matter of paying close attention to when and in which direction to get the hell out of their way. In each case, the agency of the poem took root and asserted itself.

For me, the "I" has been always the prime cause and the prime detriment to good writing but collaboration rescues me by effectively mitigating my static sense of identity and activating my dynamic sense of identity. Collaboration forces me to recognize the death of how I know myself and allows other slants of reflection to inform and re-form me.

GENE TANTA

Lessons from the Kitchen

Jim Elledge & Kristy Nielsen

Like a shiny penny, Innuendo rolls
across the linoleum. Like a cockroach,
Innuendo scurries across
the linoleum, making kissing
sounds, howling, smacking its lips.

The cat learns the hard way,
sliding into cupboards, rattling
old crocks. Innuendo is parchment-thin
if required. Then insidious gas
settles over them. The cat cleans herself.

"You know," she says, "fog like this
is a cloud touching earth," flattering Innuendo
like icing on a birthday cake, delicious all
the way down and oh, so fattening!

PROCESS NOTE

Being on opposite coasts—Kristy's near San Francisco while Jim's in Brooklyn—
we've found that e-mail works beautifully for our collaborations. Our MO is
simply this: Kristy writes a line, then Jim responds—or vice versa—throughout
the poem. But we alternate, neither of us moving forward until the other has
responded. Either of us can end a poem at any point. We trust one another, so
whatever either of us says is OK, and because we trust one another, there's no
sense of owning lines. In fact, neither of us remembers who's written what. We
don't have to. Writing is about the work itself, not about us. E-mail helps to
destroy the sense of ownership and of property—as does the act of collaboration.
But it's also more fundamental to our MO than that. Using e-mail to cross the
three-hour difference in time zones that separates us allows Jim to be up and at
'em, hammering out a metaphor, while Kristy's still slumbering, dreaming of
bird-women and water, or Kristy can be slaving away over a line break, while
Jim's nodding off, martini in hand.

JIM ELLEDGE & KRISTY NIELSEN

Ifugao Red

Nick Carbó & Eileen Tabios

Wings flare. Hawk soars
as if the sky is Ifugao red
and her wrists shake

with seven silver bracelets, each
dangling a stone etched with
memories formed as feathers,

teardrops, arrowheads. The sound
of her grandmother crushing
gabi leaves for a spell

fills the room. The window persists
with its lack of your face
supplanting the pumice stones

during the monsoon season
in Pampanga. After tasting
salt through her tears

why did you open your pores
to the temptress's curved copper
tongue? Does the witch paint

heavy verbs on your thighs? Boulders
like "ravage," "pillage," "ransack"
or "despoiled"? Peel off their signs

for sweetness: her damp eyes walking
to the front mahogany door
to answer your wing beats

discerned through the breeze.
To arrive home is to release your
armor, dropping it on ancient terrazzo.

PROCESS NOTE

Filipino and Filipino-American poets have been the bastard children of American poetry for more than a hundred years, spawned by the U.S.'s invasion of the Philippines in 1898. Although often overlooked, marginalized, disinherited, alienated, or forgotten, this rich tradition of poetry is worthy of inclusion in the main fabric of American and English literature.

Thus, Nick Carbó and Eileen Tabios collaborate on poems which include references to Filipino culture. It is their hope that non-Filipino readers read the poems and be moved to research the Filipino references (in the same way that readers are asked to research Greek, French, and other Eurocentric or Western references frequently inserted in poems that make up the literary canon), thereby learning about Filipino culture.

The collaborative nature of authorship also relates to their consciousness that English was a colonizing tool in the Philippines. Following the U.S.'s military invasion in 1898, English spread across the archipelago to solidify their imperialist rule to become the preferred language for commerce, education and politics. When Carbó and Tabios collaborate together to write poems, they do so partly to shield their autobiographical I's as forming the authors of these poems. For these poems are written in English.

On "Ifugao Red," the poets collaborated through e-mail. Carbó recollects: "One line you. One line me. One comma here. One ellipsis there. Is that my virgule dangling from your page? Ah, the ampersand has spoken and! You spun your tilde on the table."

NICK CARBÓ & EILEEN TABIOS

Logogriph

Nick Carbó & Eric Gamalinda

The river of light brought these things—
the moon, eyes in it, what we saw,

innumerable forms worming—
six poets leaping like metaphors

into the swan dive of speech! But what
does it mean? And where does it begin?

From black matter came Chronos,
a tablet of red minutes, ejaculations

of the Om, alpha-genesis, inverse
of darkness. I, too, have seen

them fondle the Ur of words,
landing topsy-turvy like children's toys

in a country of orphans. Searching
as a way of life: found loneliness.

Bending their arms like roman arches,
they encountered the apex of silence

gladly, as though they were born to it.
Can you see it now—Paraselene

and the Endymion bulge? The metronome
counting the alizarin heartbeats

like a deathwatch, bright with spectrums
that shimmer even in darkness. Look:

Einstein's ear! It dances in swirls
like matter and antimatter and enters

the range of albedos, the mathematical
fluency of God. We have the moon

opening the ancient door made of
Javanese silver, Butuan bronze,

blood of the Sri Vijaya: halation
of empires, fictive, glorious—

poignant with the brown child
of sound—our future utterances.

PROCESS NOTE

The poem was written via e-mail. I wrote the first couplet with no specific idea
what the poem was going to be about. But Nick and I easily picked up on each
other's "image-wave" and there was a consistent pull to keep the poem within
an intuited context. It soon became clear that at the same time Nick was taking
the poem one way and I was taking it another, a process that reminded me of
the prototype video ping pong games Nick and I grew up with in the 80s: we
kept hitting the images to the opposite side of the court—in this case, not to win,
but to make the match more interesting. Or, to put it differently, Nick and I
became two sides of one brain. The roles were not absolute but interchangeable,
fluid, negotiable. This tension propelled the motion of the poem. I realized Nick
was insisting on a certain sensuality, or sexuality, in the imagery; I was pulling it
back to what I thought was its contrapuntal force, some idea of "spirit." The
result was a kind of frisson between body and spirit, abstract and concrete, life
and death. But what was most interesting to me was that instinct or intuition
seemed to make us totally aware of what the other was trying to do; eventually,
the poem was being written by one mind. Months later I couldn't recognize
which were my lines and which were Nick's; I had to e-mail him back and ask.

ERIC GAMALINDA

All Saints' Day

Guillermo Castro & Ron Drummond

All over the barrio, cats' whiskers pick up
FM radios tuned to tango-only stations.
Doña Carmelita cranks up her stereo
To screaming merengue, like there's no mañana.

FM radio tuned to a tango-only station.
Her feet begin to move with ease
To screaming merengue, like there's no mañana.
"Undress the poodle, give the parakeet a sponge bath."

Her feet begin to move with ease
When Doña Carmelita reaches for more garlic.
"Undress the poodle, give the parakeet a sponge bath,"
What a crazy thing to think! And twice!, she mutters.

Doña Carmelita reaches for more garlic
Spin-wrapped in cheesecloth, strung like a dreidel.
What a crazy thing to think! And twice she mutters:
"But it has always been true."

She unwraps the strung cheesecloth, spins like a dreidel
That once blurred letters to oblivion.
And it has always been true
That the barrio cats bellow from the ledges

Where once burned letters to oblivion.
And the old saints shake their clovelike buttocks
To the barrio cats bellowing from their ledges
With hardly a high whimper or a lyric love song.

And the old saints quake their clovelike buttocks
As Doña Carmelita cranks up her stereo
From hardly a whimper to a high sung love lyric
Only the barrio cat ladies' whiskers pick up.

PROCESS NOTE

We wrote four poems using our own variation of the Exquisite Corpse. We call our version "Delicious Limb," wherein:

1. Poet A grabs book of poetry, picks one page at random, then writes down the first line of the poem on that page.

2. Poet A covers line and tells Poet B only the last word of that line.

3. Poet B writes a new line, covers it, and tells Poet A the last word.

4. Continue same process to the end of the page.

5. Poets A and B read the results aloud.

6. Poet A takes poem home to develop in any way he sees fit.

7. Poet A gives poem to Poet B for further revisions. They'll continue back and forth until they declare the piece is finished or kill each other.

8. Start again with poet B taking a line from a poem picked at random.

9. Describe the collaborating process in ten easy steps.

10. You can name your hypothetical poets other than A or B. Letters from Cyrillic or Greek alphabets are also acceptable.

GUILLERMO CASTRO & RON DRUMMOND

The Great Cuban Sculptor

Virgil Suárez & Ryan G. Van Cleave

Ebaristo only works now in brass,
its siren shine, how it blooms
in island sunlight like a conch

pinned into a pretty woman's
hair. On the palm of the great
spirit, Doña Inez–who simply

knows how to levitate baccarat
and pour aguita santa from cocos,
and he has seen her walk on water,

yes, true, the hem of her silk gown
fluttering above the surface,
a memory of a long-remembered

kiss. At an exhibit in Matanzas,
a place named after the famous
slaughter, a blind girl ran her fingers

across La Asención de Dios en Los
Labios de Doña Inez, La Pura . . .
Then asked, "Are you homesick

for the hand healer's soft hands?"
And he hurried home, through harsh
light and framboyan shade, his own

image burned and stretching in front
of him. Home finally he crawled
into gauzy sheets, pulled a cold towel

over his face, inside the cocoon
of mosquito netting, knowing full well
he could never be fresh enough, or brave.

Process Note

Ryan G. Van Cleave & I have very similar tastes in poetry, and as such we work very well together. The process was extremely organic for us. He wrote a few lines, I wrote a few lines, the poem grew, and then we took turns revising. We had already done several poems in this vein. . . it works . . . though I am sure we are not the first ones or last ones to try it.

                                                    Virgil Suárez

Sestina for Horse & Destiny

Connie Deanovich & Rachel Loden

When tubas go on sale in October
Who will buy and therefore find destiny?
Like a tan and orange animal about to eat
The day is neither free nor easy
An Italian Hercules movie may be relief, but it isn't fun
Give up something fresh for me, and make it quick

Although giving up is never quick
Especially in a month as fractious as October
When ripping leaves off artichokes is too much fun
To pass up for something prim like "destiny"
And the sullen girl whose life had seemed so easy
Is building secret ziggurats of things to eat

She does this so her mind begins to heat
And her senses go from slow to quick
In summer life is just too easy
She needs the planetary rush that is October
To free her from the extravagance of destiny
To take her someplace much more fun

Where Tilt-A-Whirls are not the only kind of fun
And cotton candy's not the only thing to eat
Where a girl can get a leg up on her destiny
That horse so fickle and so quick
It startles the delinquent meadows of October
Never caring what is comfortable or easy

And yet this brown and gentle horse named Easy
Becomes a national symbol of a more fun
United States with a new holiday in October
Whose point is not just eating
And where storytelling's witty and quick
Listen, kids, we say, "There is no destiny!"

Or at least no point in swooning over destiny
When Hercules can make things look so easy
And the race, even with tubas, goes to the quick
And keen of heart, whose random flights of fun
Include a line of crisp and patriotic eats
And thus a braver, bratwurst-free October

The same October of our bodacious destiny
Eating cherries jubilee on ice cream over easy
Quick pitted moon, the future hellbent on fun

PROCESS NOTES

The sestina is my favorite form, and a collaboration gives it a unique edge.
Rachel Loden and I have been longtime correspondents, our friendship forming
strictly by letters, phone calls, and e-mail. We have never physically met so the
idea of sitting down together to collaborate is an impossibility. We decided,
across the continent, to do a sestina together for fun. Rachel, I think, was more
serious about the task than I, and it was her intense and brilliant handling of the
language that gives the poem its dark spin. We sent the thing back and forth
through e-mails for months before calling it done.

CONNIE DEANOVICH

I'd been a fan of Connie's sestinas since I first came across her work. So it was
inevitable that this form should suggest itself when we decided to write together.
I liked the notion because it seemed somehow modular and buildable. We set
about choosing end words: Connie's were *quick, fun,* and *easy,* and mine were
October, destiny, and *eat.* What was compelling for me was how the end words
governed the feel of the poem and how psychedelic it was to try to get my often
mordant and macabre mind around these unaccountably cheerful words. It was
fun to imagine that I was thinking like Connie, whose poetic mind I'd always
found mysterious and admirable.

RACHEL LODEN

Soul #1

Julianna Baggott & Norman Minnick

Baggott:

My soul is as narrow as a fence post.
And what do I know of hate?

Minnick:

My soul is the space between fence posts.
And the closer I get, the wider the world becomes.

I can't fit my body between the posts.
My ego is balled up like a monkey's fist
full of berries stuck inside that hollowed-out tree.

Baggott:

I know the monkey well. He's a thief.

My soul was once as pungent as an orange
peeled in church, but that monkey wore a cap,
rode an organ grinder's shoulder, and stole it.

Minnick:

My soul was also as pungent as an orange,

but it fell from the branch as I reached for it
and rolled under the pew and was eaten
from the inside out.

PROCESS NOTES

As an author, I'm always looking for a way out of authority. When I'm alone with my work, I'm the bully–telling the words what they can and cannot do. A poisonous habit. And so I'm always looking for ways to take myself out of authority, allowing the work to bully me. If I'm collaborating, I'm being taken (by means of a forceful cha-cha or a jujitsu kick) to places I wouldn't have gone on my own.

JULIANNA BAGGOTT

There is an aphorism by Novalis that says, "The seat of the soul is where the inner world and the outer world meet. Where they overlap, it is in every point of the overlap." Since ours is contemplation of the soul, I imagine that two poets who are talking about the soul might be dancing, fighting, or both in this overlap.

NORMAN MINNICK

Spin

Laura Bandy & Shirley Stephenson

How could anything happen in this room? The colors
    make her dizzy. The door. Everyone gapes.
Someone's left. Beyond the window, someone just

arrived, tangle of electric wire. Fuse, meter. A steady
    churn & measure indifferent to calamity at the table.
She clutches a spoon, head nestled beside the oatmeal.

Usher of light, murk. She dreams a map, a black key.
    Maybe she's leaving. Maybe she meant escape.
A breeze has all the luck—blow through, blow out.

No, she meant: *anything like this*   & everyone
    in the orchestra knows it. The skies are jammed
with wishes for reversal. When she hears the news

her mother will turn statues to the wall. *Rouse.*
    Degas' dancer speaks from high. Watch her spin,
watch her multiply beyond herself, hands clutched

as if she's finally won, finally caught the fast ball
    that broke them all into a thousand shades, slick
& iridescent. Curtsey. When your body lies, you fall.

PROCESS NOTE

The collaborative process is in many ways like writing a solo collage poem, but
with more demanding and dissonant tensions. Sometimes the urge is to respond
to the other writer's words, and sometimes it's to lure them in a different
direction, to tempt the poem to do something it hadn't previously considered.
There's something like dancing a tango in the process—two voices move in the
same direction, focused on one another, then step apart, maybe with an air of
deviousness. And then the fizzy excitement of waiting to see what comes next.

LAURA BANDY & SHIRLEY STEPHENSON

Days of the Week

Paulette Beete & Danna Ephland

Lime sofas and gray draped felines border the room.
She writes "dry petunias" and "Yesterday, the beans in my hands felt wet, safe."
This is how days tumble now, everything only words—their rhyme and rhythm,
their heartbeat hot in her wrists, angry at her temples.
This is what fuels the song: molasses thick, a sweet, sad river of
*I used to know a man...*rising then falling.

> *Exhale.* She sees his face. *Inhale.* Another. *I am a juke box. I am a phone book. I am last year's bad report card, tomorrow's dishes left in the sink all night.* She turns her mind from failure again and again, but it stares back, asking questions, relentless.

PROCESS NOTE

We first collaborated in a Chicago Writer's Voice workshop led by Maureen Seaton, on a pantoum where Paulette introduced Heathcliff and the moors into our poem. Both of us have always been keenly interested in collaborative work (Danna, with a modern dance career/background; Paulette as an actress and singer). We wrote this poem on a humid summer afternoon in Washington D.C., seven years after we first met. There was laughter as usual, but mostly yawning and some notes compared about coping with depression in its various incarnations in our lives—good reasons for it, and no reason at all on some days, bad luck and chemistry gone awry. We came to the table with exercises to offer each other, including two Exquisite Corpses, an anaphora and I cannot recall the other. Paulette had the wisdom to let them sit a while before looking at them again, and it turned out that we had indeed written poems. We are very different women. Besides our love for language, music is a big part of what connects us. But mostly it's spirit—come hell or high water—spirit and creativity in the fine company of each other or other artists, people we meet along the way. What these encounters produce is always a surprise, shaking us from any semblance of predictability we might have been counting on in our lives. We are grateful for the upsets and what they bring and yield. We are grateful for each other.

PAULETTE BEETE & DANNA EPHLAND

Where We Live Now

Michael Hettich, Claudia Livini,
Susan Parsons & Yair Segal

This is the place we work in now:
code red, heat advisory,
animals that rise like smoke

and walk across the weathered sky
to languages for other worlds.
Rain falls every day

where we work with dust
and covered in dust,
where we work with broken things

we vaguely remember
the names for. Who are you?
Nobody   Nothing Else   Nevermind   Not.

When short people cast
long shadows, we know
the sun is going down, and soon

dark must fall. But there once was a man
who learned to sleep backward
and woke younger every day . . .

June 2002

PROCESS NOTE

A few years ago, a few of my students and I decided to resurrect our college literary arts magazine, *Metromorphosis*, which unfortunately had gone unfunded for a number of years. Though ultimately successful, the process was fraught with the kind of frustration born of too little technical knowledge, too little time, too few submissions, and too little money. These factors, combined with the challenges of communication with a multinational staff, gave the entire experience a "creative" edge that forced us all to collaborate in ways we'd never anticipated—and kept me awake a night or two along the way . . .

A week or so before we were to deliver the journal to the printer we realized that we needed at least one more poem to fill the layout we'd planned. We decided, in the spirit of our collaborative efforts on the journal, to make a collective poem. So we all wrote lines and phrases on small bits of paper, put them in a hat, shook the hat up and plucked our lines out, arranging them in the order they were retrieved. I tweaked things a little, adding some punctuation, breaking some of the sentences into lines and arranging the lines in loose stanzas. Otherwise "The Way We Live Now" exists as it came to us out of the hat, vivid in its Hebrew and Spanish accents, strangely urgent in its metasensibility.

MICHAEL HETTICH

Thirst

Alice George & Cecilia Pinto

I could tell you of my daughter's backseat lamentations,
how strange each day has its particular grief

as we leave our Maine vacation, her weeping for water,
a dry throat, a longing for the left behind, the lost.

Or my painting of my father-in-law's temporary gravestone,
how strange the way even loss lacks permanence,

the way his widow leaned over the work, politely nervous,
following the rituals of mourning, counting on the solace of duty

until I found the right botanical image: a willow.
There are other trees, lean out any window, find them and the fluttering birds.

Or the way each morning my hands can count,
number them, name them, remember

the new dead in the Middle East. But my tongue—
Robin, Blue Jay, Raven, Crow—

could turn black and nothing would change
names carved in stone. How strange that a name in stone is enough

except some settling in me, and perhaps in you.
I could tell you of tears wept under a willow, roots that go into the ground.

Instead, let's make new things to mourn, let's forget, let's eat.
Our names will remain for strangers to consider, our thirst, however, will end.

What Is She Doing Right Now?

Alice George & Cecilia Pinto

Cecilia Pinto   I.   There is a purple post-it in my handwriting at the back of the notebook I'm using. It says, "Cletus, 543-7725." Cletus is a dog. I'd like to think I could talk to him on the phone. I know him pretty well and I bet he'd have plenty to say. I'd have some questions too.

A. lent me a journal. Flipping through I find a brite pink post-it on which is written, "overheard language." Not, overheard conversation, but language. As if the note maker, I assume A. wasn't interested in context but in something else, not the gossip, not what but how; how were words chosen, how was the sentence constructed, how did it sound when spoken?

I try to imagine A.'s side of this page of writing, what is she listening to? What is she doing and how? What is she doing now?

So some questions and maybe directions too. We each have a post-it, one charts a course, the other is a dog's phone number. It seems enough for a beginning.

Alice George   **I.**   I don't know if there is a braid that can hold this ambition.

If we sit at a table together and smile and share food, then something is made. Two women, born four days apart. Living perhaps seven miles away.

When we sat talking about this endeavor, we kept laughing. Hard. Talked about back pain, yoga, our son's acne. Compared phrases we mutter in the car:
give me a fucking break
beam me fucking up

Both yang. Ready to smear and interfere with each other. What could happen if we look and see different things and then talk about it to each other?

It's so quiet, though, in this room. I could be crushed into a skillet of sautéing vegetables to make everything smell like summer. I'll e-mail C. this first entry soon.

Cecilia Pinto **II.**   Days have passed.

A. wonders what has become of me?
I'm not getting enough sleep and doze off on my son's shoulder in a waiting room. I fall asleep while reading. I sleep instead of writing.

I have slept in libraries. Many times. I remember the couches or carrels where I lay my head. There was a nice red leather one in the college library. I'm taken with the idea of dying in the library. Not now, but later: some rainy afternoon, in a big chair, in my coat, car keys in one hand (assuming I'm still allowed to drive) my mouth open. Books tucked around me, my purse at my feet. Asleep. Dead.

A. laughs whenever we talk about this business of me dying in a library. I laugh too but just because it's funny doesn't mean I'm not serious.

We've had a frost since I've last seen her. The leaves fell dramatically overnight, suddenly, unexpectedly vanquished. A frost like a pox upon the houses of the trees. Leaves maybe screaming as they fell.

And so A. and I awake, miles apart, to the same devastation and write.

There is never any screaming at the library. It's not allowed. Here and there a page turns, people whisper. I suppose occasionally someone disappears in the stacks. Trail your hand along the rows of books, still here, pages and leaves and reams, still here, waiting, serious in their intents. Faithful to you. Sleeping.

Alice George II. One of the roots of the word hard is the old french *hardir* to render bold. That's what I want from this writing right now. I summon squirrels to carry my post-its to C.–10 miles across town–but they don't come.

I read a book once where an old man's memory was distributed among written notes posted around his house.

The post-its near me right now say:
Soul
part will be in tommow no appt. needed
LOA/Check for Kay

I want to tell a story that has me and C. and our kids and our husbands in it, like building an arc, or ark, though I am not that afraid, I don't think, though fearful, surely. In that story, our boys sniff each other like dogs, and smell us, their mothers, on each other, and start laughing and sharing food and searching for ways to travel far away from us.
or
C. and I are infants and we just ate fear. We are riding on the backs of two dogs (one chocolate lab one american bulldog) naked towards the area of an impending war. The armies smell us coming and start laughing and sharing food.

I am sitting here in my backyard where I think I will die, perhaps, later. I just drew a pile of leaves using markers and graphite and I am almost ready to rest and eat lunch. My solitude is making me soft. That's why I came outside, where it's cold. And hard. If I could find a stone to wedge myself against.

Cecilia Pinto   **III.**   There is this idea of humans and animals in a boat. This very old idea that, in order to save the world, we must all get in a boat.

White tail deer populations are resurging in the eastern part of the country. Because of this, mountain lions are coming after them. The abundance of deer can only be a good thing for the lions.

What if, instead of populations dwindling, as has been predicted, species dying out. What if animal populations increase, the near extinct revive? What if, their supremacy?

This, for me is an acceptable apocalypse. This seems fair, they get to come back, the tiger, the elephant, tiniest bug.

A. is in the boat, surrounded by husband, children, goats, bees, hippos. Each child holds several bags of seeds. I shove them from the sandy shore with my foot. I will stay here, my family, here. We will guard the library for as long as we can, anticipating their return, preparing for the swallowing stampede.

Alice George III. My backyard has become a library since I last wrote towards C. Leaves tell of their home tree as they lie there on the still-green grass. In humans, each cell contains the blueprint for the entire being. Are leaves the same? Could some tree savant clutch the brittle oak leaf in his hands and know the huge old tree it came from? Do we have the proper instrumentation?

Leaves like sides of whole little houses, like faces of frightening elves (all spiked and veiny), like dead books.

Lack of money is a pox upon our house, but we are still middle-class Americans and thus safe. And thus able to contemplate backyardness, libraryness, the accumulation of tales.

Strange consolations befall this lonely work-at-home mom. Logging onto my son's history teacher's website only to discover my slacker is getting an A in this honors class, an A! And it says so on the computer. Anyone could see this, if they sat here.

The A (which was in black type on the monitor but seems red because I wrote a poem with the phrase "big red A" a long time ago) perches in my brain as I swim up and down the lanes today, again. Like I am the beginning of the alphabet flying in the water.

Cecilia Pinto   **IV.**   Some notes:

        A. says secretive. Referring to C.

        C. says generous. Referring to A.

It seems they understand something of each other's nature, and the equation in which they find themselves if not the answer.

(Secretly, C does not see herself as all that secretive. I mean really, isn't it all right here?) She puts an X to indicate where, for her friend, to be helpful, to be generous. Here, right here.

Anyway, A. wants to talk about war. She has put it here, she wants it here.

And so, we (re) turn to Napoleon. Banished to Elba, he became king. (Some people cannot help themselves.) Imagine standing on the cliffs of Elba, staring at the sea understanding the loss of life required so that you might be what you must be. Without knowing him it is still possible to imagine that he wept. Not necessarily accurate but possible.

Today there is the bite of winter in the air,
a cold bitterness remembered. We prepare with resignation.

Last night I dreamt I told everyone I met I was alone.
Anxiously I await word from Alice.
Here.

Alice George **IV.** A boat is like a room without walls. C. put me here and so I decide I must write songs, because I hate the idea of her pushing me off, of decisions like that only happening in fiction. I want to stand in a moment of decision and face huge consequences so clearly a soundtrack swells unbidden. Or write songs.

The boat is melancholy
The boat is small
The boat moves wonderful
and smells like a stall.

We must stand with our mouths wide open!
We must stand with our mouths wide open!

The boat used to be yellow
it used to be called Sallie Mae
now it carries the world inside it:
people and creatures and hay.

If it rains we must stand at the ready and drink!
If it rains we must stand at the ready and drink!

Sometimes the boat gets to leaking
and sometimes it looks like to sink
but then we bail and mend for hours
not even bothering to think.

If we are here then the world is an ocean!
If we are here then the world is an ocean!

This song is delivered to the small coastal town C. and her family are living in, delivered by dolphin. C. weeps at the contents, unsure whether she's lamenting my psychotic break or the realization that the muse came aboard <u>my</u> boat.

287

Cecilia Pinto **V.**

Brave songs require courage.
It is not every soul can shout so joyously.
Brave sailors on the lonesome sea
Search for landmarks endlessly.

We on shore wade out to greet the dolphin. Hear his news:

"Once a man taught a gorilla sign language. After, he went away. Years passed. Then, the man and the gorilla were reunited. The gorilla in his cage began signing when he saw the man. He pointed to himself and said his name, over and over."

Now, even though he said it again and again, I cannot remember the name of the gorilla. But he is surely somewhere writing it in sawdust, straw, shit.

We wade back in. The rest of the afternoon is spent thoughtfully drawing words in the sand, thoughtfully watching them wash away.

Not every sailor knows the words to every song
Still the brave shout loudly just the same.
Up in the heavens are all the mighty stars
Pray somewhere someone remembers your name.

Alice George **V.** Anxiously, I think of war. Somehow, in my Illinois, green-sheeted bed. As if it was with me, beneath the covers. But I don't want to write lyrics today towards C., who is anxious, like me and perhaps beribboned with holiday nerves. I want to act.

Marie Ponsot: "We must act in events. We must touch what we name."

My hands extend feebly towards the Middle East. The distance between my fingertips and the nearest grave filled with someone with American bullets in it is _____. (to be calculated)

I name my mood *never* and I touch black dirt.
I name my dog *lovely* and brush my foot against her warm neutered body.
I name C. and her family *companions* and send this by e-mail, o gray and flinty fingers, o harbinger of speech.

I name myself *alone* but I cannot touch it, it is the live nerve beneath my tooth, it is the poisoned chocolate, it is the avenue towards death, it is what I sometimes pray for and often lament. My body beneath trees.

Cecilia Pinto   **VI.**   She has written more than me.
She has more enthusiasm, stamina, time?

She has more words.

I have lost the way, forgotten where we started.
Something about language, dogs, the language of dogs?

Forgive me.

I dreamed I remembered nothing, not this, not anything. I stood, in panic on an unfamiliar street, looking around. I saw mountains. I said I know that word. I said, I'll start here. And began walking and began walking away.

I know there was a party,
music, children, friends
and this apparently is how it ends.

Alice George   **VI.**   Sign language requires hands, requires a lack of common throat, requires the knowledge you are alone, yet adjacent to someone, at least, who is watching.

Hail the new ye lads and lasses
Up in the heavens are the stars
Bring me some figgy pudding
Search for landmarks endlessly.

Touch what you name. C. came to my new years party with her husband and two boys. She emptied my trash, drank my soup and understood when I said her boys couldn't plug in their electric instruments. If I could touch the gorilla in her story, I could name it, perhaps, though a name is not always what's needed.

I still don't know whether I should be glad I can say *alone alone alone*. Though surely this writing back and forth should have taught me a little about isolation vs. communion. Yes. I. am. fight. for. both.

Soldier

Alice George & Cecilia Pinto

My sister tells a story from our past. She says, remember.
  She says you were wonderful how could you forget?
She was twelve and left at home with my older brother who is less able,
  whose needs have guided our family, made us plan.
A woman, hired for the weekend, was abusive to my brother
  in ways even my sister forgets, but she knows it was bad.
Scared, my sister reached me at boarding school to ask if I'd come home?
  I imagine her sitting on our parents' white bed, door closed, dialing.
I have no memory of this, nothing my sister relates is familiar,
  though I must have made a sound in my throat, I must have decided.

My sister describes me as awesome, furious as I told the woman to leave our house.
  Should my forgetting cheer me, that I could let go a starring role?
My grandparents had a backyard filled with azaleas and rhododendrons.
  Or does the forgetting cast me as some addled soldier, blank between commands?
Blazing fuchsia, pistils tipped in yellow, heavy-headed white blossoms, peeking pink.
  I remember my brother and sister, clearly, though never in that story, I remember me,
I remember this. I remember hiding amongst the plants as a girl, not found
  for minutes, or hours, perhaps, hunkered down in the fragrant damp.
I decided this was best, until someone called my name.
  I can't believe you just disappeared, my sister says. I don't remember that at all.

Process Note

We chose each other for our similarities (born within four days, same number of children, same School of the Art Institute MFA), and our differences (laconic vs. effusive, prose vs. poetry, etc.). Throughout, we've found the process very satisfying and quite challenging, as voices, ideas, tales and tongue became tangled. We keep trying new ways of mixing it up, hoping our readers will find our version of the vulcan mind-meld intriguing.

"Thirst" and "Soldier" are from the first batch of collaborations we wrote. The process was simple: we each wrote a ten-line poem and emailed it to the other, who then wrote in between the lines. We didn't define the intent too carefully . . . the general idea was to twine voices to create a new narrative or song. We wrote about eight, then gathered at Alice's picnic table and did a quick collaborative edit, and chose titles. This was a pleasure, and we owe it to Maureen Seaton, who had planted the idea of collaboration.

We wrote "What Is She Doing Right Now?" over the course of a week or so in August of 2002. It started with talking, on a sunny day, then we used email, swapping and responding to what the other wrote, picking up threads, ideas, words from each other's writing and braiding them into our own so that successive entries become more intimate and complicated and responsive. A narrative develops which is as much about what's on the page as it is what's going on between us. Placing them side-by-side on facing pages was very satisfying.

ALICE GEORGE & CECILIA PINTO

Fugitive Car

Pamela Gemin & Julie King

Them Littles, they have a pit bull now, our dad declared.
You girls stay away from Lo-Lo and that yard, it'll swallow
you up. Beware the Dog! suggested the new homemade sign,
nailed to the porch the Littles would not finish painting. Our dad
called the city hall when the dull orange stain went only as far up
as Buck Little could reach, resting on flaking blue. Our dad
called the Social Services: Lo-Lo's chest was so skinny it caved
like a shallow bowl, his hair shaved on top and long in the back,
a Mohican Mullet. Mama Shirl Little (Beware the Shirl!) whacked
at his calves with a witchy broom. Her own legs wore half-finished
tattoos of cobra snakes crawling halfway up, on the way to her wicked heart.
"Lowell T. Little, close the fucking door!" was her favorite song.
Our dad called the city hall again when Buck Little announced
his new Auto Mart Plaza—five ratchety cars rusting up on their blocks
in his weed ranch yard, their once-cherry paint jobs
flying out onto the breeze. Lo-Lo jumping from hood to hood
in just his cut-offs, holding the screaming baby Bee Ann
on his skeleton shoulders, Donny the pit bull snapping
at his heels. Our dad made a lot of official calls that seven months
laid off from Twin Disc, but we snuck to the Littles anyway.
I'll be The Fugitive, you can be two of my girlfriends,
Lo-Lo Little said, and then went and hid in the Fugitive Car
till we brought him saltines and tuna. We knew that The Fugitive's girlfriends
were never long for this world, having secret diseases or vows
or sly bonds with the law. The Quinn-Martin scripters
assured their untimely betrayal or demise.
Hey, Doctor Kimball! We know who you are
and we brought you some fish and crackers!
we yelled to Lo-Lo through the tailpipe of a Ford Fairlane.
Lieutenant Gerard came nosing to our door, but we told him
you went to Toledo. Please do not think us habitually a liar. We firmly
believe you are innocent, and so does our ailing dad.
You're allowed to stay here in this Auto Mart Plaza
and work the odd jobs, as long as we all shall live.

PROCESS NOTE

For the seventeen years we have been friends, we've also read each other's first drafts, so collaboration is natural for us. We grew up in the same kind of neighborhood, so for "Fugitive Car" we both had neighborhood characters in mind. One of us e-mailed a sketch based on a boy who'd jump from roof to roof of the junk cars his father collected in their side yard, and the other filled and colored it. And then we both fine-tuned, as we would writing on our own, e-mailed more versions, and came up with the final product. We have helped each other to navigate and negotiate life since we met—friendship seems the ultimate collaboration. Extending what we hope to be a lifetime of collaboration, we are currently coediting an anthology of women's poetry about the beauty ideal.

PAMELA GEMIN & JULIE KING

The Life

Nin Andrews & Mary Beth Shaffer

2 black Buicks, her father's, 1 red station wagon, her mother's (all used, one
   lost its muffler)
2 moves (one house, tiny, new, with yellow carpet in her bedroom, the other,
old, with windows that never closed in winter and had to be popped open in
   summer)
3 mailmen (one who limped with a bad knee)
4 schools (including nursery, kindergarten and two transfers)
1 trip to D.C. (the AC broke, and it was so hot, her mother let the wind
   blow her permed hair straight)
1 half-dead oak (the house number 328 nailed into it)
12 fire drills (8 in winter when she shivered outside with no jacket)
4 TVs (1 still working, 3 channels)
4 goldfish (soon overfed and dead)
2 library cards (1 lost)
3 bikes (hers pink and shiny, too small to ride)
1 old box of Swiss chocolates (Lindt, hidden in the closet, forgotten)
1 add-a-pearl necklace (started by her grandmother, left unfinished at her death)
1 neighbor, Mr. Card, who calls her mom 2 times a day (Is your mom
   home, dear?)
1 father, missing...

The girl could shut her eyes and count the freckles on his forehead (16) and
   not miss one, even when they fall into the folds of his crinkled brow.
She could tell where her father's favorite cufflinks were hidden (gold, a gift,
   he kept but never wore. She stole them when she knew he was leaving.)
She knows what he gave his secretary last year for Christmas (a diamond
   bracelet. It was in his sock drawer for weeks).
And why he never finished college and lied about it (even to his mother).
And exactly what time he slipped away (12:34, Sunday, January 3).
How he stood in her doorway for 48 minutes, then whispered, "Bye-bye Baby
   Girl."
He closed the front door so softly behind him, she had to hold her breath to
   hear it click.

Another Avenue

Haya Pomrenze & Brenda Serotte

I've always loved short men with short legs, like the 7 Santini Brothers
Who parked their moving van across the street, looked up at my window

When I got dressed. Contrary to rumors along the Avenue, these men made
   good lovers—
Ask Annette in 10-A—especially Vinnie, with biceps thick as marinara jars,

Calves so compact they seemed deformed. Mama Santini cooked pasta
All day, the smell wafting through the streets,

Pasta tinged with the scent of Old Spice and sweat from
One of the brothers doing the "bada bing." I knew there had to be

Escape. After all, could I stare at the moon forever while the 7 Brothers
Stared at me? I dreamed of life on finer streets

Like Madison or Fifth, where girls knew enough to shut their lights when
They stood by blowing curtains, tonguing their lips, begging

To be objectified. By day they wrote feminist manifestos,
By night, like me, they belonged to the 7 Santinis.

Would that one of those short-legged men had thrown a rope
Through my eternally open window, lassoed my beaded dress

At the waist, lowered me into their van like an acrobat at the
Big Apple Circus, I would have had that avenue of escape,

This story would have had a more unusual ending.

Process Note

When Haya asked if I'd like to collaborate on a poem, I said, sure, but I doubted I could. However, doing it via e-mail changed my mind. I'd had this idea about creating a poem based on a story a friend told me of a woman from my old Bronx neighborhood, but I couldn't come up with more than a line or two about it. I e-mailed that one line to Haya and she immediately "answered" it with a line of her own that seemed to "complete" my thought. That became "Another Avenue's" first couplet.

As far as form is concerned, I have always let the poem decide which form it wants to be: prose poem, unbroken narrative, etc. "Another Avenue" seemed just right as couplets, to both of us, and so we let it be. I think it succeeded because of the anonymity of e-mailing our lines to each other. We wrote quickly. Also, we took certain risks with ideas that we might not ordinarily have done if we were sitting across from one another trying to collaborate. We did get together a couple of times to read aloud and to tighten up the finished piece. In all, the whole process was amazingly simple and lots of fun.

BRENDA SEROTTE

She Dreams about Being Jung

Cathryn Cofell & Karla Huston

If dreaming about sex means you're horny,
then what about the halfmares,
the partial ting ting ting,
the this is it this is it this is and then
deer run across the highway,
your mom tells you to eat your peas
and something about a 9 A.M. appointment?
Some so tussled nights,
some so parched your throat is a fullback,
or the feeling of sand in your shoes,
that gritty feeling of loss.
If everyone in the dream is a version of you,
then what difference does it make who shows up,
holds a gun to your head, plays
tic tac toe with your animus, runs
a slack tongue up your thigh?

Some people wait their whole day to sleep
I sleep my whole day to wait
unfinished
one half a parentheses,
something done undone–
I think I can I think I can I think
I am snapping shut like a trap.
What about all the dreams I forgot?

Process Note

We have been friends for eons, but made the leap to collaborative poems only a few years ago at the inspiration of Denise Duhamel and Maureen Seaton. Cat had a great stanza with no legs, and Karla offered to "take it off her hands," giving it the kick-butt end it needed. Since then, there've been virtually no limits (just a few rules) as to how we create a shared work—Exquisite Corpse via e-mail or shared assignments or allowing the other to write into the other's seemingly "failed" poem; surprises show up everywhere!

CATHRYN COFELL & KARLA HUSTON

Horror Movies We'd Like to See

Ronald Koertge & Charles Harper Webb

The Thing That Wasn't There

Not invisible, exactly, and certainly not malicious.
Just not there:

Guys camping in Nevada—lights in the distance, a muted
explosion. But nothing happens.

Girls in skimpy underwear alone in an old house—
the fire gutters out, noises downstairs, a branch
scrapes the windowpane. But nothing happens.

The campers and the girls meet at a rest stop near
Barstow and talk about how uneventful their weekend
was. One of the girls takes a long time in the bathroom,
then turns up.

It wasn't there, either.

The Island of Dr. Morose

An English Professor wins the lottery and retires from BSU to his own palm-
fringed Florida Key. There he tries to turn animals into humans through constant
exposure to the world's greatest, hence most depressing, art.

When perky blonde Sabrina windsurfs to the island in search of her lost
Chihuahua, she's horrified to find her pet living in a bachelor pad, wearing
nose and scrotum rings, but refusing to stir from his doggie bed. Ms Parrot,
in the next room, shrieks "Polly wants a razor blade." Mr. Crocodile is beyond
tears. Mr. Hyena, the Doctor's star pupil, has stopped laughing, wears a bow
tie, carries a cell phone, and is deep in the study of The Law.

Devastated by what she's seen, plus the passages from *Madame Bovary* she overhears while Bartok string quartets grate and groan, Sabrina OD's on Xanax, dresses in black, makes herself up like a zombie, and is dragged, raving, from an open poetry reading by her Econ-major boyfriend.

Monsters at Their Leisure

Certainly Wolfman chasing a red ball, Dracula in a polo shirt, and Frankenstein playing badminton.

But the Banshee, too, humming as she does dishes Grendel's mother sunning on the shore of Dark Lake Medusa at Cut 'N' Curl, chatting with the other girls the Sphinx asking a group of children, "What did the mayonnaise say to the refrigerator?"

The Exercyclist

Despondent over the loss of her first love, a pretty adolescent girl named Viagra is possessed by an obese demon, "Fatty" Badway, who drives the girl to binge on pizza, Big Macs, Kentucky Fried Chicken, and macho burritos served "animal style," washed down by milk shakes and classic Coke, with fried pies and double banana/chocolate chip/whipped cream extravaganzas for dessert.

Viagra's parents send her to Family Fitness, but she vomits a gallon of green pistachio ice cream on a new Stairmaster, throws her neck out in yoga, and tells her sales associate, "Your mother sucks push-up pops in hell," before she waddles out the door.

Desperate, Viagra's parents call Pibb's Personal Training. Utilizing a combination of Perrier water, massage, and compliments, Mr. Pibb transfers Viagra's food addiction to exercise—in particular, the special seat-for-girls that he attaches to her stationary bike, which soon has even Fatty B hissing his praise.

A Perfect Saturday Night in Front of the Tube

4:00 P.M. *Doctor Naugahyde's Restless Bier*

6:00 P.M. *Fiendish Plankton*

8:00 P.M. *All Kinds of Seepage*

10:00 P.M. *The Dreadful Negligee*

Midnight *The Nose of Prince Edward Island*

Course of the Werewolf

Dear Sir: I assumed the list of "classic horror films students will view in the light of lycanthropic theory" had fallen victim to the teacher's need to type with paws. But the first class did indeed feature *Bing Kong,* the soporific tale of a hundred-foot-tall crooning ape. The next day brought *The Mommy:* a woman with four kids, buried alive in housework.

When I questioned his choice of films, the teacher snapped "Stop by my office, and we'll chew the fat." Moon being full, I didn't go.

No need to bore you with a precis of *The Bread of Frankenstein,* or *I Was a Teenaged Teenager. Dracula Has Risen from the Cake* did spark my interest when the Vampire King leapt out of a huge angelfood into a strippers' convention. *Curse of the Living Deadhead* seemed to promise Jerry Garcia, and a rockin' time for all. Instead, the class was treated to the story of a nearly submerged floating log that somehow became a woman with menstrual cramps. And all the while, the teacher thrashed on the floor, howling with delight at how he'd snookered this great penitentiary.

Charles and I chatted on the phone about the poem, and once we had the title the rest was, as they say, easy. I'd write about a horror flick that I'd like to see, then he'd take a turn. We saw each other's work-in-progress, of course, and I remember being spurred on (poets are competitive) to write my next stanza as well or better. Once we'd exhausted the process (how long can we go on without losing the reader?), we were done. Both of us are a little giddy by nature, so it was fun to send the drafts back and forth and to see how hyperbolic we could be about horror films. I just saw, by the way, *Mars Needs Women,* an icon of cheesiness.

RONALD KOERTGE

Term

Kate Gale & Terry Wolverton

Between your thighs I cracked eggs, blood spilled out
coming at me, filling my eyes–what to do with all that blood?
Vinegar rinse, cotton towels and still your eyes followed mine.
We're not going to make it, I thought, eyes avoiding the trashcan.

And who was the little girl whose soul slipped through the window?
Who will inherit my Barbies now? I think she is hiding in the tree
above my head, shooting tiny arrows through the screen door.
Meantime, you forget the dreams from which you can't wake up.

Dreams of cloudy days sipping something, wearing silk; in movies
women look like queens for ransom, alone, waiting. My fingers sticky,
counterpane cracked, potted geranium aches with broken soil and rot,
random sour milk smells spill across cement, what's left.

I type this garbled message to the future. In case you find it,
remember I was more than a rag doll, cotton squooshing
from my busted seams. Remember that my mouth, though painted on,
was capable of shattered testimonies.

While you and I cleaned the floor, my hands touching your hands, fluids,
unnameable leakages, our fingers holding pieces of little selves.
The smell was onion and liver frying from lunch
the sound was grunting from next door; that's how they did it.

Testament

Kate Gale & Terry Wolverton

Repression is the kiss that gags you
J'ai soif, Jesus said, then was given vinegar
his tongue swelled like a balloon to be
carried through the streets in a parade
Mary Magdalene weeping, her dress alight
with its own happiness, a speaking dress
stained with the semen of presidents
fetid with desperate sweat and lies
Golgotha, the soldiers played cards
nobody won; the game went on under sky
Mary Magdalene never wept, her eyes
hardened by the heat of screams
Jesus reached down from the cross
Mary in his arms, whispered in her ears.
You and my mother are one, she heard
and repeated it to herself as she floated.
Because the thorns were bright red,
the revelers drank more wine, rolled
old bone dice, chanted, "Who's your Daddy?"
Next day, all was quiet, grave mouth open
air held its yellow breath, the disciples moaned
anyone could hear them if they cared.
Querulous cock of subjugation won't stop
crowing; I push the snooze button, turn over.
Sweet cabbage, she's a quiet person
doesn't like to be deserved, fingers her rosary
Jesus hangs above the bed, quiet, resting probably.
Someday soon, we will all be on our knees
genuflecting to the sacred bomb.
Dinner's ready, daddy's in the hall, brother's in the closet
mother's counting change. The counting house is closed.
Let's pray before dinner, close your eyes.
Now open them.

Process Note

When I received the invitation from the editors to write a collaborative poem with another poet, Kate was the first person to come to mind. We conducted the entire exercise by e-mail, over the course of a few months, eventually coming up with four poems. One of us would offer some beginning lines and the other would respond with lines of her own. I looked forward to her e-mails, waiting for the new batch of gems, the next challenges. There was a way in which we could have kept going forever. At the end, we performed only the tiniest amount of editing, and Kate swears, "Every line seems like it could have been written by either of us."

TERRY WOLVERTON

Jangling

Joshua Beckman & Matthew Rohrer

Money cannot find me.
I try to be reasonable but money is horridly banal.
Money, blow and blow is what I think about you.
Street urchins make more than me.
Water tastes funny without cups.
How far will I go?
Jingle jingle jingle.
Despite holes that compromise living rooms, friends visit.
Money money and more holes to look into.
You are dangerously close to falling.
The money said nothing.
The neighbors called up to us, "Your whole system sounds cockeyed!"
They suck the life from each other and we pay the bill.
Money always whispers,
"You pathetic humans don 't know my true name."
I know my own name.
It is something exaggeratedly French.

Architecture Believes in Formalism

Joshua Beckman & Matthew Rohrer

Half dome drifting structurally above the abandoned piazza
with speckles along its outer ridges.
Beautiful marble colonnades
fell beside beautiful marble women.
As tailors find exquisite hems, exquisite shoulders, and exquisite inseams
beneath crowds of scholars' sports coats, architects' work shirts, and belabored
proletarian pajamas, customers demand headroom when showing up clothed.
As busses tunnel wantonly through urban rubble, authorities watch from afar.
High.
Your trellis believes I'm you.
Beginning with concrete lions and sandstone pools
the library contains books which speak.
In rotundas everywhere pigeons feel supreme religious duty.
There among turnstiles children advance freely.
With zero gravity buttresses buoy armadas of designs and remain there.
About 1300 a wazier named Hakim thought he could design a palace of
      sugar cubes
with cubes of salt. Hakim believed.
About this plaza he told subordinates nothing
but one evening while stoned in Tunisia he scribbled down schematics
for something he dreamed would resemble all palaces.
His ceiling seemed to expand and his curtains seemed shivery.
Today we don't fear Hakim.
We found blueprints.
We found nails.
We found his ever-present skeleton.
Our architecture resembles little.
In Sumerian plazas demons are sewing drapes each evening
for their landlord's girlfriend's bedrooms.
On frescos found in refrigerators behind Canada
a tourniquet seemed poorly rendered.
Believe the lies.
Our gnosis.
Our slippers.

Our nightlights.
Don't stop believing.
Journey towards Chicago.
There within Masonic Temples the pigeons consort.
Flashes of religious knowledge seductively flatten and thoroughly cleanse you.
With striking familiarity women's gaits reveal women's pretensions.
Where have all the flowers hidden themselves?
Where have all the dancers' boyfriends' disdainful looks accumulated?
Pillars fell beside marble women.
Beneath this truth there exists a frightening bowling alley.
Inside the bowling alley there will be no forgiveness.
Where forgiveness notices itself forgiveness lifts off.
Beneath forgiveness and regret there settles a delicate cabin
filled quickly with little flowers.
I believe Sumerian guilt is pointless.
Before giants wandered Brooklyn a device for preventing wandering giants
from Brooklyn wanderings stood centrally and proudly.
Our leaders perished.
Our device went to pieces.
Our beautiful neighborhood fell over onto another couple.
Our courthouses are reminiscent.
Our trolley cars disappeared.
Giants. Giants.
Our horse can't escape.
Beneath Brooklyn a bigger Brooklyn shines secretly.
Beneath that dome you felt active.

A Note on Process

Joshua Beckman & Matthew Rohrer

[being an improvised attempt at disclosure–done one word at a time. central park, late july]

A flag unknown to us walks past. We talk into our microphone about what is important about this flag. Central Park is confusing. Flags often unknown to us walk past. We notice different things. Sometimes. Sometimes we converge. These birds pecking. Horses carrying tourists. Sunlight. Bellies with adornments. We enjoy New York. We enjoy narratives. Space age experiments. Industrious modes of alienation trouble us. We respond bilingually. Let's explain some-thing about something: first I say something and then he says something. Skiing is usually interrupted by falling. Second, I say one line and then he does the same. First we thought rhyming would work because Allen Ginsberg and Kenneth Koch said so. We rhymed poorly. We suffered thoroughly. Soon we abandoned rhyme. Different joggers keep time differently. Next we tried using formal constraints that would help the two of us improvise. We record every-thing. Sometimes losing is also winning. An alternative to rhyme was useful. Two guys saying stuff gets them nowhere fast. Two guys saying stuff into micro-phones gets repetitive, but forms keep them busy and they feel productive. Sunlight comes through leaves burning the skin of joggers. Water fountains are useful but hard to find. We walked all over New York. We walked around. We sat on everything. We rode the subways and ferries and recorded our secret findings. Public swimming pools. Boardwalks. Piers and docks. Parks that smelled. Parks that were abandoned. Bars, bridges and waiting rooms. Why did we write this together? The park is full of people who talk without recording it. We have a problem. We have recorded everything for some of our friends. When both of us told our mothers about this they were moderately excited. We must make money. Our mothers would be pleased if you bought about two hundred copies. Why did we sit on this rock? Surely there is no more reason-able place. When the poems are good, we are happy. When we see kids, we are happy. When the poems are bad we happily hide behind each other. Sometimes we write the best line together accidentally. Sometimes it doesn't feel good. If we bought roller skates and started roller skating, wouldn't we be home by now? Sometimes we feel tired, but sometimes there is another twenty dollars in our wallets. We saw things move more often than we would've liked. We got behind trees and recorded what we saw. We saw our dreams talking. We saw our stories in rivers. Sometimes neighbors added chili powder. Sometimes heat causes intellectual perspiration. Sometimes heat just knocks us down. Much ado about nothing is plenty. Our method turned us into another guy. Light falls through tourists' hair this afternoon. Light coming down from that divine cloud we call New York turned us on. Leaves turn. Summer tries to confuse America but that's already happened. Dreams begin in New York and today we are in New York.

PROCESS NOTE

Everything you see (including the note) was written one word at a time, going back and forth between us into a tape recorder—very little editing (almost none).

JOSHUA BECKMAN

Equitable Deviation

William Fuller & Tom Raworth

there is no definitive answer
no license can assure
to a culture of their own
the enlivening element
breathing room pressure
when diverse unavowed purposes
purse and politics for the murderers
involve an erroneous standard
primary chaos repairing a marketing point
of actual not deemed death
influence pledges to abide
feeding and hydration courtesy of Mars
cultivating that corner of wilderness
child and putative father

a ration of melted sheep
the seedbearing bugalu
rarely gives up storage mechanisms
invokes <u>in terrorem</u>
planted by a christmas basket
soberly enticing heirs
a spin cycle of glum capers
to reap their fill
between direct sounds blur
with diamond-like clarity
the image elimination game-show
three sick pigeons
before black becomes a safe place
greet them at home

Zombie Dawn

Tom Clark & Anne Waldman

Does any of the meaning you think at times you see
disappearing ahead of you just out of your reach
actually materialize once you're gone (no longer looking)
Long white nights insomniac alone save
for your stupid fears dull recursive woes inventories
of chronic fuckups defects in the code the world
cup flickering mute on nocturnal tube midnight
to zombie dawn (get a life) later back to books
Henry IV Part One Falstaff a recognizable
human like you takes bribes carries bottle
into battle not gun dismisses honor as a mere
word empty and then Tacitus on globalization
in Britain 2000 years ago the legions of Rome
raptores orbis plunderers of earth prophetic world
dot com fable of profit motive (what else is new)
Then as sun comes up Sunday paper for the obits
wherein growing older you discover your familiars
today Jean du Lac master of the orotone (photo repro
on glass) born in France died in San Francisco ashes
scattered off Marin coast "The majority of his life
a mystery" he "left behind a single key
to a solitary padlock The location of the padlock
is unknown"

Does any of your poet's philosophy, sketchy text both
light modern you stray into unaware ever just out of
reach (no longer looking), does any of it—in reproductions
himself splendid on glass—a not very dominant alpha male
dark with urge and playing the wicked *Richard III* blame
nostalgia—does any of him add up here? the company
of rude mechanicals ailing, who's got scratch to take in a show
although you can't say enough about a kingdom for a full house
as elderly immigrants get the slot machine blues,
free chits in Atlantic City no excuse for better one-more-time

314

globalization policies (they are hungry immigrants)
where jealousy is mere passing and jumpy
disquiet because house empty again house empty again
adjacent to 3 A.M. altercation you reading Cymbeline
down the block in new Snitch Mode police arrive
to lock up noisy hormonal teen (girl?) who wants to break glass
all over the lawns the worst crime is lack of
imagination wherein growing older she's got fires to burn
water to waste drought to countenance hell to pay
the Armageddon that is bolder these days, smoke on the mountain

Synchronicity stranger than fiction tv shows off-beat cinema night of the living
dead beating off the poetry ghosts like Odysseus at the fosse Orpheus Eurydice
O nervous raven queen O caring world saver which you is you
middle of night brings out truth horror you like urge-dark doesn't-add-up him
splash yourself despite yourself hands incarnadine on wasted-time Rorschach
paper tiger wounded alpha boring mister wrong (again) stands indicted
in arid mammal power vocabulary not very dominant alpha male like not
very wet water oxymoronic easy reductivist wordgame must we poets stoop to that
kids' mirror-language turning-the-word-inside-out
"jumpy mechanical altercation 3 A.M. house empty again
a kingdom in reproduction who wants the slot
machine chit splendid dark wicked you police arrive"
arrest you (me) lame shooter-back of cheap shot
3:41 A.M. take meds try not
to wake sleeping wife whose fault this isn't then whose
arrow points back at self who's talking
go comb fleas out of silky fur of big beautiful black
and white male happily not very dominant cat
catch two crush look down oops fingernail stained with red flea blood

the meds were dead. the light extinguished. I walk outside.
Moon. Moon mooner than full, I mean rose water, I mean Sphinx
In the play about the asphyxiated I will retire.
I am wound all over again. I am silky fur, I
walk the mile in my way to get nails done
Get mails done! get nails done sooner: okay!
semi-colon marks for the long suffering I beg of you
because otherwise we rot and burn our only thorns

not enemy erratics when—go for it—Chaucer aka Richard III
intuit the erratic, fear no and fear again no, no
The Diet wars subside in the low-cost lost calendar
I penciled in marks as one who would strive, love
Another kingdom to follow? stay here, my friend—
before I die to hound you. Life is short. They
had been marked by color and by problematic love
you wonder you lose sleep, sent to the Meditator offering the notion
that "time is smooth"
it is, and then the Roshi dies and you are done now, night

fears, never again, go off and hound warlock day for now we are at peace
though the inky dictates of this Memphis nightshade dawn keep plucking
at the reins of the ghost riders in the sky who drag red roses across this moon
as if the dark and wicked Richard traded his kingdom for their horses
blood or rose water pale-faced and perturbed silent sister cold
governess of floods and vitreous watery beams, forget the stars fruitless
O Sphinx explain nothing in this long Nile night pour your allegory on our banks
worldly night green and glowing then red then touched with charcoal
Long Nile night pour your augury on our blanks   O problematic love
what flowers are these at my feet in this sleeping forest
not sent by you, tender and ever growing in your Roshi desolation
to which we come in homage I know you are there
fair regent of the Nile O night shade terror gloom queen
The tail of the great Sphinx flicks and swishes across my chest
eternity is greeted with an empty handed salute damned or blessed
all the same in the end just or unjust, absolutely equal
to the great Sphinx, it's only you who insists on getting excited
in this time of the government of shadows

lovely that, and dark yet a government that in recalcitrant
not bending-mode scorns and insults its citizens, will not
make appraisal of "right" thing to do it's more we're right not them
the voters fickle in the night of endless desert war, right you say?
and water the amniotic flows through his embalmed veins, the teacher
that in lambent mode—pain or balm?— lies down his Roshi stick
isn't water to be born in? isn't water the end to all our drought & thirst?
isn't she, the watery one, just our style? won't water
drown your sorrows? and the water that follows wine ease this

headache? and nurture the poor Miss Manners in the yard, the lilies,
of the field brought to the desert, water the red feather grass,
the purple sage, all a bouquet in Roshi death
Richard storms the stage again tonight, bad boy leather-clad
where's the retribution? kill the leaders and get not horse
quixotic Trickster Sphinx who does not take our cares away
& dwells in mystery and back-alley shadow, what we do to each other

say it again: do to each other

Interview (an interlude)

**1. Tom I ask you how did we meet? I know it happens thru mail and the
publications of poetry in major and precious small literary magazines and
the dock at the boat the day you come to our city and are welcomed. And
a day of DMT at the apartment of the poet who turns art critic, is that
correct? What is a first impression? tell me again Who are we? What is time
and destiny?**

Memory, as one gets older, has an amazing way of revealing its stored "frames"
in the form of palpable moments still clear and tangible "as day" even nearly
forty years down the line, in the great otherwise dark of the otherwise endless
(but not quite) night. I have two moments here. One is a postcard I get from
you in England, that is I'm in England, you in N.Y., sometime in the winter of
1966-67. I am holding it in my hand and looking at it in my memory. (The card
itself is long gone, I took no mail back from England with me.) It says, "Do you
go all the way?" The other memory or stored frame contains the day in
February 1967 when I get off the ocean liner United States in New York. This
is an absolutely clear and vivid memory of that whole day, almost minute by
minute. It starts in the saloon (bar) of the ship, where I'm dressed up for entering
the Empire, waiting, as we cruise past the Statue of Liberty and up the river to
the harbor of the great city of the Empire of Birth and War which I haven't seen
in nearly five years. As I wait among the other passengers I am nervous and
excited, a little scared, and beginning to feel the effects of a massive dose of
powdered Swiss pharmaceutical LSD which I have, as I wait, nibbled out of the
quicks of my fingernails, where I've intended to store it as I pass through
customs—a bad idea I've decided, thus the nibbling (that too a bad idea, as
I now look back on it, though at the time...). So anyway, here in the huge

imperial customs shed, my steamer trunk full of books is being thoroughly and closely searched because they've noticed my collection of Olympia Press books, this takes what seems like hours, finally I am admitted to America and as I approach the gate I am greeted by—this is actually a complete not to say welcome surprise—three charming and dear long-haired youthful instant poet-friends, who, I soon learn, are Jim Brodey, Lewis Warsh and yourself. My first impression is you're all marvelous-looking and you've made this terrifically generous gesture of hospitality and greeting on behalf of (or in despite of) America. I am moved and amazed. I also realize you've been waiting here quite a while, in this vast dark and tiresome theater of horrors U.S. of America customs shed. Your impatience to get the show on the road doubles my amazement at the patience you've already shown. We all get in a taxi. The taxi takes us to the Third Street ground-floor apartment of the poet later art critic Peter Schjeldahl. Peter too has wonderfully long hair, though he is otherwise quite well groomed and well dressed. Lewis's and Jim's hair is not as long as Peter's. Your hair is longer than Peter's and so is mine. (Peter's wife Linda, who has the longest hair of all, isn't home at the time.) We sit around at Peter's. Ted comes over. Ted's hair is almost as long as Peter's but he is much less well dressed in, as I remember, army fatigue pants. Some one of Ted's charming street hippie connection friends has lately bestowed upon him some substance which, Ted charmingly explains, contains belladonna, but only of a most benign kind—or, perhaps, Ted adds as a bit of a tease (also a bit of the truth) it is not belladonna but INK, however—anyway some of us take some of this. The moment of the taking of it is BLACK OUT (temporary blind spot in the otherwise vivid stored frame). Next, Lewis and you leave. You have to go back to work at your job at Poetry Project and Lewis is going to go home to St. Mark's Place to chill out (as kids would now say though can you do that on DMT?). Peter has turned down the belladonna/ink and now grows visibly impatient though I have now generously produced my Jimi Hendrix records and would happily settle in, however taking cue from Ted I pack up, we—Ted, Jim & I—leave, outside black kids' transistor radio plays "Heatwave" (Martha & Vandellas), it's bright hot & sunny though only February, at corner of Third & 1st Ave. we pause at light, Ted nonchalantly says "Jim now we go this way (pointing south) you go that way" (pointing east). Jim obeys. Ted takes me off to begin official Lower East Side monument tour including Frank's ex-apartment where we stand outside while Ted gives his Frank lecture, Joe's apartment where we go in and Joe perfectly gracious yet nervous and slightly impatient at being interrupted in midst of making paintings for big upcoming first Fischbach show serves us Pepsis as Ted gives total lecture on Joe's complete works, on down through the illuminated rest of that day, Fiorello La Guardia and ending up chez Bernadette. Bernadette not that thrilled to be included in the tour (by now it's night) hooray for Bernadette, I don't blame her. First impression, everyone is absolutely wonderful but who are we? What is time and destiny? How can we have put up with ourselves and each other down through these many years? How can and have other people put up with us? Did they and do they? What can we (together) really do for them? Will it really help them? Does it make any difference? Can we make up now for everything we've done wrong before? Am I using the royal We? Should I have adopted that kitten with no tail who followed me on my way home tonight? Why can't it all work out right?

2. Tom I ask: What is our poetics? What do we share and did share?

Without meaning to evade this question I'm a little bit (superstitiously) afraid of risking stepping on the toes of our poem-in-progress (which has better manners than me, but at least I'm trying), or scaring it into hiding, by even so much as whispering about poetics in its presence. Keats spoke of a line in Shakespeare as being so delicate "one's very breath while leaning over these pages is held for fear of blowing this line away—as easily as the gentlest breeze Robs dandelions of their fleecy Crowns." (He was talking about *Troilus & Cressida*, Act One, "...the seeded Pride / That hath to this maturity blowne up..." etc.) Aileen Ward, the best of K's biographers, called "La Belle Dame Sans Merci" a poem so delicate one fears to breathe on it lest one blow it away. Our poem is nowhere near that delicate but you're trying and I'd like to live up to that example by not taking one wrong rude blunt breath right here. (The Sphinx, upon hearing the words which a human has dared to utter in its presence, begins not to speak but to sing—in total silence.)

What we *do share and did share*, I'd like to think, is taking joy in and having love and thus respect for poetry, that thing which presented us the opportunity to know one another in the first place and which now presides over the opportunity for us to get to know one another in the long run even better, hopefully for the good of ourselves (I don't want to get carried away here) as well as of others, "not forgetting animals" (to quote the current favorite author in our house, Nancy Mitford). As to the vulgar details of poetics, I'd never speak (lightly) of them in public, but as we're in private here, I have a strong sense that in this department we probably did and do share more in common than either of us knows or would want to admit. I've always been a little bit more interested in constructing sentences than you and you've always been a little bit more interested in getting to the point. This too long answer can stand as evidence of the superiority of your way, ergo why I'm enjoying learning from you as we go (though they say the old are very slow at language learning).

At any rate, if anything has ever stood between us at any time in life (see #3 below & reply), how sad that would be but it wouldn't I bet be poetics. And just to elaborate on that for one moment, I find, latterly, as I compare the work of my contemporaries with that of the poets I teach (Wyatt, Jonson, Donne, Herrick, Marvell, Keats, Pound), that I place you as a "traditional" formalist by *instinct*, by which I mean merely that in poems that seem to begin as *mere* formal exercises—I think here of "a perfectly clear liquid"—you seem to be able to reach also the top of YOUR form (personality & truth). As I consider this a strong compliment I'm obviously honored to get invited behind the screen to peek at your poetics "from the inside" as a collaborator (because he or she who shares "authorship" is both uniquely privileged, and necessarily forced, to do so). But of course when I do get in there and feel your mind at work now, I feel it as a strong and active formal *interrogation*—as indeed I feel with this "interview." This voice becomes my inquisitor, its rhythms the rhythms of a beautiful and delicate interrogation ("isn't water to be born in?") which moves from questioning moment to questioning moment within its formality, with sense of "lengths" of "lines" of question as refractory waves that *break back*—as, in fact, do the refrain lines in "a perfectly clear liquid." Wyatt, of course, would have admired that: *I speak from memory* here of your amazing triolet which is not so much an exercise—and as you of course know triolet is the ultimate degree-of-difficulty French fixed form, achieved fully in English only by Thomas Hardy before you—as an act of formal distancing wherein the fixed-form "tuning" removes one (you) from the painful moment with your mother in the hospital sufficiently to allow you to make a poem of it. This DISTANCING is also the effect of the formalization of the interrogation. It's this distancing which I find in questions #3 and #4 below, making them almost bearable. (Almost but not quite—thus inevitable and "telling"—see Q. #5 below & reply.)

But in writing those sentences, you'll see, I've both finally bowed my head and begun to give an honest answer to your questions, and in doing so not only rudely breathed upon our poem, but perhaps—to use a verb my student Micah Ballard latterly introduced me to, relating Lyn Hejinian had once done it to him in a wet dream—"ralphed" on it.

3. Tom, please tell me, if you will, the urge to settle. The urge to write.

Is this a "personal" or a "general" (?) question? Urge of dark wicked Richard returning to haunt the personal (grudge) field of our poem again with his dense lines of argument by night or urge of weak day?

If you mean, to settle with and write to you, I am telling you the answer to that question in our poem as we go (see below). I can't further tax the patience of our longsuffering silent third partner in this collaboration Angelica by saying more at the moment but of course if you want to know more, call me up some night & I'll tell all. (See answer to question #4 below.) (Do you go all the way?)

If you mean, to settle something else, or write something else, I have those urges all the time, but unlike with this, I usually don't act on them, if you get what I mean here kid.

4. Tom: how does love last?

On a wing and a prayer and by my keeping this short.
Or, by shaping up. (As our poem suggests, love is problematic by nature.)

5. Tom, as investigative poet and biographer and memoirist what is the "telling" line? What drives these heroic tales?

My dear, it's 5:12 in the morning, and the first half of your question has squeezed the truth out of me at last: "as" all of those things you list, I'm hung out to dry forever (as you must know), and furthermore, this work (answer to interrogation) represents my last words ever of any kind (if our poem survives these embarrassments & exposures it's got more nerve than I have).

However, as "me" (ailing geezer who reads poetry for consolation & deep pleasure late at night), "I" believe the "telling" line is the inevitable line that gives the game of the universe away by revealing it repeating itself endlessly. Poetry is like the universe and of the universe. Its formality is a way of pawing the ground in place, to use the phrase of the anarchist maniac Blanqui. In infinity, eternity performs, imperturbably, the same routines. The wave keeps breaking back. The refrain lines recur over and over and over again. They are inevitable and telling, the ghosts that haunt the structure (the house in *The Night of the Living Dead*), and the tale they tell is inevitably haunting. The weird recursiveness of this formal interrogation itself, in fact, both slyly imitates and perhaps shrewdly invokes poetry. I'm going to leap on the latter possibility before the sun comes up and I lie down again in my coffin. New line of argument:

say it again: do to each other and here again love enters the picture
problematic, but also like suffering our teacher who says
confess, do admit the wrongs you have done for knowledge
is the Negative One, all we know is our suffering
our joy is what we do not know for in the moment of knowing it
we fuck it up, in this darkness which is the size of Africa yet cold, cold
and we don't dare whisper a word in the presence of this frozen Sphinx
everything is torment perhaps we'll get to the end of this world
come out at the other end without this agony in which we begin to die
but quiet women friends bring soup, we shall live a sort of half life
in our nice little house with pain killers on hand yet the struggle
up the slope of the glacier is tedious, we must be kind
we don't wish to hurt people's feelings but Americans haven't got any
"leaning slightly to pick up a book I had a pain like the
end of the world" (Nancy Mitford) or more to the point
remember her heroes Scott, Wilson who made the appalling winter journey detour
sixty miles along the Antarctic coast to Cape Crozier
in utter darkness and one hundred degrees of frost solely to find
the egg of the Emperor Penguin ("man" searches for knowledge the supposed
"missing link" between bird and fish but the real goal the knowledge
the suffering stupid "solely to know"), Oates who staggered out into the blizzard
endless winter night to die so his comrades might survive
no one survives this journey to the end of the night (steering by Jupiter)
the darkness profound invariable day/night in this total blackness quite arbitrary
frozen stiff in one's clothes by sweat which turns to ice and everything slow, slow
each of us humans wants to be tested wants to prove to ourselves how much
    we can endure
how much we can know

like the end of the world: aerosol sprays, aircraft noise, arsenic, automobile exhaust
like the end of the world: benzene, beryllium, carbon dioxide, carbon tetrachloride
like the end of the world carcinogens, chlordane, chlorobenzenes, chromium
like the end of the world you say coal smoke, dichlorides, DDT, dieldrin, dioxin
like the end of the world: endosulfan, ethanes, ethylene glycol, ethylene oxide
like the end you say who sent me here

like the end of the world: fenoxaprop ethyl, fluorocarbons, fungicides, gasoline
at the end: heptaclor, herbicides, hydrocarbons, industrial particulate matter,
isocyanuric acid
as an end to : lead paint
like the end of the world: leptophos
like the end, and is it? mercury, mining waste
then: napalm, nitroso compounds, noise, nuclear waste: like the end, and was it?
paraquat dichloride, parathion, pesticides, radionuclides
the end it was & my friends came weeping: sewage sludge, sulfur oxides,
    tobacco smoke, toxic waste
ultraviolet radiation, vinyl chloride, wood smoke rising
pain like the end of the world or reading the world as a book
she bends her hero-pioneers to the task, like us, readying for the launch
the stars are out out of their canisters, earlier I phoned many senators to
stop a war on Iraq: Boxer, Kerry, Feingold, Biden, Helms have mercy on us, I,
    citizen beg of you, and may your voices be as mine—mine of the
poets resembling Kurds living in a no fly intersices: who sent us here?
for rant and comment, see my new space station replete with space weapon dock
loading up for the millenniums and the moons of Jupiter in their
    checkerboard houses, I live chez the young poets of the past it is the
    hour of the day crossing the time frame, no war this time it is whatever
    you say it is, but I say it is no war this geezer hour of the night

consciousness hath murdered sleep, I mean vigilance hath
in this summer of pro bono and cultural reparations
I get so little sleep, I'm able to memorize
the 4 A.M. BBC world news soccer results for Diogo
Olympia over Sao Caetano in Copa dos Libertadores
Sao Paolo, Ailton scores in the first half
for the faery tale Sao Caetano side but Olympia
comes back on a series of furious crosses
in the second half, wins on penalty kicks
when two Sao Caetano players lose their nerve
I identify with them and send Diogo an e-mail
Anne, only our poem knows what will happen
in the great field of play which is the field of the Lord
to whom we say, Lord not among these people
after Seferis who meant the Germans occupying Greece
whereas we mean the people getting ready to invade Iraq

or is it the people who are firing missiles into apartment houses in Gaza
each particular combination of materials and people
must be repeated thousands of times to satisfy the demands
of infinity, a death in this world is also a death in another
what I write at this moment in my cell at dawn as the birds begin to speak outside
on paper with a pen, clothed as I am now, in circumstances like these
I have written and shall write throughout eternity

sports was a body once and kicked the ball, sitting in the biker bar
all the rules collapse in color and does this world cup bring out
the beesties or what narcissism? bump it up, flip the bird, slam on "other"
As the categoria pequena baseball kid in Cuba said re: "American"
athletes "They play only for the millions. A real player plays
because he likes baseball and doesn't need that much money to lead a
normal life" & we would love that sense of normal, that sense of life,
        wouldn't we—passing the buck?
Marina Tsvetayeva of "Insomnia" responds: "But I have looked too
long into human eyes./ Reduce me now to ashes Night, like a black
sun." And you might agree looking that hard into what only our poem knows
me too the night-dawn shift, was it the piece on pre-cogs? or the
American turned toward Iran, now revealed (beard off) in
"Kandahar", was I reading Chaucer in my sleep again, dawn #10 or so
in this poem the alchemy parts or listening to Poulenc, the ongoing
syncretic life parts, Sikelianos' "borderguards" thinking that's what we are at
        this weird juncture,
at this divide: keepers of the lines, how read the world map once again for the
next bright day without rain, garish light, we turn back into the desert
caked earth underfoot & last night a drumming Macbeth set the lines back,
        what they would not let the words speak of themselves, double double
        toil and trouble
& the headline speaks of a ban on sofas so the kids don't go crazy and torch
        them don't go crazy don't go crazy , what are those birds, Tom, what kind?

for TC:

What about the poet-heroes of yesteryear? What do you see on the horizon
in that realm? Reading your Dorn book struck once again by the diversity
of the older poets lives, more hard-scrabble...and now?

Those birds, Anne, are ravens saying nevermore, loons saying someone wants to read this, and Emperor Penguins trumpeting to us from a cold, dark nether-world of confused and confusing hypertextuality, where I'd fear to tread water and toward which we are, it now seems, headed in one's handbag.

Yes, the heroes of yesteryear are definitely both diverse and dead and WE are so NOT hard-scrabble anymore, Toto.

I've all along suspected (reminded here by the wording of your question, "horizon of that"—or is it "horizon in that—realm") that the reconstruction of dream-realm elements, in the horizon moment of waking up, provides a good paradigm for the construction of poems. Thinking of the ballad of Thomas Rymer, who could remember only vague bits of his seven years away in the faery kingdom of the horse-riding woman who abducts him in his dream, reminds me poems too are necessarily faulty reconstructions. Like dreams in their state of incomplete recovery, the area of this making which we and our goofy-geezer doubles do is riddled throughout infinite universes with error, contingency-process unreason, in short it is that penetralium of the mystery, or by another way of saying, that jungle of utter endarkenment we call chance. Night and chaos have descended upon Zombie Dawn.

Coda
[wherein the "line of argument" turns upon itself, beginning to die out]

He: Talking to yourself like hello stranger friends to one another late slightly
    dotty handbag poem,
forgetting to remember and remembering to forget, you tell me
Life is short.

She: It sucks. They are ruining it for us. They aren't my people my tribe my government. They never had my vote or approval. In fact they stole all the horse power. You know the Trickster stories: birth in the form of a rope, avoiding thunderbolts, killing a shark which is thrown up to the Milky Way. All these I would do to undermine their reign of terror. And so on.

He: Before I die to hound you shall I become you,
drown your sorrows? And the water that follows wine ease this
cup of sorrows flickering mute on nocturnal tube tonight? Time grows smooth,
word empty sketchy text marked both by color and by problematic Love

325

the quixotic trickster Sphinx who does not take our cares away,
his jealousy mere passing and jumpy his arrow points back at a mystery "he"
    who's talking

She: & "he" who is the guy inside, the watcher?—mapping the galaxy. It wakes
and slumbers, this one in our head. It emits Nebulae. The absorption nebula
contains dust that scatters starlight and hides stars from our view. In her hand-
bag: a cosmic mirror you cannot see, Dark Age Makeup for the new
Millennium.

He: Moon of your forgetting and mooning fuller than full
not seen by miners inundated 100 hours in the dark, won't your rose
water (isn't water to be born in?) drown their sorrows, what flowers are these
    at my sleeping feet O moon
of shadow market's swoon and crash, Tokyo index down two hundred points
    at opening
who dwells in mystery? What do we do to each other beneath the earth in
    the dark
worldly night green and glowing then red and touched with charcoal?

She: We do the best we can, touch each other gently through impulse of sound
that a poem might be that a poem is, we mark time in hours otherwise
consumed by rage, despair, and loneliness. We take the green version with the
red, we lie down with the river and the corn, with the boulders and the snakes.
We look up.

He: The stars are out
for rant and comment, blue immigrants vulnerable in this elephant graveyard
    when they dream
what I write in this moment in my cell as the birds

She: (what kind? here it's jays and crows)

He: begin to speak

She: (yammer)

He: outside
while quiet women friends bring soup at zombie dawn

She: and caution: hush.

Coda [once more, with feeling]

Talking to yourself like hello stranger friends to one another late slightly
    dotty handbag poem,
forgetting to remember and remembering to forget, ·you tell me
Life is short. Before I die to hound you shall I become you,
drown your sorrows? And the water that follows wine ease this
cup of sorrows flickering mute on nocturnal tube tonight? Time grows smooth,
word empty sketchy text marked both by color and by problematic Love
the quixotic trickster Sphinx who does not take our cares away,
his jealousy mere passing and jumpy his arrow points back at a
mystery "he" who's talking
Moon of your forgetting and mooning fuller than full
not seen by miners inundated 100 hours in the dark, won't your rose
water (isn't water to be born in?) drown their sorrows, what flowers are these
    at my sleeping feet O moon
of shadow market's swoon and crash, Tokyo index down two hundred points
    at opening
who dwells in mystery? What do we do to each other beneath the earth in
    the dark
worldly night green and glowing then red and touched with charcoal? The
    stars are out
for rant and comment, blue immigrants vulnerable in this elephant graveyard
    when they dream
what I write in this moment in my cell as the birds begin to speak outside
while quiet women friends bring soup at zombie dawn

327

PROCESS NOTE

A useful, well-informed and relatively disinterested process note has been supplied by Angelica Clark (a friend to both collaborators and specific enabler of the production):

Tom begins the exchange by sending Anne the opening lines, ending on the mysterious padlock; she then replies, addressing him (?) as Richard III in the second "clump" or block of verse (the elderly immigrants getting slot machine blues, etc.). Tom fires back, addressing Anne as "nervous raven queen...caring world saver," etc.; she then brings in death of the Roshi as calming influence. Tom comes back with the "Memphis nightshade dawn / Sphinx / government of shadows" stanza; Anne comments in hers, "lovely that, and dark..."–which leads into her "interview" with Tom. He fields/dodges the questions, and then introduces "New line of argument": Scott's doomed trek and the quest for knowledge. In response to that Antarctic stanza by Tom, Anne explodes into a list-rant about the evils of the world. In his next stanza, Tom circles back to the World Cup, then branches out to Gaza and eternity. Anne replies with "sports was body once," etc., and then slides back into quizzing Tom. Tom ducks out from under the latest round of quizzes, then heads for exit/Coda. His Coda is interrupted by lines from Anne (Tom turns this into a "he"/"she" dialogue); finally he "reinstates" the Coda as he originally intended it–i.e. as "poem." The whole work was done via e-mail in July-August 2002.

ANGELICA CLARK

This was a salutary way to be back in touch with Tom Clark–a rapprochement of sorts–I felt we were on a similar wavelength, picking up and extending each others' language, phrasings and thinking in a sustained way. Kobun Chino Roshi, a Japanese Zen teacher close to the Naropa University community had recently died, and was on my mind.

I appreciated the opportunity to probe and the graceful way Tom responds in the interview section which is an interesting slice of history. I wrote my sections–intentionally–in the middle of the night in keeping with the insomniac "theme". Skanky Possum published a lovely edition in 2003, with a noirish cover by Tom.

ANNE WALDMAN

Riparian

Andrew Schelling & Anne Waldman

Basho dogs us here
albeit "Pets
          Not Aloud"
and five miles down
the grocery store has frozen pizza
The St. Vrain roars
          chortles and roars
past the billboard advertising
smoked trout
Are there trout in there?

"Fan"
the St. Vrain speaks
"oven"
daylight valley walls of burst
granite
ponderosa pine
          but by night . . .

          sentimental curtains with
          pussycats
          at the windows

All over Colorado
into alpine lakes and cold rivers
trout rain from helicopters
Every spring they dump them from helicopters,
and what senator speaks for the trout?

Who was St. Vrain?
Consult *High Country Names*
          Louisa Ward Arps & Elinor Eppich Kingery–

what was Cache la Poudre?
What were the French up to?

1848 keeping their
powder dry

Eagle Canyon
Clap trap houses displace the eagle
dislocation
driving through subdivisions
named for what they displace

Golden Eagle where is thy eye
(and vanishing)
Bald Eagle thy claw?
(prospering, replete with road kill)
Who dwelleth yet in Eagle Canyon—?
  wise philosophers

      knotted
  should we say
     twisted
  the
 ways
   of
    this
   road

 staked out

You think watching a small tv
the same as listening to
quiet music?
or a book with fine print?

Gold   *Light*

I'd get up and turn off that fan if I could

      −I will

turn off the refrigerator if I could

           −not sure I can do that

      crab apples are ornamental

           and St. Vrain is not a Christian holiday?

Bring back Basho & temper the
      lane, the light, her dawn

Basho hears a horse piss near his head
Basho sees a dream waver on the autumn field
Basho gives his youth to homosexual love
Basho shaves his head
Basho builds a hut and assumes a pen name
Basho takes on students
Basho hates the poetry scene

The capital Edo is like New York

He comes to loathe it
      flees it in riparian
      twist & turn

−I am not a poet of Edo
−Not a New York School poet
−We are not poets with any name exactly
     though half of us is a New York School poet
−I am not a New York School poet
−You are when you collaborate that half
−Collaboration was not invented in New York
     nor in Edo
−I missed a beat O yes & proud of it

Bring back the golden eagle of five syllables

*

Dusk by the creek

this is a little haiku—

the rabbit
eyes the idling
Subaru

add another haiku—

What loneliness
the rabbit
eyes the newly arrived Honda

Can't get a word in edgewise, ceded to river

and another—

Move your fingers
and count syllables
the old man

*

Catch us if you can

blue & red in the rocky mountain

slant light / sun set

Waiting for you in a swing by the St. Vrain
what I always knew poetry could do

shoring up for the millennium

so many thousands before us

doing the same with their broken syllables

"tremble"

the river it's the river

I'm just going to walk over to it

PROCESS NOTES

Riparian: of, on, or relating to the banks of a creek or river. The St. Vrain drains the east slope of the Rockies near Lyons, Colorado. Up there are the remains of an Ice Age glacier. Both creek and glacier are named for a French trader who set up a post where Indians could swap buffalo hides for sugar loaf or a looking glass. Anne Waldman and I took a pocket notebook. We parked the Subaru near the creek's bank and passed this poem back & forth as we wrote. Nearby stand some recreational cottages, and many lines of the poem refer to the cabins and hastily built subdivisions in this narrow canyon below Estes Park. "Pets not aloud" we obviously took from a sign, the cats sat in a distant window, & Basho was my reading matter. From there we were off and going. For the most part we scrawled six or eight lines each before handing off the notebook, but at times went faster— as in the rapid-fire exchange about Basho and poetry schools. Later I typed up the poem, edited it lightly (probably using *High Country Names* for reference), & then Anne did her own light retooling. It is very difficult now to know who wrote what. The dedication to Philip Whalen seemed necessary—he was in the hospital and much in our thoughts. Later, based on the title-word "riparian," we thought we'd cover the range of western landscapes—shrubland, foothills, tundra, high plains—but the only other one we ever did was "Montane."

ANDREW SCHELLING

"Riparian" was actually handwritten written by a stream at a place called Shelly Cabins near Estes Park, Colorado, moving a notebook back and forth. It appeared as a small printed edition for the Winter Solstice of 1997 for family & friends. It was possibly best thing to come out of this troubled relationship.

ANNE WALDMAN

As If I Was a Cloud Expert

Anselm Berrigan, Edmund Berrigan & Karen Weiser

if the wine cellar can't be bombed
other, colder rooms will work
this makes perfect sense from a viewmaster stage
that cooked a whole gargoyle
unrelated to a possible variety
of the Unified Stacks of salamis
and salt-cured feets
down four point four percent
from the thawed cast of *No, No Nanette*
Patricia stowed chickadees in the ids
of lawyers and analysts in a standalone grain elevator
so don't risk that special day-glo bunion
on some cheap imitation of sweet glaze
aren't your family and friends
worth seventy-five cents more?

I Think You Get the Privilege 0

Anselm Berrigan, Edmund Berrigan & Karen Weiser

A row! Arrah a row exclamation point
The virgin be blessed a row!
Plunge in with ye, out there all alive
In that misshapen antichamber
(ten page fragment on whaling goes here)
And I hurled a heavy heartball in the passage
With the meat and wine of the war
Greeting a tribe of toast; thin pink
Using Roget's be(a)st cutlery
With a vengeance—cris rash I was tea in a bat
There goeth the gib hypen say, yes
I have heard something lugubrious on that score
I hereby expectorate the whales
From the wish of my knowledge

PROCESS NOTE

The three of us took turns at the computer, transcribing lines that the others
shouted across the room from various sources including the self and whatever
else is handy. We then each took a turn at editing. The third poem has since
been destroyed by fire.

EDMUND BERRIGAN

from **Cartographic Anomaly**

Terri Carrion & Michael Rothenberg

May 10, 2003

Hollywood, Florida to Bonifay, Florida, gouache baroque floral
economy Motel, refurbished like Spanish Riviera.
Plaster mermaids caste in Dothan, Alabama
adorn the three stroke swimming pool.

Sushi served by blonde college drones.
Orgasm under stars (sunroof).
Misguided penetrations is the phrase of the day.

May 13

Orange, Texas.
Stop in Baptist Orange Hospital
parking lot where a giant billboard hovers over a field.
"Some people call them trash, other people call them babies."

Road stress up and down emotions & sinus

Michael on computer, in bed, blue glow
from screen on his face like TV image.

Big Bend National Park.

Inflorescence, scape, floral scape, bracts, flower petals
Ocotillo
Hectia scariosa
Agave havardiana (century plant)
Manzanita, mesquite, cottonwood, dead minnows, red mud bank of Rio Grande
102 degrees, peanut butter & jelly sandwich
Jack rabbit
silvery salmon snake ribons curve dip road into purple prickly pear

hail knocks flowers off yucca plant, sweet rain smell
"That peak out there ought to have a name"

I name the mountain outside our window,
"The Sleeping Gypsy"

May 15

2 PAIRS OF SUNGLASSES

On pool step, swept hat floats
While Michael stretches out wet
On hot, peach concrete
Cold grainy dust on jacuzzi bottom
Hot diet coke can
Between plastic lounge chairs
And red necked bird singing
On top of palm frond stump

White winged dove on palm frond stump
Swimming pool Travelodge
Sable palm fronds hellacious rattle
Swallows glide sideways in sky stream
Between Interstate 10 and 4 dollar carwash.

Lunar eclipse gravel road behind landfill east of El Paso

Glowing golf ball, egg, pearl, eyeball.
Red-pink glow nipple moon.
Strange round lights bouncing around in the sky. Planes?
Strange flight patterns. Military or UFOs.
We share binoculars and compose bad haiku.

Wind storm last night blew lawn chairs to the edge of roof
Sweet dark clouds promise rains, fulfill drought
La Placitas through Abiquiu, try to find Ghost Ranch

June 3

The Dalles.
Stories of Indians catching salmon off the waterfall.
Dam built, goodbye Celilo Indians.
Look for longhorn on the side of road.
I feel very lost suddenly.

June 4

Arlington, OR pop. 850
Morning. Watch mallard couple in the river.

Walla Walla, Washington.
Onions and asparagus and wheat.
Blue mountains and wineries
Make it downtown to eat at deli in strange mall.
Find Beat bookstore.

Silos everywhere, a procession (family) of cows followed by a llama.

June 5

Arrive Orofino, Idaho.

Air full of moths.
Steelhead trout and hunting.
Men with prize antlers and skinned cougar.

Road backed up due to horse trailer colliding
with truck full of cows on their way to slaughter.

June 8

Can't get my days straight.

Make it to Badlands, off 14 then to 200
Roosevelt Park. Sandstone, shale, coal formations,
concretions (Big eggs. I think Dali).
Buffalo, lounging around
on damp grass and in the middle of the road.
I rise up out of the sunroof to take pictures.
Buffalo gather around the car.
We're surrounded.

June 9

"JOURNEY TO THE HEART OF THE BOG"

Crimson Columbine,
dragonfly, bog, mosquito, American Blue Vetch,
Wild (False) Lily-Of-The-Valley, Marsh Marigold,
Starflower, Moccasin Flower (Stemless Lady Slipper),
Cala Lily,
black striped biplane dragonfly,
Sedge, Horsetail, Tamarack, Black Spruce,
Bunchberry, Pitcher Plant,
Dragon's Mouth Orchid,
Buckbean, Labrador Tea, Giant Reed Grass,
Sweet White Violet,
sphagnum moss,
Cinnamon Fern,
Blue Flash Iris,
Sundew,
red mushroom (looks like rusty nail),
Dwarf Raspberry,
bog water, Bog Rosemary,
"The bodies of long dead or mummified
animals remarkably well preserved are found
buried in peat bogs",

Serviceberry,
Crested Fern, Oak Fern, willow,
Bog Cranberry,
bumblebee,
Twin Flower, Gold Thread...
Red Hat Ladies
                    at
Country Club
Purple-Breasted Beer-Bellied Minnesotan walks black & white spotted Chihuahua

June 14

Lost on highway looking for bed, fight w/ Terri
High tide? Low tide? Slack tide?
Bay of Fundy same level of St. John River
Engines of the world stop, shout "Fuck You!"
Courtenay Bay Motel, we find a bed.

June 16

Cinnamon roll at Cream Puff Bakery, Sussex

            Hwy 114 to
Fundy National Park
Maritime Arcadian Highlands
Red Spruce Trail to Point Wolfe Cove
Driftwood, pine cones, mussel shells
Skip blue, red, green, yellow, orange, white stones on Bay of Fundy
Alma, Tides Restaurant, shrimp & scallop gumbo, pilaf & lobster roll
Bunchberry, Starflowers, Ferns
Moose on the road

June 17

        curly fries, gems, home fries, french fries,
        American fries, wedges, hash browns,

mashed potatoes, baked potatoes, sour
cream potatoes, poutine

Welcome to MAINE: "The Way Life Should Be"

Augusta, "The Governer's Restaurant" Peppy, tanned waitress

"Is it real chicken?"
"Oh, yes."

June 18

Outside Bangor, ME, Waterville Budget Host Inn, full night of dreams.

stabbing pain in head
cartographic anomaly in Rand McNally

New Hampshire, Connecticut, Rhode Island . . .
Bumper to bumper through the Bronx
Maze of roads, bridges, 10:30 P.M. rush hour

"Poetry in Motion" The video.

New Jersey Turnpike (Philadelphia exit). Fat. The Gross Realization.
Fried clams, cole slaw, chicken & mashed potatoes w/gravy,
cranberry sauce, blackberry frozen yogurt sugar cone.

Road repair & rain every ten feet.
2 A.M. Stretch. Still fat.

June 19

Cheese grinder in Richmond
Magnolia trees I don't remember
10 years ago drunk on a bike through the snow

June 20

South Carolina morning, humid, mosquito bites on arms & neck
          drove me crazy all night. Canadian mosquito bites.

"A Window In Time" Rachmaninoff.

The sign on the front door of Pedro's Firework store says,
"YES, WE SELL AMERICAN FLAGS."

Arrive Miami.

Things to do

        1. Clean gutters
        2. Gulf Stream cover
        3. Add up receipts
        4. Prepare syllabus
        5. Hurricane insurance
        6. Change oil
        7. Stop flood

May 10th-June 20th

PROCESS NOTE

"Cartographic Anomaly" was created from travel journals that each of us kept when we took a road trip around the US, literally circling the entire country. Six weeks and 12,000 miles later, we typed out our journals, printed them, cut them into strips according to daily entries and spread them all out on the pink rug in a two long rows parallel to each other. We quickly went down each row and pulled out strips we felt didn't work or were just plain boring. We then rearranged them into one row, alternating each other's entries, and keeping the chronology. We went ahead and pulled out more pieces that didn't hold. Then it was all retyped in its new form and titled. The title actually came out of one of the journal entries, a moment on the road when we discovered the road atlas we were using didn't match up to the actual surroundings. A "Cartographic Anomaly in the Rand Mc Nally." had been found.

TERRI CARRION

from **TRI / VIA**

Veronica Corpuz & Michelle Naka Pierce

Postscript

The aim of the
letter is merely to
bring in a personal
hyphen between
the person writing
and the person
written to.

Poem as letter as email as collaboration as conversation as discourse as interchange as collection as accumulation as copious pages as manuscript as so on and so forth as et cetera as trivium as effluvium of minutiae as the usual details as in trivia as in *TRI / VIA* as in three ways as in *ménage à trois* as in Hermes in bed or Hermes at the crossroads as in point of exchange as in, dare say, commerce as thief as trickster as technology as annotation as footnote as distance as expansive gaps as suspension of time as interval or hiatus or procrastination as sabbatical as Sabbath as sin or pathos or relations as in sex[es] as in playing footsie in an affair as inter[sexed]actions as dialogues as epistles as in *this* as dispatch.

♠Q & A

1. Does this mean there is magic in the act of love?

    a. If you close your eyes, you may pull a rabbit out of a cat or a cat out of a carpetbag or a carpetbag from your sleeve or a sleeve from a tree or a tree out of a dinghy or a dinghy out of a compass.

    b. If you close your eyes, Prince Charming may be Sleeping Beauty who may be the frog who may be the woman who lived in a shoe who may be Robin Hood who may be Cinderella who may be all seven dwarves who may be the rabbit who may be you.

    c. If you close your eyes, I'll be gone.

    d. If you close your eyes, everyone will swap pronouns, and you will be the only one wearing a slender "I" wrapped around a buxom "you."

2. That sex, as in the art or craft of it, requires technical skill or trickery?

    a. tool box

    b. magic wand, cape, and woman to be sawn in half

    c. deck of marked credit cards

    d. scatology

3. What does it take to get someone to love you?

    a. bribes

    b. cash on the nightstand

    c. matrimony

    d. a quick hand shake

4. To have sex with you?

    a. All

    b. of

    c. the

    d. above

5. In other words, what does it take to balance⇄ long distance relations?

    a. musical scales

    b. pharmaceutical scales

    c. fish scales

    d. none of the above

Medical History

1. What is the nature of your visit?

    a.   Divine. I rarely make house calls to tell a woman she has immaculately conceived the Messiah.
    b.   I followed the white rabbit.
    c.   A tornado, a house, a pair of ruby shoes one size too small.
    d.   I can't quite get rid of this itch.

2. How long since your last period?

    a.   Two sentences ago.
    b.   What's being punctual got to do with it?
    c.   Three...
    d.   None of the below.

3. Do you smoke?

    a.   Socially.
    b.   Only when I dress in tuxedos.
    c.   Depends on what you mean by "smoke."
    d.   Smoking is inconsequential to this investigation. The epistolists do not smoke.

4. Do you practice any of the following?

☐ unsafe sex   ☐ sexual taboos   ☐ laissez faire
☐ forgiveness   ☐ abstinence   ☐ adultery
☐ commitment   ☐ religious fanaticism   ☐ the piano

5. Have you experience any of the following symptoms?

☐ amnesia   ☐ influenza   ☐ deafness
☐ bruises   ☐ tinnitus   ☐ kinesis
☐ aphasia   ☐ alcoholism   ☐ constipation
☐ cowardice   ☐ blindness   ☐ fever
☐ homophobia   ☐ dysmenorrhea   ☐ diarrhea

𝒫 Anatomical Quiz

1. *organ of the ethical*

   a. Mine?
   b. Yours?
   c. For the masquerade of division?
   d. Where have I heard this before?

2. *areola*

   a. Was it ever?
   b. Shall we have some dinner?
   c. How do you feel about girlfriends?
   d. Can her frame be a syllogism for bruises?

3. *umbilicus*

   a. Is that a chart or axis?
   b. Can our lives be marginalia?
   c. Would you?
   d. Did *you* loosen your exterior skin?

4. *la bouche*

   a. Why not try some of your language to seal the deal?
   b. Want 'em, need 'em, don't want 'em?
   c. When did it get in the way of connubial alliances?
   d. You're not hurt, are you?

5. *scatology*

   a. What incest?
   b. Do I look for your irregular verbs and change them into gerunds?
   c. Lipstick?
   d. Is six too many in bed?

PROCESS NOTE

One of our many goals in creating *TRI / VIA* consisted of dismantling traditional notions of author, text, and meaning. Michel Foucault's questions about authorship as well as Brion Gyson and William Burroughs's activities into "third mind" shaped our own ideas about collaboration—approaching the collaborative act from the perspective that our processes could actually merge.

Based in part on the epistolary conceit running through the book, we also worked to create an open-ended text in which, as Michael Palmer states, "the reader is an active part of the meaning, that the reader completes the circuit." The writer creates the poem, but for the poem "to be resolved" as Palmer refers to it, "calls for a dwelling in the poem. You [the reader] have to decide what your relationship to the poem is."

In addition, Victor Shklovsky's concept of defamiliarization coupled with Ron Padgett's premise that "play is healthy," served as influences on the body of work.

As for the actual writing process, we began with poems as letters and responded to each other's texts. We then experimented with various word and syntactical replacements, knitting the poems together with inquiries into relationships, sexuality, gender, religion, and textual interchange. We broke open the form by introducing a set of meditations and variations on the epistolary, along with theoretical jargon and questionnaires. Finally, we shaped a landscape of linguistic juxtapositions, interweaving the personal with the theoretical, all the while blurring the lines between us as well as between us and our readers.

VERONICA CORPUZ & MICHELLE NAKA PIERCE

from **Braided Creek**

Jim Harrison & Ted Kooser

Under the storyteller's hat
are many heads, all troubled.

At dawn, a rabbit stretches tall
to eat the red asparagus berries.

The big fat garter snake
emerged from the gas-stove burner
where she had coiled around the pilot light
for warmth on a cold night.

Straining on the toilet
we learn how
the lightning bug feels.

For sixty-three years I've ground myself
within this karmic mortar. Yesterday I washed
it out and put it high on the pantry shelf.

All I want to be
is a thousand blackbirds
bursting from a tree,
seeding the sky.

Republicans think that all over the world
darker-skinned people are having more fun
than they are. It's largely true.

Faucet dripping into a pan,
dog lapping water,
the same sweet music.

The nuthatch is in business
on the tree trunk, fortunes up and down.

Oh what dew
these mortals be.
Dawn to dark.
One long breath.

The wit of the corpse
is lost on the lid of the coffin.

PROCESS NOTE

From *Braided Creek:*

When asked about attributions for the individual poems, one of the authors
replied, "Everyone gets tired of this continuing cult of the personality . . . [.]This
book is an assertation in favor of poetry and against credentials."

Alaska

Tom Breidenbach & Nathan Kernan

That's when a lot of the craziness
is out there gleaming
in shells, our hope for it
cut off and enlarged
sun. The plain floods in
and micro-articulated flatness
playing tenderly around in it
triangle of chance vision
on the shoulder and bake-sale joke
where foreground lines waver
the bridge. The quiet favorite
expand and come forward.
everything's fine and always has been
nor either edge is visible:
sewn the dark pact it takes
a kind of flesh
side, bleeding into its mirror. Mom's

My favorite brick wall
interrupts, cupping the distant
intervals and increments
a first kiss, under berries in
burnished into ochre specificity
with people we love and forget
monumental in the imperfect
walking up, friendly slaps
between here and there
faces, so much fire under
against which it seems to
brings its smell and blouse eyes
Neither top nor bottom
in, the interlude's botches having
as backdrop it's perfect
to rescue you, who sleeps out-
colored scrim, ocean or air,

speech or travelogue,   calling, gusts handing us toward

the porch, to the roof, over trees.   or someone else's silence.

The Slave

Tom Breidenbach & Nathan Kernan

I never   I blend what I am in it

and it gives me some. The police   even liked you

now I miss   come, lisps and fire.

I don't hold it against one. It   not you but something

about the way I   told me so and roots. I'm its

favorite and breathe you, who goes   didn't like you, or

didn't like the   back in me where I am

our little friends. They go   part of me that

did like you, after   home and want to stay

longer, blah blahing   all. You'll start to

tell me why there   in the corner. Yup

and yep, pills, the kiss whisper   are too many, oh,

things in this   or pliers. They exchange hands

to let go, a cold morning   room, the world, and

it's I who never gets out.   for faces. It's on our clothes.

PROCESS NOTE

What we did was each write an independent poem, (at the same time, in the same room) of a predetermined number of lines, with the idea that each line would become, alternately, the first or second half of the projected full line in the collaboration. Once the two separate poems had been spliced together, we made some, but very few, adjustments. We liked the stuttering conversational quality of the new poem. Not to detract from this we retained, typographically, the "spine" formed by the separations between our half-lines, as well as both contributions' internal punctuation. The intertwining structure of the collaboration led us to call the form "Helices."

Tom Breidenbach & Nathan Kernan

Ghazal As Menu or with Adumbration

D. A. Powell & Rachel Zucker

Love seldom lingers as long as the taste of goat: men
Dine anyway. A swan-white throat, salmon

Pink lips, intimate digestion. Taste this, she begs
Somewhat smoked and muttering. Afterward, stoat, gammon,

Pickled herring, red bliss potatoes and an onion gratin.
His insatiable sampling, a snifter and portion, wild-oat ken—

Pray, sir, anything not on the menu?
She twines spaghetti round her fork. Outside, the boatmen

Play guitar in bateaux-mouches. Sitting inside a giant fog
Their thoughts float between quote and quote. Seine

Colored cufflinks stud his chest and pucker his sleeves
She leaves. But not without a negative vote: men

Are the wild onions that spoil the taste of milk. Perhaps
Next time a slower boil, forbearing eye: note when

Bubbles first appear—even the least fire turns flesh to fiber.
Such alchemy: black water, sugar, a checkered coat. Amen.

I think it was I who wanted to write a poem together. But it was certainly Doug who suggested the form since, until then, I'd never heard of the Ghazal. We communicated mostly through e-mail and to myself I pronounced the thing we were writing, Guzzle or Huzzy. I suggested that we write two Guzzles simultaneously because the initial lines seemed to determine the flavor and nature of the poem. I was inspired by the practice of playing two simultaneous games of backgammon. I'd played this double backgammon with my husband in order to break out of the rut where each person's distinct style leads to an overly predictable game. I predicted that the poem Doug started would be a Doug poem with a little bit of Rachel and the poem I started would be a Rachel poem with a little bit of Doug. Not so. Soon, I was forgetting which lines I had written and which he had done. The writing proceeded slowly, over the course of a few months although I'm not sure why it was so slow going. Sadly one of our two poems floundered at line 8. Doug ended a line with "like Piper Laurie in *Carrie*." I felt that it was irresponsible to finish the line without having seen the movie.

RACHEL ZUCKER

See, there's a good example of the difference between our outlooks. Me, I'd never feel irresponsible about jumping into the poem without knowing what that creature was that was swimming around in the water. It's a poem, for Pete's Sake. *It's process.* But as Sammy Cahn wrote the year I was born: *Call Me Irresponsible.* At any rate, the collaboration has been truly enriching. As anyone who has listened to the last few recordings of Frank Sinatra knows, duets can go horribly wrong. What you hope for is the perfect combination, the person who senses where you're going and goes there with you, almost before you even know yourself where you are headed. I was Billie Holiday, strung out and faltering. Rachel was the tenor saxophone of Lester Young, smooth and delicate. Together we did *I Can't Get Started* in two takes, and the result was a kind of music I don't think either of us knew we were capable of making. I think we should tour.

D. A. POWELL

Now It's Tomorrow As Usual

Maggie Anderson & Lynn Emanuel

An Epistolary Poem with James Schuyler

Of course when I found the letters I read them. You wouldn't have hidden them if they weren't interesting

Dear M,
Where are you?
On some Northern Scene, like a postcard?
Brilliantly the azure vaginas
of the fjords and you!
Saucers, cups, eating pastries in Denmark,
you periwinkle!

My plangent, bittersweet one,
I write from an island in the Baltic,
my insouciant balloon, my full-of-hot-airs—

I'm reading James Schuyler.
Who is Libby Holman? Mother of

—Lorenz Hart?

And where are my steps and when?

And what, may I ask, is a sazerac? A meal, a disease, a priest?

Shadrach, Meschach, Abednego and Sazerac? The fourth one walking through
the fire.

A verb? To take a sharp turn on two wheels: Sazerac.

Sazerac
near rhymes with entr'acte
                    heart attack
                    amphibrach

For Jimmy do you think the daily
was sufficient?

Drooping like an unwatered flower
above his selected I feel

the blizzard of lithium must have been
awful and monumental and also

the dark and sloppy decks he walked,
adrift on the Seas of Depressions.

August 15

The rain this morning is the prozac pearl rain I love—the blue and white
seersucker cocktail: the shaker, the ice, the olives, the slippery capsule that
keeps me from the crystal lithium.

Joubert is wearing his pink dressing gown.

Jimmy in flannel and terry cloth.
And what are you wearing today,
my words, my wrist, my sweet vernacular?

The crystals inside my blue and white mental health are soft—ash from the
World Trade Center, ash from my used-to-always-be-a-cigarette. I emptied 15
pills onto the table. A mound of sand: seaworthy, flowery, saxophone, cocaine.
I blew on the powder and it flew through the room, dust on the dog and my
poems and my telephone. I had thought to put this dust in the blender, make
a milkshake with it, and little sprinkles of xanax and deseryl on top for decoration.

August 16

For lunch I ate "oriental" rice with
yellowish stain of egg and confetti of pork.

I will write you a letter:

Dear M., Dear Blue Chevrolet,
you're all in a mood; I can see, your chromium
winking at me under the blinding sun

and the children screaming on the hot vinyl

and the parent poking the cigarette back in its face

and pulling it out again.

It is the afternoon of landscapes of the past.

The clay-stained lawn of the house across.

I dawdle here until the real matter overtakes me
What might that be?

What might that be?

It is steamy August now, with thighs and eyes to match.

the throng of crows going about
their dark and iridescent business

my whole seeing among

tuftedness,...the pattern of its later shading

359

Understory, the clouds fly by
        above the house which is pickled in primness
        and that car blue as smeared makeup.

A crow laughs.
The engine throttles.

It is, at last, the morning of the poem:

Here is our theme:

Things should get better as you get older, but that is not the way.

Over to you M. chatting among the shards of high tea.

——————————————

                As I was telling John David,
to be an author with an endowment, a painter with a patron...

                      Could I be endowed?

All my life, completely taken care of so that I might practice my craft or sullen
art in the still night?

                Or in the open air, where the wide spaces of
                imagination appear, can open out for the writer

who does not have to think about cash.

Here comes a cloud bank, thick gains
        high interest, slow returns

        herring and black bread
        ship flags, white and red

stock market going up and down and down and down
and up and down and down

             Anodyne of heartbreak, another thing done wrong.

You're all in a mood:
        ...entrapped in
a lobster pot.
Carapace and claws snapping and thrashing, mottled stormily.

Do you remember the little synagogue in Amsterdam? Lost, we only crossed the Amstel once. Or three times? Not the right number to get home, dear. Lost on the canals, in the grasshopper bars.

And Mandy was so sad she could write only by crutching along from syllable to syllable like an invalid

and so became a Formalist!

             Are you my handrails? What kind of form are you?

             I've made more false starts than anyone since
             Homer was a pup.

—says Jimmy

It is our signature these days, the Hoboken Clam House motto, the red sky over the George Washington Bridge, the west side of Kent, the South Side of Pittsburgh, the afternoon, hot, steamy with rain, *oh my bright particular*

Jimmy says

        Dearest l,
        you are still in my thoughts
        today in lower case, a hum, not yet a word but
        flinders and shards of pre-word
        an initial, a start.

––––––––––––

October 17

It's me again—
Lena Horne is singing "Mad About the Boy"

––––––––––––

        The tops of the trees at the edge of the sky.
        Edging. Aging.
        Metal-threaded tapestry.
        Selvage. Savage. Salvage.

––––––––––––

The trees are turning, slightly red sumac, slightly auburn, sazerac...

the light, what light
        there is...
        light lighting up
the scrub
        in red...,

––––––––––––

                —as Jimmy said.

Process Note

In the summer of 2002 we were both reading the poems of James Schuyler. Maggie was on the Danish Island of Bornholm in the Baltic Sea; Lynn was in Pittsburgh. We took notes on our reading and wrote letters to each other with Schuyler as a referent. In the fall we worked on the poem through e-mail and on the phone. On January 17, 2003, Maggie drove from Kent, Ohio to Pittsburgh in the snow. We worked in Lynn's attic studio cutting and pasting and combining sections of our own lines and Schuyler's. The result is "Now it's tomorrow as usual: An Epistolary Poem with James Schuyler." You should know that some of what is attributed to Maggie Lynn wrote and vice versa. As we were working we felt that we were creating two characters and a dramatic situation and implied biographies.

MAGGIE ANDERSON & LYNN EMANUEL

Sprung Flung

Douglas Kearney & Harryette Mullen

Laura lie. Black bottom on the rocks.
She sigh. Wren sing. Suite
or bitter notes sent by air to where
up on her tongue. A string of purls
or tender stitches knit from her
sweat. Her body wound in the sun's stroke.
Heart stricken with such heat
and aw the aws of awe and all the ands of thee,

the means and ends of all my awestruck luck
plucked like blossoms gawking at the sheer -ness of
shears sharpened for such a purpose—
to leave off the poses, posies, poesy purpled
stained and straining to express
a scrambling of scents. This nose, open.

PROCESS NOTES

Exchanging lines by e-mail, Douglas Kearney and I wrote ["Sprung Flung"]
between February 5 and March 5, 2003.

HARRYETTE MULLEN

Harryette Mullen invited me to participate in a collaborative sonnet. I agreed
and she suggested I begin the process. Feeling a bit intimidated, I e-mailed her
two different lines, giving her the option to choose which she'd like to build
from.

She responded to each, and sent each back.

So I responded to each, and sent each back.

After about 7 such volleys, Harryette suggested we splice the two develop-
ing poems. Thus began a little literary turntablism. We adjusted the sequencing
back and forth. We tweaked a line break here and there. And when we saw what
we had done, she gave the title "Sprung Flung."

My inspirations were double-talk, signifyin', *Buhloone Mindstate* and my
esteemed collaborator.

DOUGLAS KEARNEY

About the Contributors

Keith Kumasen Abbott is an associate professor in the Writing and Poetics department at Naropa University. Publications include the novels *Gush, Rhino Ritz, Mordecai of Monterey,* and *Racer,* and the short story collections *Harum Scarum, The First Thing Coming,* and *The French Girl.* His memoir of Richard Brautigan, *Downstream From Trout Fishing in America,* was published in 1989, and he wrote the *Introduction to Richard Brautigan: The Edna Webster Collection of Undiscovered Writings,* (Houghton Mifflin, 1999). His writing has appeared in five languages, most recently in an international anthology *Rimbaud aprés Rimbaud* (Paris: Intermedia, 2004). His work has been selected for over thirty anthologies, including *Richard Brautigan Essays on the Writings and Life* (McFarland, 2006) for which he chaired a symposium and contributed an essay. His story "Spanish Castle" was optioned by Ziji Productions and he co-wrote the screenplay. His articles, journalism and reviews have appeared in the *Los Angeles Sunday Times, Tri-Quarterly, Rolling Stone,* and the *San Francisco Chronicle,* and he won a Sigma Delta Chi award. He has twice been Artist in Residence at the Djerrassi Foundation and among his awards are a Squaw Valley Scholarship, two Poets Foundation Awards and a CCLM Award.

He teaches Brush Calligraphy at Naropa University and has received several solo and group shows of his art, Western and Asian calligraphy and collages. His Zen brush art appears regularly in *Shambhlala Sun* and *Buddhadharma magazines.*

Samuel Ace (formerly L. Smukler) is the author of two collections of poetry: *Normal Sex* (Firebrand Books) and *Home in three days. Don't wash.,* a book and multimedia project with accompanying CD-rom (Hard Press). His work has been widely anthologized, and he is the recipient of numerous awards in poetry and fiction including the 1997 Firecracker Alternative Book Award in Poetry. He has received fellowships in poetry from the New York Foundation for the Arts and the Astraea Foundation. He is the co-owner of Gallery Katzenellenbogen, in Truth or Consequences, New Mexico.

Opal Palmer Adisa writes what writes her. Her newest collection of poetry and essays is *Eros Muse* (Africa World Press) 2006. Her newest collection of stories is *Until Judgment Comes* (Peepal Tree Press, 2006). Other works include *Caribbean Passion* (poems, Peepal Tree, 2004) and *It Begins with Tears* (novel, Heinneman, 1997). Visit her website at www.opalwriters.com.

Maggie Anderson is the author of four books of poems, most recently *Windfall: New and Selected Poems.* She teaches in the northeast Ohio consortial MFA program through Kent State University where she also directs the Wick Poetry Center and edits the Wick Poetry Series of the Kent State University Press.

Nin Andrews is the author of several books including *The Book of Orgasms, Why They Grow Wings, Spontaneous Breasts,* and *Any Kind of Excuse.* She has a new book forthcoming from BOA Editions. She has been collaborating with Mary Beth Shaffer off and on since they graduated from the MFA program at Vermont College where Mary Beth studied fiction, and Nin studied poetry. Their first collaboration, *The Divorce Notebooks,* was a published contest finalist in *Quarter After Eight* (for their annual prose contest).

John Ashbery has published more than twenty collections of poetry, including, most recently, *Chinese Whispers* (FSG, 2002) and *Where Shall I Wander,* (Ecco Press and Carcanet, 2005). His *Selected Prose* was published in 'fall 2004 by Carcanet and the University of Michigan Press. Since 1990 he has been the Charles P. Stevenson, Jr. Professor of Languages and Literature at Bard College in Annandale-on-Hudson, New York.

Julianna Baggott's first book of poems, *This Country of Mothers,* was published in 2001. She is also the author of four novels—*Girl Talk, The Miss America Family, The Madam,* and a collaborative novel with Steve Almond entitled *Which Brings Me to You*—as well as a series of novels for younger readers, *The Anybodies,* under the pen name N. E. Bode, whom she also considers a collaborator. She teaches at Florida State University's Creative Writing Program.

Joshua Beckman is the author of *Things Are Happening,* which was selected by Gerald Stern to receive the first American Poetry Review/Honickman First Book Award; *Something I Expected to Be Different; Nice Hat. Thanks.* (with Matthew Rohrer); *Your Time Has Come;* and *Adventures While Preaching the Gospel of Beauty,* an audio CD of live collaborations with Matthew Rohrer. His latest collaboration with Matthew Rohrer was a ten-hour nonstop improvised collaborative poem performed at the Bowery Poetry Club in New York City in May 2004.

Paulette Beete's poems, fiction, and nonfiction have appeared in journals including *Crab Orchard Review, Callaloo, Provincetown Arts,* and *Willow Springs.* Her work garnered an Intro Award from the Association of Writers & Writing Programs (AWP), as well as a Pushcart Prize nomination. In 1999-2000, she was a Winter Writing Fellow at the Fine Arts Work Center in Massachusetts; she has also held residencies at the Atlantic Center for the Arts and the Ragdale Foundation. She holds a Creative Writing MFA from American University where her collection, *A Sacristy for Hunger,* received the Myra Sklarew Prize for Outstanding Thesis in Poetry. She was also selected as one of two Outstanding Scholars at the Graduate Level in 2004. Currently, Paulette lives in Silver Spring, Maryland.

T Begley is a poet and teacher. Her publications include *Sappho's Gymnasium*, a collected volume of poems, and *Open Papers*, translations of the selected essays of Greek poet, Odysseas Elytis, both with Olga Broumas. Since 1989 she has created lyrical environments for writers as teacher and founder of an evolving workshop series that spans *By Heart, Meridian*, and *Dive*.

Dodie Bellamy is the author of several books including *Pink Steam* (Suspect Thoughts, 2004); *Cunt-Ups* (Tender Buttons, 2001), which won the 2002 Firecracker Award for Poetry; and the novel *The Letters of Mina Harker* (reissued by University of Wisconsin Press, 2004). *Academonia*, a collection of essays, is forthcoming from Krupskaya. She lives in San Francisco.

Martine Bellen has published numerous collections of poetry including *The Vulnerability of Order* (Copper Canyon Press) and *Tales of Murasaki and Other Poems* (Sun & Moon Press), which was a winner of the National Poetry Series. Her most recent collection, *GHOSTS!*, was published by Spuyten Duyvil in December 2006. She is a contributing editor of *Conjunctions*.

Bill Berkson's many books of poetry include *Fugue State, Serenade*, and most recently *Gloria*, with etchings by Alex Katz (Arion Press). His criticism has been collected in *The Sweet Singer of Modernism & Other Art Writings*, and Tuumba Press has just issued his epistolary collaboration with Bernadette Mayer, *What's Your Idea of a Good Time? Interviews & Letters 1977–1985*.

Anselm Berrigan is the author of *Zero Star Hotel, Integrity & Dramatic Life*, and *Some Notes on My Programming*, all published by Edge Books. He was raised and lives in the East Village of New York City.

Edmund Berrigan has been writing and publishing poetry for over twenty years, and also performs music regularly as the musical group I Feel Tractor.

Ted Berrigan (1934–1983) was the author of more than twenty books, including *The Sonnets* (1964); *Bean Spasms*, with Ron Padgett and Joe Brainard (1967); *Red Wagon* (1976); and *A Certain Slant of Sunlight* (1988). In 2006, the University of California Press released *The Collected Poems of Ted Berrigan*, edited by Alice Notley, with Anselm Berrigan and Edmund Berrigan.

James Bertolino's recent or forthcoming magazine publications include poetry in *Indiana Review, Spoon River Poetry Review, Luna, Stringtown, Cranky*, and *Writing It Real—*

which also published his essay on collaboration. He has had nine volumes and twelve chapbooks of poetry published, including *Snail River* (Quarterly Review of Literature Award Series, 1995), *Greatest Hits: 1965–2000* (Pudding House Publications, 2000) and *Pocket Animals: 60 Poems* (Egress Studio Press, 2002). Bertolino and Boyle have coauthored a series of collaborative books: *Tavern Writings* (2000), *Pub Proceedings* (2001) and *Bar Exams* (2004), all from Egress Studio Press. He teaches creative writing at Western Washington University.

Anita K. Boyle's publications include poetry in *Indiana Review,* the *Raven Chronicles, Crab Creek Review, Arbutus, Stringtown, Cranky, Stirring, Margin: Exploring Modern Magical Realism,* and *Jeopardy,* as well as an essay on collaboration in *Writing It Real.* Her chapbook of poems, *Bamboo Equals Loon,* was published in 2001 by Egress Studio Press. The Willard R. Espy Literary Foundation awarded her an artist residency in 2003, and she was a winner of the Red Sky poetry chapbook competition in 2004.

Tom Breidenbach's book of poems *The Double Whammy* was published in 2001 by Didymus Press. He lives in Brooklyn.

Carson Brock is a junior at Hume-Fogg Academic High School in Nashville, Tennessee. He participates in soccer and sings and dances in his school show choir, The Blue Notes. His essay on the electoral college, which he wrote in the eighth grade, won a citywide competition.

James Brock is the author of three books of poetry, the most recent being *Pictures That Got Small.* For his poetry, he has won fellowships from the National Endowment for the Arts, the Alex Haley Foundation, the Tennessee Arts Commission, and the Idaho Commission for the Arts. He currently directs the Graduate Program in English at Florida Gulf Coast University.

Olga Broumas was born and raised in Greece, and migrated to this country for college and beyond in 1967. Her first book in English, *Beginning With O,* was the first Yale Younger Poets selection by a poet for whom English was a second language. She has published seven books of poems, collected in 2000 in *Rave,* and three translations of the Greek Nobel Laureate Odysseas Elytis, collected in *Eros, Eros, Eros,* in 1999. She is a bodywork therapist, and director of Creative Writing at Brandeis University.

Michael Brownstein is the author of nine books of poetry and three novels—*Country Cousins, The Touch,* and *Self-Reliance.* His latest book is the antiglobalization manifesto *World on Fire.*

Nick Carbó is the author of three books of poetry, the latest being *Andalusian Dawn* (Cherry Grove, 2004). He has also edited and coedited four anthologies of poetry and fiction from the Philippines, the latest being *Pinoy Poetics* (Meritage, 2004). He has taught at several MFA writing programs, the latest being Columbia College, Chicago and the University of Miami.

Tom Carey was born in Santa Monica, CA, the scion of three generations of cowboy actors. He is the author of one book of poems, a novel, and a play. He is a Franciscan brother and Episcopal priest and lives in New York.

Terri Carrion was conceived in Venezuela and born in New York to a Galician mother and a Cuban Father. She has lived in Los Angeles and Miami and currently nests among the redwoods in Northern California. She is the assistant editor and art director of *Big Bridge,* an online magazine of poetry, art and everything else. Her own poetry, prose, and photography has appeared and disappeared in various publications.

Guillermo Castro's work appears in *La Petite Zine, Frigatezine, Barrow Street,* and other journals, as well as the anthologies *The New Breed, Margin,* and *Short Fuse,* among others. His musical theater piece with composer Doug Geers, *How I Learned to Draw a Sheep,* for which Castro wrote the book and lyrics, was presented in the Spring of 2004. He's the author of a chapbook, *Toy Storm.*

Susan Cataldo was born in the Bronx, New York City, on September 15, 1952 and died there on April 25, 2001 of cancer, having spent most of her intervening adult years living in Manhattan's East Village. In the late seventies she began her close involvement with the Poetry Project at St. Mark's Church-in-the-Bowery where she first participated in workshops and later taught. Besides her three books of poems published by Telephone Books (*Brooklyn-Queens Day, The Mother Journal,* and *drenched*), her poems have appeared in numerous poetry publications as well as in the anthology *Out of This World.*

Maxine Chernoff is the author of six poetry collections including *Evolution of the Bridge: Collected Prose Poems* (Salt Publications, 2004). She has also published six works of fiction including *Some of Her Friends That Year: New & Selected Stories* (Coffee House Press, 2002). Coeditor of *New American Writing,* she teaches at San Francisco State University.

Tom Clark is the author of many volumes of poetry, including *Sleepwalker's Fate* (Black Sparrow), *Empire of Skin* (Black Sparrow), *White Thought* (Hard Press/The Figures), and *Night Sky* (Deep Forest), as well as a number of literary biographies, including *Jack Kerouac* (Thunder's Mouth), *Charles Olson: The Allegory of a Poet's Life* (North Atlantic), and *Edward Dorn: A World of Difference* (North Atlantic). Since 1987 he has lectured on Poetics as a core faculty member at New College of California.

Cathryn Cofell's work can be found in such places as *Prairie Schooner, Laurel Review, Phoebe, Fireweed Collective,* and *Rattle.* She is the author of four chapbooks including *Sweet Curdle,* released in late 2006 by March River Editions. Cathryn Cofell and Karla Huston's collaborative poems have been published in *Margie, Rhino,* and *Indiana Review.*

Jeffery Conway is the author of *Blood Poisoning* and coauthor of *Phoebe 2002: An Essay in Verse,* a collaboration with Lynn Crosbie and David Trinidad. He lives in New York City. His most recent book of poems is *The Album That Changed My Life* (Cold Calm Press, 2006).

Dennis Cooper is the author of *The George Miles Cycle,* an interconnected sequence of five novels that includes *Closer* (1989), *Frisk* (1991), *Try* (1994), *Guide* (1997), and *Period* (2000), all published by Grove Press. *The Dream Police: Selected Poems 1969–1993* was published in 1995. His most recent books are the novels *The Sluts* (Void Books, 2005) and *God Jr.* (Grove Press, 2005).

Veronica Corpuz has taught and guest lectured at Kelly Writers House of University of Pennsylvania, New York University, Naropa University, and Chatham College. Her work has appeared in the journals *Chain, Shiny, Aufgabe, Interlope,* and *Cities of Chance: Experimental Poetry from Brazil and the United States.* She is the coauthor of *TRI / VIA* (Erudite Fangs /PUB LUSH, 2003) with poet Michelle Naka Pierce.

Lynn Crosbie is a Toronto poet who teaches at the Ontario College of Art and Design. Her latest book is *Liar* (House of Anansi Press, 2006). She has a PhD in English literature and an unrecognized doctorate in Joan Crawford studies.

Connie Deanovich is the author of *Zombie Jet* and *Watusi Titanic.* She has been a recipient of a Whiting Writers Awards, a GE Award for Younger Writers, and has work in numerous anthologies.

Tom Disch has written work in a number of forms and venues, but at the age of 67 he is generally considered unpublishable. His old books have long been out of print, and friends of days gone by do not return his phone calls.

Margo Donaldson was born in 1959, in Brooklyn, New York into a family of renowned eccentrics. Her uncle, Itche, was a member of the Polar Bear Club. He ate raw onion for breakfast, and swam in the Atlantic during the winter. When not in training, he wandered the streets in his bathing suit exclaiming, "I'm a lost little girl," over and over. Margo credits him with helping her deconstruct gender identity. She is the co-owner of Gallery Katzenellenbogen, in Truth or Consequences, New Mexico.

Ron Drummond's poems have appeared in *Northwest Review, Borderlands, Columbia Review,* and *Global City Review,* and in the anthologies *Poetry Nation, Latin Lovers, Literature as Meaning, Poetry After 9/11,* and *This New Breed.* He has received writing fellowships from Blue Mountain Center, Virginia Center for the Creative Arts, and Ragdale Foundation, and was one of the founding editors of *Barrow Street. Why I Kick at Night,* his first collection of poems, was the winner of the 2004 Portlandia Press Chapbook Contest.

Stephen Dunn is the author of thirteen collections of poetry, including *Different Hours,* which won the 2001 Pulitzer Prize.

Jim Elledge's books include, most recently, *A History of My Tattoo,* a book-length poem (Stonewall, 2006) and *Masquerade: Queer Poetry in America to the End of World War II* (Indiana University Press, 2004). A number of his individual poems have also recently been published by *jubilat, American Letters & Commentary, Hayden's Ferry Review, Margie, Washington Square,* and others.

Lynn Emanuel is the author of three books of poetry, *Hotel Fiesta, The Dig,* and *Then, Suddenly*–which was awarded the Eric Matthieu King Award from the Academy of American Poets. Her work has been featured in the *Pushcart Prize Anthology* and the *Best American Poetry* series numerous times, most recently in 2005. She has been a poetry editor for the *Pushcart Prize Anthology,* a member of the Literature Panel for the National Endowment for the Arts, and a judge for the National Book Awards.

Danna Ephland lives in Kalamazoo, Michigan. She is a teaching-artist, poet, and dancer. She earned her MFA at the University of Notre Dame, and her poems have been published in *Indiana Review, Mothering Magazine,* as well as *Folio, Rhino,* and *Permafrost.*

Elaine Equi is the author of *The Cloud of Knowable Things* from Coffee House Press. She has also published many other collections of poetry including *Surface Tension, Decoy,* and *Voice-Over,* which won the San Francisco State Poetry Award. Her work is widely anthologized and appears in *Postmodern American Poetry: A Norton Anthology* and in The *Best American Poetry* 1989, 1995 and 2002. She teaches in the MFA program at the New School and in the graduate program at City College.

Thomas Fink, a Professor of English at CUNY-LaGuardia, is the author of three books of poetry, most recently *After Taxes* (Marsh Hawk Press, 2004) and two books of criticism, including *A Different Sense of Power: Problems of Community in Late Twentieth Century U.S. Poetry* (Fairleigh Dickinson UP, 2001). His paintings hang in various collections.

Charles Henri Ford (1913–2002) was an American poet, editor, filmmaker, photographer, and collage artist. His novel *The Young and Evil*, co-written with Parker Tyler, was banned in the United States and abroad. His first full-length book of poems appeared in 1938 and was called *The Garden of Disorder*, with introduction by William Carlos Williams. Ford's later books of poetry include *The Overturned Lake, Sleep in a Nest of Flames, Spare Parts, Silver Flower Coo, Flag of Ecstasy, Om Krishna*, and *Out of the Labyrinth*.

Joanna Fuhrman is the author of three books of poetry, *Ugh Ugh Ocean* (2003), *Freud in Brooklyn* (2000), and *Moraine* (2006) all published by Hanging Loose Press. A native of New York City, she attended the University of Texas and the University of Washington. Since returning to New York, she has been involved with the Poetry Project at St. Mark's church, running a reading series from 2001–2003 and organizing video and theater events there. Currently, she poetry in the public schools and works as a private tutor. She has taught poetry at the University of Washington, the Poetry Project, homeless shelters, and Korean delis.

William Fuller is the author of a number of books and chapbooks, including *byt, The Sugar Borders, Aether, Sadly*, and most recently, *Watchword*. He lives in Winnetka, Illinois.

Kate Gale is the President of PEN USA 2005-2006. She is the Managing Editor of Red Hen Press, the Editor of the *Los Angeles Review* and the Director of the Los Angeles Summer Institute. She is the author of one novel, one children's book, five collections of short stories, and the libretto *Rio de Sangre*, an opera by Don Davis.

Eric Gamalinda published a book of poems, *Zero Gravity*, with Alice James Books, and was given the Asian American Literary Award in 2000. His most recent novel, *My Sad Republic*, won the Philippine Centennial Prize in 1998 and is published by the University of the Philippines Press.

Pamela Gemin is author of *Vendettas, Charms, and Prayers* (New Rivers Press) and editor of *Boomer Girls* (with Paula Sergi), *Are You Experienced?*, and *Sweeping Beauty*, poetry anthologies from the University of Iowa Press. Her poetry and anthologies have been featured on NPR's *Writer's Almanac, All Things Considered*, and *Morning Edition*. She teaches poetry at the University of Wisconsin Oshkosh.

Alice George's work has appeared in journals such as *Diagram, Denver Quarterly, New Orleans Review,* and *Sentence;* she is an editor of *RHINO.*

Amy Gerstler is a writer of poetry and nonfiction living in Los Angeles. Her most recent book of poems is *Ghost Girl* (Penguin, 2004). She teaches at the Bennington Writing Seminars, Bennington College, in Vermont.

Allen Ginsberg (1926–1997) was born in Newark, New Jersey, a son of Naomi and lyric poet Louis Ginsberg. As a student at Columbia College in the 1940s, he began close friendships with William Burroughs, Neal Cassady, and Jack Kerouac, and he later became associated with the Beat movement and the San Francisco Renaissance in the 1950s. After jobs as a laborer, sailor, and market researcher, Ginsberg published his first volume of poetry, *Howl and Other Poems,* in 1956. *Howl* defeated censorship trials to become one of the most widely read poems of the century, translated into more than twenty-two languages, from Macedonian to Chinese, a model for younger generations of poets from West to East. Ginsberg was a member of the American Academy of Arts and Letters, was awarded the medal of Chevalier de l'Ordre des Arts et des Lettres by the French minister of culture, was a winner of the National Book Award (for *The Fall of America*), and was a cofounder of the Jack Kerouac School of Disembodied Poetics at the Naropa Institute, the first accredited Buddhist college in the Western world. He died in New York City in 1997. In 2006, HarperCollins Publishers released Ginsberg's *Collected Poems 1947–1997.*

Lisa Glatt's novel, *A Girl Becomes a Comma Like That,* and a collection of short stories *The Apple's Bruise,* were both published by Simon & Schuster. Her poetry collections include *Shelter* and *Monsters & Other Lovers.* Visit her website at www.LisaGlatt.com.

Kendra Dwelley Guimaraes is a retired gypsy. She now lives in South Lake Tahoe, California where she teaches English.

Marilyn Hacker lives in New York and Paris. She is the author of twelve books of poems, most recently *Desesperanto* (W.W. Norton, 2003). She is also a translator of contemporary French poetry, including Venus Khoury-Ghata's *She Says* (Graywolf Press, 2003).

Jim Harrison's most recent novel is *True North,* and his most recent volume of poems is *Saving Daylight,* both from Copper Canyon.

Stacey Harwood is a policy analyst for the New York State Public Service Commission, the government agency that regulates electric, gas, telephone, and water utilities in New

York. She received an MFA in writing and literature from Bennington College and lives in New York City.

David Hernandez's poetry collections include *Always Danger* (Southern Illinois University Press, 2006), winner of the Crab Orchard Series in Poetry, and *A House Waiting for Music* (Tupelo Press, 2003). His poems have appeared in the *Missouri Review, Ploughshares, FIELD, TriQuarterly, AGNI,* and the *Southern Review.* In 2007, HarperCollins will publish his first novel, *Suckerpunch.* Visit his website at www.DavidAHernandez.com.

Michael Hettich has published a dozen books and chapbooks of poetry, mostly with very small presses. His two most recent books were released in 2005: *Swimmer Dreams* (Turning Point) and *Flock and Shadow: New and Selected Poems* (New Rivers Press).

Paul Hoover has published nine poetry collections including *Winter Mirror* (Flood Editions, 2002) and *Rehearsal in Black* (Salt Publications, 2001) and the essay collection *Fables of Representation* (University of Michigan Press, 2004). He won the Jerome J. Shestack Award for the best poetry to appear in *American Poetry Review* in 2002. He is editor of the anthology *Postmodern American Poetry* and, with Maxine Chernoff, the literary annual *New American Writing.*

Lita Hornick (1927-2000) was a publisher and literary critic, who for more than twenty-five years fostered collaborations between artists and writers through *Kulchur Magazine.*

Karla Huston's poems have been published in *Cimarron Review, Eclectica Magazine, 5 A.M., North American Review,* and *One Trick Pony.* Winner of the 2003 *Main Street Rag* Chapbook contest, she is the author of five chapbooks of poems, including her most recent from Marsh River Editions called *Catch and Release.* Cathryn Cofell and Karla Huston's collaborative poems have been published in *Margie, Rhino,* and *Indiana Review.*

Jacqueline Johnson is a native of Philadelphia, PA, and is the author of *A Gathering of Mother Tongues,* on White Pine Press. She has just completed work on a new poetry manuscript *The Place Where Memory Dwells.*

Douglas Kearney believes in repetition, revision and remix. Red Hen Press is publishing his first book, *Fear, some.* He lives in Glendale, California with his wife and dog.

Nathan Kernan is a poet and art critic who lives in New York. He is writing a biography of James Schuyler.

Kevin Killian is the author of *Shy, Bedrooms Have Windows, Arctic Summer, Little Me, Argento Series,* and *I Cry Like a Baby.* For the San Francisco Poets' Theater he has written thirty-odd plays, including *Island of Lost Souls, Often* (with Barbara Guest), and *Stone Marmalade* (with Leslie Scalapino). With Peter Gizzi he is editing the complete poems of Jack Spicer (1925-65).

Julie King lives in Albuquerque with her husband, two dogs, and four cats. She just received her MFA from Queens University of Charlotte, quit her university teaching job of fifteen years, and stars in B horror films.

Kenneth Koch published eighteen books of poems, two books of fiction, five books of plays featuring many that were performed off-off-Broadway, six books about the teaching of poetry, and a book of comics (*Art of the Possible: Comics Mainly without Pictures,* Soft Skull, 2003.) Koch's *Collected Poems* and *Collected Fiction* were published by Knopf and Coffee House Press, respectively, both in 2005.

Noelle Kocot's most recent book, *Poem for the End of Time and Other Poems,* was published by Wave Books in 2006. She lives in Brooklyn.

Ron Koertge is a poet and fiction writer for young adults. His latest book of poems is *Fever,* from Red Hen Press. His latest piece of fiction for young adults is *Boy Girl Boy* from Harcourt.

David Lehman's sixth book of poetry is *When a Woman Loves a Man and Other Poems* (Scribner, 2005). With James Cummins he collaborated on a book of sestinas called *Jim & Dave Defeat the Masked Man,* published by Soft Skull Press in 2005. Lehman has collaborated on poems with Cummins, Sally Dawidoff, Stacey Harwood, Ron Horning, Nikki Moustaki, Karen Pepper, William Wadsworth, and others.

Joseph Lehman is a senior at Franklin Pierce College with a double major in history and criminal justice. In the 1990s poems of his appeared in Mitch Sisskind's magazine the *Stud Duck.*

Timothy Liu is the author of six books of poems, most recently *Of Thee I Sing* (University of Georgia Press, 2004) and *For Dust Thou Art* (Southern Illinois University Press, 2005). He lives in Manhattan.

Reginald Lockett has published three books of poetry. His work has appeared in more than fifty periodicals, anthologies, and textbooks. He teaches at San Jose City College and lives in Oakland.

Rachel Loden's *Hotel Imperium* (Georgia) was a *San Francisco Chronicle* poetry pick. Recent news includes a Pushcart Prize, a California Arts Council Fellowship, and poems in *Jacket* and *Iowa Review*, both of which also published interviews. A new chapbook, *The Richard Nixon Snow Globe*, has been published by Wild Honey Press.

Chris Martin is the author of *American Music* (Copper Canyon, 2007), which received the Hayden Carruth Prize. He hails from Colorado, Minnesota, California, New Mexico, and Brooklyn. With dear friends, he edits the online journal *Puppy Flowers.*

Bernadette Mayer is the author of numerous books of poetry and prose, including *Scarlet Tanager* (2005), *Two Haloed Mourners: Poems* (1998), *Proper Name and Other Stories* (1996), *The Desires of Mothers to Please Others in Letters* (1994), *The Bernadette Mayer Reader* (1992), *Sonnets* (1989), *Midwinter Day* (1982), *The Golden Book of Words* (1978), and *Ceremony Latin* (1964). From 1972 to 1974, Mayer and conceptual artist Vito Acconci edited the journal *0 TO 9*. With writer and publisher Lewis Warsh, she edited United Artists Press. She has taught writing workshops at the Poetry Project at St. Mark's Church in New York City for many years and she served as the Poetry Project's director during the 1980s.

Jeffrey McDaniel is the author of *The Splinter Factory, Alibi School,* and *The Forgiveness Parade.* He teaches at Sarah Lawrence College and lives in Brooklyn.

Jane Miller's book-length sequence of poems, *A Palace of Pearls,* was published in 2005 by Copper Canyon Press. She's recently completed *Seven Mediterraneans,* a fanciful memoir of the same period from which the excerpt in this anthology arose.

Norman Minnick grew up in Kentucky. He earned a BA in Art from Marian College in Indianapolis and an MFA in Creative Writing from Florida International University in Miami. His poems have appeared in such journals as the *Christian Science Monitor, Notre Dame Review,* the *Seattle Review, Chelsea,* and the *Texas Observer.* His book *To Taste the Water* will be published by Mid-List Press in 2007.

Harryette Mullen has published six poetry books, most recently *Blues Baby* (Bucknell University, 2002) and *Sleeping with the Dictionary* (University of California, 2002). She met Douglas Kearney thanks to the synergetic· collaboration of Toi Derricotte and Cornelius Eady who founded Cave Canem Poets.

Eileen Myles divides her time between NY and SD. Teaches at UCSD. Her opera *Hell* is currently traveling around the world. She's finishing a novel, *The Inferno,* and putting some books of poems together. Last books: *Skies* and *on my way.*

Kristy Nielsen's work has been published in *Mid-American Review*, the *Madison Review*, the *Prose Poem: An International Journal*, *Kalliope*, and *Spoon River Poetry Review*, among others. Her poems have been nominated for the Pushcart Prize and her fiction recently won an honorable mention at *Literal Latté*. She's currently revising her third novel manuscript, *Throw Me a Bone*.

Pat Nolan, born 1943, Montreal, Quebec, Canada, has been published in *Rolling Stone*, the *Paris Review*, *Exquisite Corpse*, the *World*, *Hanging Loose*, and *Big Bridge*. He is the author of fourteen books of poetry, all out of print or in hard to find limited editions. His most recent, *Fly By Night: Selected Poems 1975–1992*, was published by Re:Issue Press (Monte Rio, 2006). He has written renku (haikai no renga) for over twenty years with numerous other poets including Gloria Frym, Steve LaVoie, Joen Eshima, Joanne Kyger, Don Guravich, and Karen Elizabeth Gordon. Since 1993, he has collaborated with Sandy Berrigan on a Rainbow Renku sequence, and since the mid '80's, with the so-called Totem Pole School (Keith Abbott, Maureen Owen, Michael Sowl) he has authored over a dozen renku, some of which have been published in *Hanging Loose* and *Jack's Magazine*. *All Ears* was published by Empty Head Press (Monte Rio, 2004) in a limited edition of thirty-six, with woven reed covers, imported Japanese endpapers, and hand bound using a tortoiseshell stitching. Pat Nolan resides in Northern California among the redwood wilds along the Russian River.

Alice Notley, American poet based in Paris, is the author of around thirty books, including the epic poem, *The Descent of Alette*, and *Mysteries of Small Houses*, Pulitzer-prize finalist and winner of the *Los Angeles Times* Book Award. Her book-length poem, *Disobedience*, won the Griffin International Prize. Notley recently edited *The Collected Poems of Ted Berrigan*, with coeditors Anselm Berrigan and Edmund Berrigan. She is also the author of *Coming After: Essays on Poets and Poetry*. *Grave of Light: Selected Poems 1970–2005* (Wesleyan) and *Alma, or The Dead Women* (Granary Books) are her most recent volumes. Of *The Descent of Alette*, Steve Silberman wrote in *Hotwired*, "The kind of major poetic achievement that comes along once in a generation . . . ."

Sarah A. Odishoo, a professor of English at Columbia College in Chicago, has had her work published in *New Letters*, *Confrontations*, *Laurel Review*, *Aura Literary Arts Review*, *Berkeley Fiction Review*, *Florida Review*, *Fugue*, *Georgetown Review*, *Jeopardy Magazine*, *Laurel Review*, *Left Curve*, *Libido*, *Limestone*, *Lynx Eye*, *Pikeville Review*, *Portland Review*, and *RiverSedge*. She was also nominated for a Pushcart Prize, 1996.

Douglas Oliver (1937–2000) was one of the most important British poets of his generation. Volumes in print include *Arrondissements* (ed. by Alice Notley); the double prose memoir of himself and Louise Michel, *Whisper Louise*; and *Selected Poems*.

Maureen Owen is the author of ten books of poetry; her title *Amelia Earhart* won a Before Columbus American Book Award and her selected poems, *American Rush*, was a finalist for the *Los Angeles Times* Book Prize. A special selection of poems from her title *Erosion's Pull*, in collaboration with the stunning art of Yvonne Jacquette, has been published by Granary Books, New York City. Her complete collection of *Erosion's Pull* was published by Coffee House Press in Spring 2006. She currently teaches at Naropa University in Boulder, CO. Her awards include grants from the Foundation for Contemporary Performance Arts, Inc. and a Poetry Fellowship from the NEA. Andrei Codrescu notes, "Her exuberant style and tremendous energy shine in her strongly feminist works."

Ron Padgett's many books include *You Never Know* (poems) and two memoirs, *Oklahoma Tough: My Father, King of the Tulsa Bootleggers* and *Joe: A Memoir of Joe Brainard*. Padgett is the editor of *The Handbook of Poetic Forms* as well as the translator of Blaise Cendrars's *Complete Poems*. Forthcoming are two collections of poems, *If I Were You* (collaborative works) and *How to Be Perfect*. For more information, visit his website at www.ronpadgett.com.

Michael Palmer was born in New York City in 1943. He is the author of numerous books of poetry, including *Codes Appearing: Poems 1979–1988* (2001), *The Promises of Glass* (2000), *The Lion Bridge: Selected Poems 1972–1995* (1998), *At Passages* (1996), *Sun* (1998), *First Figure* (1984), *Notes for Echo Lake* (1981), *Without Music* (1977), *The Circular Gates* (1974), and *Blake's Newton* (1972). Palmer's work has appeared in literary magazines such as *Boundary 2, Berkeley Poetry Review, Sulfur, Conjunctions,* and *O-blek*. His honors include two grants from the Literature Program of the National Endowment for the Arts, a Guggenheim.Foundation fellowship, and most recently the Wallace Stevens Award. In 1999, Palmer was elected a Chancellor of the Academy of American Poets. He lives in San Francisco.

Karen Pepper lived in Paris for ten years. She received her MFA at Bennington College and has had work in such magazines as *Pharos*.

Jean-Paul Pecqueur's first book, *The Case Against Happiness,* was published by Alice James Press in 2006. Jean-Paul currently lives in Brooklyn where he teaches at the Pratt Institute.

Michelle Naka Pierce has taught at the University of New Mexico, Bard College, and Naropa University–where she is director of the Naropa Writing Center. Her poems and interviews have appeared in *Shiny, Traverse, Rain Taxi,* and *Teachers and Writers Magazine*.

Co-written with Veronica Corpuz, *TRI / VIA* is her first book of poems (Erudite Fangs/PUB LUSH, 2003).

Cecilia Pinto's prose has appeared in places like *Esquire, Fence,* and *Quarter After Eight,* and she is a writer-in-residence in the Poetry Center's Hands on Stanzas program. Cecilia and Alice met as graduate students and have been collaborating for more than two years.

Haya Pomrenze's poetry has been published or is forthcoming in the anthology *Irrepressible Appetites, Poetica, Zeek, Pearl,* and *Gulfstream.* She teaches creative arts in the mental health field where she first worked on the collaborative process for a group poem.

D. A. Powell is the author of three extraordinary books: *Tea* (Wesleyan), *Lunch* (Wesleyan), and *Cocktails* (Graywolf). He is the recipient of many prizes and awards and the receptacle of an eclectic group of recipes (many involving Jell-O or soda pop). A patient and thorough teacher, Mr. Powell coached me via telephone through my first attempt at making Shake 'N Bake pork chops. He also teaches poetry to some lucky students at Harvard. His soft Southern speech has, over the years, become increasingly inflected with Yiddishisms some of which he charmingly mispronounces. In addition to being a loyal and generous friend, he is one of the most important poets of his generation. His poems—funny, sorrowful, achingly soulful, impeccably crafted—are treasured by his readers. —*As told by Rachel Zucker*

Lawrence Raab is the author of six collections of poems, including *What We Don't Know About Each Other* (winner of the National Poetry Series, and a finalist for the National Book Award), *The Probable World,* and most recently *Visible Signs: New and Selected Poems.* He teaches literature and writing at Williams College.

Tom Raworth is shorter and older than he was. He still lives in Cambridge, England.

Matthew Rohrer is the author of *A Hummock in the Malookas,* which won the 1994 National Poetry Series; *Satellite; Nice Hat. Thanks.* (with Joshua Beckman); *A Green Light;* and *Adventures While Preaching the Gospel of Beauty,* an audio CD of live collaborations with Joshua Beckman. His latest collaboration with Joshua Beckman was a ten-hour nonstop improvised collaborative poem performed at the Bowery Poetry Club in New York City in May 2004.

Joe Ross is the author of ten books of poetry, most recent being *EQUATIONS = equals* (Green Integer Press, 2004). He lived in Washington, DC for fourteen years where he co-founded the In Your Ear poetry reading series and was the Literary Editor of the *Washington Review*, before moving to San Diego, CA, where he worked in politics and co-founded the Beyond the Page reading series. In 1997 he received a National Endowment for the Arts Fellowship Award for his poetry. He presently resides in Paris, France.

Michael Rothenberg is a poet, songwriter and editor of *BigBridge* (bigbridge.org). His most recent book of poetry is *Unhurried Vision* (La Alameda/University of New Mexico Press). He is also the editor of *David's Copy: Selected Poems of David Meltzer* (Penguin, 2004). His most recent editorial projects include *Way More West: Selected Poems of Edward Dorn* (Penguin), and *Collected Poems of Philip Whalen* (Wesleyan University Press), both due out in 2007.

Leslie Scalapino is the author of thirty books, most recently poetry collections titled *New Time* and *Zither & Autobiography* (both Wesleyan University Press); *It's go in/quiet illumined grass/land* (The Post-Apollo Press); and *The Tango* (Granary Books). Fiction includes: *Dahlia's Iris* (FC2).

Andrew Schelling: poetry, ecology, mountaineering, Sanskrit studies. Recent books include *Two Elk: A High Country Journal;* the essay collection *Wild Form, Savage Grammar;* a translation of the 101 poems of the eighth-century Sanskrit *Amarushataka* under the title *Erotic Love Poems from India;* and he is the editor of *The Wisdom Anthology of North American Buddhist Poetry.* He teaches at Naropa University in Boulder, Colorado.

James Schuyler (1923–1991) was the author of *A Few Days* (1985); *The Morning of the Poem* (1980), which earned him the Pulitzer Prize; *The Home Book* (1977); *The Fireproof Floors of Witley Count: English Songs and Dances* (1976); *Song* (1976); *Hymn to Life* (1974); *The Crystal Lithium* (1972); and *Freely Espousing* (1969). With John Ashbery he also published a collaborative novel, *A Nest of Ninnies* (1969). His *Collected Poems* was published in 1993.

Brenda Serotte has published poetry and Ladino (Judeo-Spanish) translations in various literary journals and anthologies, most recently in *Tigertail: A South Florida Annual,* the *Atlanta Review,* and the *Meridian Anthology of Contemporary Poetry, Vols. I* and *II.* Her memoir, *The Fortune Teller's Kiss,* was published by University of Nebraska Press in 2006. She teaches writing at Nova Southeastern University in Fort Lauderdale, and is at work on a novel about Peru.

Mary Beth Shaffer is a writer and therapist in Milwaukee. She has been published by the *Indiana Review, Diagram,* and *Quarter After Eight.* She has been collaborating with

Nin Andrews off and on since they graduated from the MFA program at Vermont College where Mary Beth studied fiction, and Nin studied poetry. Their first collaboration, *The Divorce Notebooks,* was a published contest finalist in *Quarter After Eight* (for their annual prose contest).

In 1996, at the age of twelve, **Daniel Shapiro** wrote a series of poems inspired by Jasper Johns' "Seasons" series, which Johns then reprinted in new colors, responding to Shapiro's poems, for a limited edition portfolio of lithographs. Collaborative poems between Daniel Shapiro and his father David Shapiro have appeared in *Pataphysics,* the *World,* and other publications. He is currently a senior at Columbia University.

David Shapiro is a poet and art critic, and the author of ten books of poetry, including most recently, *The Selected Poems of David Shapiro* (Overlook Press, 2007).

Reginald Shepherd is the editor of *The Iowa Anthology of New American Poetries* (University of Iowa Press, 2004). He is also the author of four books of poetry, all from the University of Pittsburgh Press, including *Otherhood* (2003) and *Some Are Drowning* (1994), winner of the 1993 AWP Award in Poetry.

Rod Smith is the author of *Music or Honesty, The Good House, Poèmes de l'araignée* (France), *In Memory of My Theories, The Boy Poems, Protective Immediacy,* and *New Mannerist Tricycle* with Lisa Jarnot and Bill Luoma. He edits *Aerial* magazine and publishes Edge Books in Washington, DC. Smith is also editing, with Peter Baker and Kaplan Harris, *The Selected Letters of Robert Creeley* for the University of California Press.

Violet Snow is a journalist, herbalist, photographer, librarian, actress, etc. When she wrote the piece in this anthology with her husband, Sparrow, she was a computer programmer. She is currently enjoying an obsession with making fermented foods.

Michael Sowl lives in Northeastern Minnesota. He occasionally paints. Interior and exterior. His hobbies include reading brochures and walking in far places. He hopes to catch a rainbow trout before the season closes. He has a cricket someplace in his house. The Chinese may think this is lucky, but he's not so sure.

Sparrow has run for President of the United States four times. He is a substitute teacher in Boiceville, New York. Sparrow lives with his wife, Violet Snow, and their daughter Sylvia in a doublewide trailer. A rabbit, Bananacake, lives just outside, in a hutch. Sparrow is the author of *Yes, You Are a Revolutionary!; Republican Like Me: A Diary of My Presidential Campaign;* and most recently *America: A Prophecy: The Sparrow Reader;* all published by Soft Skull Press.

Christina Springer is a text artist who uses poetry, dance, theatre, film and other visual expressions. Recent dance-theatre scripts include: *Living Ancestry* and *Kikombe Cha Umoja: A Kwanzaa Myth* produced by Umoja African Arts Company, and *The Splooge Factory*, produced by Composer's Collaborative. Recent poems have appeared in *The Complete Idiot's Guide to Slam Poetry, Gathering Ground, Janus Head, Femspec*, and *Callaloo*. Until she moved to England, Springer was the co-founder and Executive Director of Sun Crumbs, a nonprofit that gave emerging artists a positive yet firm nudge in the behind. Currently, she unschools her son and teaches creative writing at CityLit College in London, England.

Shirley Stephenson's poetry has appeared in *Crazyhorse, Black Warrior Review, North American Review, New Letters, Hayden's Ferry Review*, and other journals. She has been twice nominated for Pushcart Prizes, and recently received an Artists Fellowship Award from the Illinois Arts Council.

Terese Svoboda's fourth book of poetry is *Treason* (Zoo Press, 2002); her fourth novel is *Tin God* (University of Nebraska Press, 2006). She has received many awards for her poetry, novels, short stories, plays, essays, and videos but she is particularly excited to toss around words with veteran collaborateur Maureen Seaton, the woman in the dark glasses. Svoboda is currently Writer-in-Residence at Fordham and will be teaching poetry for SLS in Kenya this Christmas.

An artist, educator, writer, and activist, **Ginny Sykes** has exhibited in Chicago, the U.S. and internationally, and has completed many permanent outdoor public art works. Ms. Sykes received an Honor Award from the Illinois Chapter of the American Society of Landscape Architects for her 1999 Percent for Art mosaic "Rora," located on the Chicago River. She is included in the books *Chicago Murals* and *Urban Art Chicago*.

Eileen Tabios has released ten collections of poetry, a short story collection, and a collection of art essays. Her most recent poetry books are *I Take Thee, English, for My Beloved* (Marsh Hawk Press, 2005) and *The Secret Lives of Punctuations, Vol. 1* (xPress(ed), 2006). She is the publisher of Meritage Press (www.meritagepress.com) and lives in St. Helena, CA.

Born in Timisoara , Romania in 1974, **Gene Tanta** immigrated to Chicago in 1984 with family. He earned his MFA in Poetry from the Iowa Writers' Workshop in 2000. He also translates contemporary Romanian poetry and makes visual art with found materials. Mr. Tanta's publications include: *Epoch, Ploughshares, Circumference Magazine, Exquisite Corpse, Watchword*, and *Columbia Poetry Review*. Currently, he is a PhD student in

Creative Writing (Poetry) at the University of Wisconsin at Milwaukee where he is also the Art Editor for *Cream City Review*.

Mike Topp was born in Washington, DC. He is currently living in New York City unless he has died or moved.

George Tucker grew up in the Ozarks of Arkansas where he learned to dowse for water and the right way to kill a chicken. He received his MFA in creative writing from Florida International University. He's currently at work on a novel about archaeologists.

Ryan G. Van Cleave most recent books include a poetry collection, *The Magical Breasts of Britney Spears* (Red Hen Press, 2006), and a creative writing textbook, *Behind the Short Story: From First to Final Draft* (Allyn & Bacon/Longman, 2006). He teaches creative writing and literature at Clemson University.

For more than a decade **William Wadsworth** was the executive director and public face of the Academy of American Poets. His poetry has been published in the *Paris Review* and the *Yale Review* and was selected by A. R. Ammons for *The Best American Poetry 1994*.

Anne Waldman has received a National Endowment for the Arts award, the Shelley prize for poetry, and several residencies. Directing the Poetry Project at St Mark's Poetry Project over a decade, she co-founded the Jack Kerouac School of Disembodied Poetics with Allen Ginsberg at Naropa University in 1974. She currently is a Distinguished Professor and Chair of Naropa's celebrated Summer Writing Program and is Director of the Study Abroad on the Bowery project for Bowery Arts & Sciences in Manhattan's Lower East Side. Author and editor of more than forty books and small-press editions of poetry, she has been working for over twenty-five years on the epic *Iovis* project (two volumes published by Coffee House Press, 1993, 1997) and her most recent books are *Marriage: A Sentence* (Coffee House, 2000), *In the Room of Never Grieve: New & Selected Poems* including a CD collaboration with Ambrose Bye (Coffee House, 2003), *Dark Arcana: Afterimage or Glow,* with photographs by Patti Smith (Heavenbone Press 2003), and *Structure of the World Compared to a Bubble,* a long Buddhist poem (Penguin, 2004). She also coedited the anthology *Civil Disobediences: Poetics & Politics in Action* (Coffee House, 2004). She is currently working on a new volume of the *Iovis* project and *Beats at Naropa,* an anthology. She makes her home in New York City and Boulder, Colorado.

Charles Harper Webb's most recent book of poems, *Tulip Farms and Leper Colonies,* was published in 2001 by BOA Editions, Ltd. *Hot Popsicles,* his book of prose poems, was published by the University of Wisconsin Press in 2005. Recipient of grants from the

Whiting and Guggenheim foundations, he teaches at California State University, Long Beach.

Karen Weiser lives and writes in New York. Her chapbooks include *Placefullness* (Ugly Duckling Presse, 2004), *Eight Positive Trees* (Pressed Wafer, 2002), and *Heads Up Fever Pile,* (Belladonna, 2005).

Benjamin Weissman is the author of two collections of short fiction, *Headless* and *Dear Dead Person.*

Bernard Welt is the author of *Serenade* (Z Press, 1980). His work appears in *The Best American Poetry 2001* (Robert Hass, ed., Scribner, 2001) and other anthologies, and in art catalogues including *Raymond Pettibon: A Reader* (Philadelphia Museum of Art and the Renaissance Society of the University of Chicago, 1998). His essays for the Los Angeles art journal *Art issues* are collected in *Mythomania: Fantasies, Fables, and Sheer Lies in Contemporary American Popular Art* (Art Issues Press, 1996). He is Professor of Academic Studies at the Corcoran College of Art and Design in Washington, DC, and a member of the board of directors of the International Association for the Study of Dreams.

Annabel Wheeler is a writer, an actress, and a student at the Francis Parker School in Chicago.

Jack Wheeler is a writer, sports enthusiast, and student at the University of Michigan.

Susan Wheeler is the author of four collections of poetry and a novel.

Terence Winch's most recent book is a nonfiction collection called *That Special Place: New World Irish Stories* (2004, Hanging Loose), which centers on his experiences playing traditional Irish music. His last book of poems is *The Drift of Things* (2001, The Figures). Winch's work has appeared three volumes of *The Best American Poetry* series, as well as in *Verse,* the *Paris Review, American Poetry Review, New American Writing,* et al. See also www.terencewinch.com.

Terry Wolverton is the author of five books: *Embers,* a novel in poems; *Insurgent Muse,* a memoir; *Bailey's Beads,* a novel; and two collections of poetry, *Black Slip* and *Mystery Bruise.* She has edited fourteen literary anthologies, most recently *Mischief, Caprice, and Other Poetic Strategies.* A new poetry collection, *Shadow and Praise,* will be published in early 2007.

Wonder Woman is an armchair quarterback compared to **Rachel Zucker**. Poet, Novelist, Memoirist, Essayist, Editor, Photographer, Wife, Mother, Jet Setter, Sex Kitten, Brisket Enthusiast. I get exhausted thinking about the sheer energy of her production, as awe-inspiring as the Hoover Dam, as multidimensional as a Bucky Fuller building. And the maddening thing is that she does everything so well. Her poems are the finest being written today. Her kids are the cutest. Her essays the most incisive. And, oh, that brisket. It could melt your heart. I'm honored to be friends with someone so rare, so talented, so present. She makes me want to be a poet. —*As told by D. A. Powell*

Acknowledgments

A sincere attempt has been made to locate all copyright holders and make all required acknowledgments. If any acknowledgments have been omitted, or any rights overlooked, it is unintentional. Unless otherwise noted, permission for the inclusion in this anthology of the following material has been graciously granted by the authors, who hold the copyright. The publishers and entities listed below granted additional permissions as indicated. Our gratitude to all who made this collection possible.

"International Chainpoem" by Charles Henri Ford et al.: Appeared in *New Directions*, 1940. To the best of our knowledge, this work is in the public domain.

"Pull My Daisy" by Neal Cassady, Allen Ginsberg & Jack Kerouac: From *Pull My Daisy*; copyright © 1971 by City Lights Publishers. Reprinted by permission of City Lights & (for Ginsberg) HarperCollins Publishers.

"Masterpiece" by Jack Kerouac & Lew Welch: From *Trip Trap*; copyright © 1973 by City Lights Publishers. Reprinted by permission of City Lights.

"A Postcard to Popeye" by John Ashbery & Kenneth Koch. Reprinted by permission of John Ashbery and the Estate of Kenneth Koch.

"Crone Rhapsody" by John Ashbery & Kenneth Koch: Appeared in *Locus Solus*, 1961. Reprinted by permission of John Ashbery & the Estate of Kenneth Koch.

"The Car" by Jane Freilicher & Kenneth Koch: Appeared in *Locus Solus*, 1961. Reprinted by permission of Jane Freilicher & the Estate of Kenneth Koch.

"St. Bridget's Neighborhood," "Song Heard Around St. Bridget's," "St. Bridget's Efficacy," & "Reverdy" by Bill Berkson & Frank O'Hara: From *Hymns of St. Bridget & Other Writings* (The Owl Press, 2001). Copyright © 1975, 2001 by Bill Berkson & the Estate of Frank O'Hara. Reprinted by permission of Bill Berkson.

"Waves of Particles" by Bill Berkson, Michael Brownstein & Ron Padgett: From *The World of Leon* (Big Sky, 1974) and *Enigma Variations* (Big Sky, 1975). Copyright © 1974, 2006 by Bill Berkson, Michael Brownstein & Ron Padgett. Reprinted by permission of authors.

"Within the Dome" by Ron Padgett & James Schuyler: Reprinted by permission of Ron Padgett & the Estate of James Schuyler. Appeared in the *Germ*.

"Inner Landscapes" & "Noh" by Ted Berrigan & Ron Padgett: "Inner Landscapes" is previously unpublished. Included by permission of the Estate of Ted Berrigan & Ron Padgett. "Noh" was published as a broadside by Lines Press, 1969. Reprinted by permission of the Estate of Ted Berrigan & Ron Padgett.

"S.O.S." by Dennis Cooper & David Trinidad: Appeared in *Mirage*, 1986.

"Strawberry Blonde" & "Anger Turned Inward" by Bob Flanagan & David Trinidad: From *A Taste of Honey* (Cold Calm Press, 1990).

"Graphic Winces" by Allen Ginsberg, with Bob Rosenthal & Brooklyn College MFA Class. Reprinted by permission of HarperCollins Publishers.

"Cataract" by Allen Ginsberg, Lita Hornick & Peter Orlovsky: Appeared in *To Elizabeth and Eleanor: Great Queens Who Loved Poetry* (Giorno Systems, 1993). Included by permission of the Estate of Allen Ginsberg.

"White Mink" by Lita Hornick & Ron Padgett: Appeared in *To Elizabeth and Eleanor: Great Queens Who Loved Poetry* (Giorno Systems, 1993). Included by permission of Ron Padgett.

"Hot Pink" by Alice Notley, Douglas Oliver & Ron Padgett: Included by permission of Alice Notley & Ron Padgett.

"All Ears" by Keith Abbot, Pat Nolan, Maureen Owen & Michael Sowl: Previously unpublished.

"Renga" by Martine Bellen, Elaine Equi & Melanie Neilson: Appeared in *Conjunctions*.

"Tenebrae" by Dodie Bellamy & Kevin Killian: From *Argento Series*; Krupskaya; copyright © 2001 by Kevin Killian. Also appeared in *Black Bread*.

"A Lover's Complaint" by Samuel Ace & Kevin Killian: Appeared in *Gargoyle*.

Excerpt from *Sappho's Gymnasium* by T Begley & Olga Broumas: From *Sappho's Gymnasium* and *Rave*; both Copper Canyon; copyright © 1994 and 2004 respectively by T Begley & Olga Broumas.

Excerpt from "A Library Book" by Norma Cole & Michael Palmer: Appeared in *Chain*.

"Chinook, 7 Poems (Like Non-existence)" by Joe Ross & Rod Smith: Appeared in *Membrane*.

"The Secret" by Cindy Goff & Jeffrey McDaniel: From *Alibi School*; Manic D Press; copyright © 1995 by Jeffrey McDaniel.

"Listening to a Storyteller" by Robert Bly & Yorifumi Yaguchi: Appeared in *Poetry*, 1998.

"In the Cities of Someone Else's Anxiety," "The Bluest Day," "The Night She Removed Her Pearls," "Sky" & "The Other Side of the Sky" by Stephen Dunn & Lawrence Raab: From *Winter at the Caspian Sea*; Palanquin Press; copyright © 1999 by Stephen Dunn & Lawrence Raab.

"Dental Records Prove We Were All Children" by Joanna Fuhrman & Jean-Paul Pecqueur: Previously unpublished.

"To My Kidney Near My House" by Joanna Fuhrman et al.: Previously unpublished.

"Four Attempts toward a Theory of True Names" by Joanna Fuhrman & Chris Martin: Previously unpublished.

"The Singing Animal World" by Joanna Fuhrman & Noelle Kocot: Previously unpublished.

"Waiting for the Cat Food to Come" by Violet Snow & Sparrow: Previously unpublished.

"Dollar Store" by Sparrow & Mike Topp: Previously unpublished.

"The New Prosperity" & "Art in America" by Thomas Fink & Timothy Liu: Previously unpublished.

"Derivative of the Curve: 2" & Robotics" by Kendra· Dwelley Guimaraes & George Tucker: Previously unpublished.

"Cereal Monogamy" by Maureen Seaton & Terese Svoboda: Appeared in *Big Bridge*, 2003.

"Somonka" by Jacqueline Johnson & devorah major: Previously unpublished.

"Somonka" by Patricia A. Johnson & Christina Springer: Previously unpublished.

"A Game of Chance" by Opal Palmer Adisa & Reginald Lockett: Previously unpublished.

"Romeo's Half-Wake" & "Screen Memory" by Reginald Shepherd & Gene Tanta: Appeared in *Indiana Review*, 2005.

"Lessons from the Kitchen" by Jim Elledge & Kristy Nielsen: Previously unpublished.

"Ifugao Red" by Nick Carbó & Eileen Tabios: Previously unpublished.

"Logogriph" by Nick Carbó & Eric Gamalinda: Previously unpublished.

"All Saints' Day" by Guillermo Castro & Ron Drummond: Previously unpublished.

"The Great Cuban ·Sculptor" by Virgil Suárez & Ryan G. Van Cleave: Previously unpublished.

"Sestina for Horse & Destiny" by Connie Deanovich & Rachel Loden: Appeared in the *Hat*, 2005.

"Soul #1" by Julianna Baggott & Norman Minnick: Previously unpublished.

"Spin" by Laura Bandy & Shirley Stephenson: Previously unpublished.

"Days of the Week" by Paulette Beete & Danna Ephland: Previously unpublished.

"Where We Live Now" by Michael Hettich, Claudia Livini, Susan Parsons & Yair Segal: Previously unpublished.

"Thirst" & "Soldier" by Alice George & Cecilia Pinto: Previously unpublished.

"What Is She Doing Right Now?" by Alice George & Cecilia Pinto: Appeared in *Quarter After Eight*, 2004.

"Fugitive Car" by Pamela Gemin & Julie King: Previously unpublished.

"The Life" by Nin Andrews & Mary Beth Shaffer: Appeared in *Indiana Review*, 2005 (as part of a story titled "The Queen of Hooky."

"Another Avenue" by Haya Pomrenze & Brenda Serotte: Previously unpublished.

"She Dreams about Being Jung" by Cathryn Cofell & Karla Huston: Previously unpublished.

"Horror Movies We'd Like to See" by Ronald Koertge & Charles Harper Webb: Previously unpublished.

"Term" & "Testament" by Kate Gale & Terry Wolverton: Previously unpublished.

"Jangling," "Architecture Believes in Formalism" & "A Note on Process" by Joshua Beckman & Matthew Rohrer: From *Nice Hat. Thanks.*; Verse Press; copyright © 2002 by Joshua Beckman & Matthew Rohrer.

"Equitable Deviation" by William Fuller & Tom Raworth: Appeared in *A Box for Tom & Val.*

"Zombie Dawn" by Tom Clark & Anne Waldman: Appeared in *Jacket*, 2003. Also published as a chapbook by Skanky Possum, 2003.

"Riparian" by Andrew Schelling & Anne Waldman: From *Riparian*; Erudite Fangs Editions; copyright © 1997 by Andrew Schelling & Anne Waldman. Also appeared in *Conjunctions*, 2000.

"As If I Was a Cloud Expert" & "I Think You Get the Privilege O" by Anselm Berrigan, Edmund Berrigan & Karen Weiser: Previously unpublished.

Excerpt from "Cartographic Anomaly" by Terri Carrion & Michael Rothenberg: Previously unpublished.

Excerpt from "TRI / VIA" by Veronica Corpuz & Michelle Naka Pierce: From *TRI / VIA*; Pub Lush Press; copyright © 2003 by Veronica Corpuz & Michelle Naka Pierce. "Poem as a letter . . ." also appeared on the Poetry Project at St. Marks' web site, 2002.

Excerpt from *Braided Creek* by Jim Harrison & Ted Kooser: From *Braided Creek*; Copper Canyon; copyright © 2003 by Jim Harrison & Ted Kooser. Reprinted by permission of poets and Copper Canyon Press.

"Alaska" & "The Slave" by Tom Breidenbach & Nathan Kernan: Previously unpublished.

"Ghazal As Menu or with Adumbration" by D. A. Powell & Rachel Zucker: Previously unpublished.

"Now It's Tomorrow As Usual" by Maggie Anderson & Lynn Emanuel: Previously unpublished.

"Sprung Flung" by Douglas Kearney & Harryette Mullen: Previously unpublished.

About the Editors

Denise Duhamel has collaborated with Maureen Seaton on three volumes: *Little Novels, Oyl,* and *Exquisite Politics.* Her latest solo books are *Two and Two, Queen for a Day: New and Selected Poems* (both from University of Pittsburgh Press), and *Mille et un sentiments* (Firewheel Editions). A winner of a National Endowment for the Arts grant, she teaches at Florida International University in Miami.

Maureen Seaton has been collaborating with Denise Duhamel since 1989. Her solo collections include *Venus Examines Her Breast* (Carnegie Mellon UP, 2004), winner of the Publishing Triangle's Audre Lorde Award; *Little Ice Age* (Invisible Cities Press, 2001), which was nominated for a National Book Award; *Furious Cooking* (University of Iowa Press, 1996), winner of the Iowa Poetry Prize and the Lambda Literary Award; *Fear of Subways* (Eighth Mountain, 1991), winner of the Eighth Mountain Poetry Prize; and *The Sea among the Cupboards* (New Rivers, 1992), winner of the Capricorn Award and the Society of Midland Authors Award. The recipient of a National Endowment for the Arts fellowship and the Pushcart, she teaches at the University of Miami.

David Trinidad's last two books, *Plasticville* (2000) and *Phoebe 2002: An Essay in Verse* (2003), were published by Turtle Point Press. His other books include *Answer Song* (High Risk Books/Serpent's Tail, 1994) and *Hand Over Heart: Poems 1981-1988* (Amethyst Press). He is also editor of *Powerless,* the selected poems of Tim Dlugos (High Risk, 1996), and with Maxine Scates, *Holding Our Own: The Selected Poems of Ann Stanford* (Copper Canyon Press, 2001). Trinidad currently teaches poetry at Columbia College Chicago, where he coedits the journal *Court Green.* His next book of poetry, *The Late Show,* is forthcoming from Turtle Point Press in 2007.

Printed in the United States
by Baker & Taylor Publisher Services